Mass Movement and Power of Media

MASS MOVEMENT AND POWER OF MEDIA

Rajesh Kumar

PRASHANT PUBLISHING HOUSE
DELHI-110094

Published by :
Prashant Publishing House
C-34, 28 Foota Road, Gali No.-3,
West Karawal Nagar, Delhi-110094
Phone : 011-22963970, Mob. : 9810396373

Mass Movement And Power of Media

First Published 2012

ISBN 978-93-80565-29-3

PRINTED IN INDIA
Published by Mr. R.K. Jha M/s Prashant Publishing House and Published at **Dynamic Printers, Delhi**

Preface

The media coordinator must be someone who is personable, can succinctly articulate the issues, and is willing to spend a great deal of time on the telephone. This person makes sure press releases go out on time, keeps media lists updated, makes press calls, and works actively behind the scenes during events. The media coordinator should become as well-known behind the camera as the organization's spokesperson is in front of it. One person handling press calls can cultivate important relationships with assignment desk personnel, news producers, and camera people. These people are key to getting the coverage of events you need, and the kind of coverage you want.

During the recent years mass media has invaded the life of a common man in a big way. Upto seventies, mass media mainly remained confined to cinema, newspaper and radio. It was in the early eighties that audio-visual electronic medium in the form of television invaded the Indian scenario in a big way. The Government created huge infrastructure for spread of television network in the country. During this decade itself, advent of computers and Video Cassette Recorders (VCR) also supplemented the audio-visual media, putting well established medium of cinema to shade. During the early nineties, satellite television revolutionised the audio-visual media by reaching most of the households in the urban areas.

The latest invasion of audio-visual electronic media has suddenly increased the demand for professionals in journalism, technicians and other service individuals. These careers not only offer excellent opportunities, salaries, challenge and satisfaction of work, but also provide an opportunity for self-employment in various fields.

In some societies, an antagonistic relationship between media and government represents a vital and healthy element of fully functioning democracies. In post-conflict or ethnically homogenous societies such a conflictual, tensionridden relationship may not be appropriate, but the role of the press to disseminate information as a way of mediating between the state and all facets of civil society remains critical. Some of the most important questions to consider when designing media support activities that strengthen democracy are, "Who holds the power to communicate in a society, who has access to the means of communication, and who is communicated to?" Answers to these questions will help to shape media sector support strategies by targeting obstacles and pinpointing opportunities for reform.

Governments and press are widely perceived as mutual adversaries. Freedom of the Press-the right of the press to report and to criticise the wrong doings of the powerful without retaliation or threat of retaliation-is the cornerstone of democracy. Freedom of the Press in the United States is more than a legal concept-almost a religious tenet. The First Amendment to the US Constitution states clearly and unequivocally that the "Congress Shall Make No Law. Abridging Freedom of Speech or of the Press". The Indian Constitution does not have similar provision, but Art 19 (1) (a) protects the right to freedom of speech and expression subject to reasonable restrictions as mentioned in Art 19 (2) Though many governments vouch for protecting the freedom of the press, there are instances galore of throttling the press. There are several agencies in various countries which fight for the cause of press freedom. Be that as it may, governments themselves are also major users of mass media for putting across their messages.

The book discusses the basic concepts and techniques of Mass Movement andPower of Media in a student-friendly manner.

—Editor

Contents

1

Introduction to Mass Media

GENERAL CHARACTERISTICS

India is the world's largest democracy. Its mass media culture, a system that has evolved over centuries, is comprised of a complex framework. Modernization has transformed this into a communications network that sustains the pulse of a democracy of about 1.1 billion people. India's newspaper evolution is nearly unmatched in world press history. India's newspaper industry and its Westernization-or mondialisation as French would call it-go hand in hand. India's press is a metaphor for its advancement in the globalized world.

The printing press preceded the advent of printed news in India by about 100 years. It was in 1674 that the first printing apparatus was established in Bombay followed by Madras in 1772. India's first newspaper, Calcutta General Advertise, also known as the Hicky's Bengal Gazette was established in January 1780, and the first Hindi daily, Samachar Sudha Varshan, began in 1854. The evolution of the Indian media since has been fraught with developmental difficulties; illiteracy, colonial constraints and repression, poverty, and apathy thwart interest in news and media. Within this framework, it is instructive to examine India's press in two broad analytical sections: pre-colonial times and the colonial, independent press (which may, again be classified into two: preceding and following the Emergency rule imposed by Indira Gandhi's government in 1975). The post-Emergency phase, which continues at the present, may be the third independent phase of India's newspaper revolution (Jeffrey).

HISTORICAL TRADITIONS

"Newspaper history in India is inextricably tangled with political history," wrote A. E. Charlton (Wolseley). James Augustus Hicky was the founder of India's first newspaper, the Calcutta General Advertiser also known as Hicky's Bengal Gazette, in 1780. Soon other newspapers came into existence in Calcutta and Madras: the Calcutta Gazette, the Bengal Journal, the Oriental Magazine, the Madras Courier and the Indian Gazette. While the India Gazette enjoyed governmental patronage including free postal circulation and advertisements, Hicky's Bengal Gazette earned the rulers' wrath due to its criticism of the government. In November 1780 its circulation was halted by government decree. Hicky protested against this arbitrary harassment without avail, and was imprisoned. The Bengal Gazette and the India Gazette were followed by the Calcutta Gazette which subsequently became the government's "medium for making its general orders" (Sankhdher 24-32).

The Bombay Herald, The Statesmen in Calcutta and the Madras Mail and The Hindu, along with many other rivals in Madras represented the metropolitan voice of India and its people. While Statesman voiced the English rulers' voice, The Hindu became the beacon of patriotism in the South. The Hindu was founded in Madras as a counter to the Madras Mail.

Patriotic movements grew in proportion with the colonial ruthlessness, and a vehicle of information dissemination became a tool for freedom struggle. In the struggle for freedom, journalists in the twentieth century performed a dual role as professionals and nationalists. Indeed many national leaders, from Gandhi to Vajpayee, were journalists as well. Calcutta, Madras, Bombay and Delhi were four main centers of urban renaissance which nourished news in India. It was only during and after the seventies, especially after Indira Gandhi's defeat in 1977, that regional language newspapers became prevalent.

There were nationalist echoes from other linguistic regional provinces. Bengal, Gujarat, Tamil, Kerala, Punjab and Uttar

Pradesh produced dailies in regional languages. Hindi and Urdu were largely instrumental in voicing the viewpoints and aspirations of both Hindus and Muslims of the Northern provinces. As communalism and religious intolerance increased before and after partition, Urdu remained primarily the language of Muslims, as Pakistan chose this language as its lingua franca. After partition, the cause of Urdu and its newspapers, suffered a setback as Hindu reactionaries began to recognize the association of Urdu with Islam and Pakistan.

DIVERSITY AND THE LANGUAGE PRESS

Naresh Khanna summarizes the trends in circulatory growth and decline varied in regional language papers during 1998-2000: In the three-year period from 1998-2000, circulation of dailies in the country increased marginally from 58.37 to 59.13 million copies. This represents a growth of 1.3 percent on the basis of data published by the Registrar of Newspapers for India in its annual reports.

In this time, two distinct groups of newspapers emerge-the first including five languages that have collectively grown in circulation by a healthy 5.65 percent and representing a combined circulation of 43.35 million copies. Amongst these newspapers, those in Malayalam and Bengali grew fastest at 12.9 percent and 12.8 percent respectively, while Hindi dailies grew by 5 percent and English dailies by 4.7 percent over the three-year period. Although Marathi newspapers increased circulation by 2.75 percent over the three years it would seem that they are in danger of falling out of this group and perhaps entering the phase of stagnation and circulation decline (Khanna 2002).

The second group of stagnating and declining circulations includes newspapers in seven languages with a combined circulation of 14.8 million copies in 2000. These dailies lost almost 1.8 million copies (10.62 percent) of their combined circulation in the last three years. Daily newspaper circulation plummeted most dramatically in Telugu, which fell from 2.28 million to 1.68 million copies, a fall of more than 26 percent. Urdu newspaper circulation fell by more than 12 percent and Tamil dailies' circulation declined by 10.8 percent with circulation of Gujarati dailies falling by 10.5 percent. Over the same period circulations of Oriya dailies declined by 2.8 percent and that of Punjabi dailies by 3.2 percent.

Although over the three years Kannada newspapers show an insignificant fall in circulation they seem to have entered a period of stagnation and decline of their own. It would seem that in spite of new editions being added by Hindi, English, Malayalam and Bengali dailies, the print media is losing its dominance of advertising market share to television, radio and outdoor media (Khanna 2002).

ECONOMIC FRAMEWORK

India's language newspapers enjoy a relatively new entrepreneurial prowess. A mutually convenient relationship between the owners and capitalists keeps a financial balance between local/regional and national spheres in both private and public sectors.

"Like coral in a reef, newspapers grew and died in a process inseparable from the creation of a 'public sphere' in the classical liberal sense. Individual proprietors sometimes brought to their newspapers a crusader's zeal for a particular cause or a diehard's loathing for a rival" (Jeffrey 105). The Second Press Commission in 1982 tried to liberate the press from the monopoly houses. In 1995 the Audit Bureau of circulations had 165 newspapers as members, with a combined circulation of about 16 million copies a day. The top ten newspapers control roughly 50 percent of daily circulations in all languages. Bennett Coleman and the Indian Express own roughly 20 percent of daily circulations (Jeffrey 108).

While capitalists sustained national newspapers, the big houses, Dalmias, Jains, Goenka et al., monopolized and corrupted free journalism. The family and caste controlled small newspapers regionally maintain their freedom from big monopolies, thriving on their loyal supporters in north and south India. Diversity of ownership is reflective of cultural variation in India's multilingual landscape. Twenty-one newspapers control two-thirds of all circulations.

PRESS LAWS

Much of India's legal framework is built upon its colonial legacy. Legal statutes and regulations have been undergoing certain changes as India's democracy grows. India's freedom came at a high cost. The country was divided. India's border conflicts with two hostile neighbors, which forced at least three large scale wars, eclipsed other political issues. The democratic process, corrupted by criminals, unscrupulous bureaucrats and politicians, created a social climate that widened social and economic inequality. Freedom of speech and expression is a constitutionally guaranteed fundamental right of the Indian people. Article 19 (1; a) ensures the implicit freedom but Article 19 (2) qualifies this in explicit terms. The Parliamentary Proceedings (protection of Publication) Act of 1977 and the Prevention of Publication of Objectionable Matter (Repeal Act) of 1977 further reinforce and restrict these freedoms. While constitutional guarantees ensure freedom of the press and expression, press and media are obligated by a self-regulatory system of ethics that protect individuals and organizations from libelous behavior. "Freedom of the press is an institutional freedom," wrote Sachin Sen (19). The Press Council Bill of 1956, introduced in the Indian parliament, stipulated the establishment of the Press Council of India representing working journalists, the newspaper management, literary bodies and the Parliament. The Indian Press commission accepted the following postulate: "Democratic society lives and grows by accepting ideas, by experimenting with them, and wherc necessary, rejecting them...The Press is a responsible part of a democratic society" (quoted by Sen 42).

While The Central Press Accreditation Committee seeks to ensure quality and self-renewal, The Press Council of India was established in 1966 to uphold editorial autonomy. Restrictions on free speech were imposed after Indira Gandhi's infamous Emergency rule. The Press Council of India was abolished after editor George Verghese's criticisms of the Indira government. The Ministry of Information and Broadcasting carefully regulates the press and its liberties. The Maintenance of Internal Security Act (MISA) was enforced to intimidate reputedly autonomous newspapers in the seventies. The Press Council, resurrected in 1979, has no legal standing to impose penalties. The Indian press, generally believed as "managed," is a self-restrained institution generally reluctant to take on the governmental policies. All India Radio (AIR) and its management exemplify this "man-aged" system.

THE NATURE OF THE AUDIENCE

While a majority of the poor working people in rural and urban areas still remain oppressed and even illiterate, a significant proportion of people-roughly about 52 percent of the population over 15 years of age were recorded as being able to read and write. That breaks down to 65.5 percent of males and an estimate of 37.7 percent of females. After the liberalization of the economy, the growth of industry, and a rise in literacy, the post-Emergency boom rekindled the world's largest middle class in news, politics, and consumerism. Since private enterprise began to sustain and pay off, mass communications picked up as a growth industry. In 1976, the Registrar of Newspapers for India had recorded 875 papers; in 1995 there were 4,453. Robin Jeffrey comments: "Newspapers did not expand simply because the technology was available to make Indian scripts live as they had not been able to live before. Nor did newspaper grow simply because more people knew how to read and write. They grew because entrepreneurs detected a growing hunger for information among ever-widening sections of India's people, who were potential consumers as well as newspaper readers. A race began to reach this audience advertising avenues were the prizes and these would come largely to newspapers that could convince advertisers that they had more readers than their rivals. Readers, meanwhile, were saying implicitly: 'We will read newspapers that tell us about ourselves and reflect our concerns." Common contenders for readership and advertising are: the National Herald, the Hindustan Times, Time, Illustrated Weekly, e Pioneer, and Filmfare.

THE REGISTRAR OF NEWSPAPERS

The Registrar of Indian newspapers, among these official and professional agencies, regulates and records the status of newspapers. Electronic news, Web sites, magazines and house publications, and a number of professional organizations (like Editors Guild of India, Indian Language Newspapers' Association, and All India Newspapers Editors' Conference etc.) enrich the self-renewal process of the news enterprise. Educational and training programs are gaining importance as professionalization of specialized fields is a prioritized activity under the privatization process.

THE OFFICE OF THE REGISTRAR

The Office of the Registrar of Newspapers for India, popularly known as RNI came into being on July 1, 1956, on the recommendation of the First Press Commission in 1953 and by amending the Press and Registration of Books Act (PRB Act) 1867. The functions of RNI involve both statutory and non-statutory functions.

Statutory Functions

The RNI compiles and maintains a register of newspapers containing particulars about all the newspapers published in the country; it issues certificates of registration to the newspapers published under valid declaration. It scrutinizes and analyzes annual statements sent by the publishers of newspapers every year under Section 19-D of the Press and Registration of Books Act containing information on circulation, ownership, etc. The RNI informs the District Magistrates about availability of titles to intending publishers for filing declaration and ensures that newspapers are published in accordance with the provisions of the Press and Registration of Books Acts. It verifies under Section 19-F of the PRB Act of circulation claims, furnished by the publishers in their Annual Statements and Preparation and submission to the Government on or before September 30 each year, a report containing all available information and statistics about the press in India with particular reference to the emerging trends in circulation and in the direction of common ownership units.

Non-Statutory Functions

Non-statutory functions of the RNI include the formulation

of a Newsprint Allocation Policy-guidelines and the ability to issue Eligibility Certificates to the newspapers to enable them to import newsprint and to procure indigenous newsprint. The RNI assesses and certifies the essential needs and requirements of newspaper establishments to import printing and composing machinery and allied materials. From April 1998 to February 1999, RNI scrutinized 18,459 applications for availability of titles, of which 7,738 titles were found available for verification, while in the remaining applications, titles were not found available. During the same period, 2,693 newspapers/periodicals were issued Certificates of Registration (2,145 fresh CRs and 548 revised CRs) and circulation claims of 1536 newspapers/ periodicals were assessed.

NEWSPRINT

Until 1994-95, newsprint allocation was regulated by the Newsprint Control Order (1962) and the Newsprint Import Policy announced by the government every year. Newspapers were issued Entitlement Certificates for importation and purchase from the scheduled indigenous newsprint mills. However, Newsprint Policy is modified every year depending upon the import policy of the government. Newsprint has been placed under 'Open General License' with effect from May 1, 1995, and all types of newsprint became importable by all persons without any restriction. Under the latest newsprint policy/guidelines for the import of newsprint issued by the Ministry of Information and Broadcasting, authentication of certificate of registration is done by the Registrar of Newspapers for India for import of newsprint, on submission of a formal application and necessary documentary evidence.

DE-BLOCKING OF TITLES

For the first time in the history of RNI, a massive work of de-blocking 200,000 titles was undertaken. As per the decision, all such titles of newspapers were certified till December 31, 1995, and those publications which had not registered with RNI have been de-blocked. The work of entering registered titles has been completed and the lists have been dispatched to state governments. Nearly 150,000 of unused titles have become available for allocation to other newspapers from January 1, 1999.

PRINTING MACHINERY

The RNI is the sponsoring authority for the import of printing machinery and allied materials at the concessional rate of custom duty available to the newspapers. During April 1998-February 1999, applications of four newspaper establishments were recommended for import of printing machinery and allied equipment.

CENSORSHIP

Even though India is committed to the freedom of the press, censorship is not unknown to the media. With increased privatization and entrepreneurial advancements, colonial and bureaucratic censorship no longer exists. However, the nexus of criminal politics and unethical monopolies continue to threaten the freedom of press. Nehru famously said: "I would rather have a completely free press with all the dangers involved in the wrong use of that freedom than a suppressed or regulated press" (quoted by Kamath 272). After 1977 people's interest and involvement in regional and national affairs increased dramatically. This development helped promote the dualism of India's patriotic passions marked by linguistic chauvinism and national unity.

STATE-PRESS RELATIONS

A Public Grievances Cell is functioning in the Main Secretariat of the Ministry headed by the Joint Secretary (Policy). In order to tone up the Grievance Redressal System of the Ministry, its time limits have been fixed for completion of various activities coming under the purview of the grievance redressal mechanism. Grievance Officers have been appointed in all the subordinate organizations of the Ministry who have been made responsible for timely redress of grievances. Keeping in view the need for effective monitoring of the progress in the grievance redressal, the Ministry has developed a computerized Grievance Monitoring System. The grievances received in the Ministry are sent to the concerned Grievance Officer in the attached subordinate offices of the Ministry. Periodical review meetings are held in the Ministry to ensure that the grievances are processed within a stipulated time limit.

ATTITUDE TOWARD FOREIGN MEDIA

India is a founding member of the United Nations Educational, Scientific, and Cultural Organization (UNESCO). UNESCO's main goal is to promote international cooperation in the field of education, science and technology, social sciences, culture and mass communication. In order to promote the communication capabilities of developing countries. The 21st Session of the General Conference of UNESCO in 1981 approved the establishment of an International Program for the Development of Communication (IPDC).

India played a significant role in its inception and has been a member of the Inter-governmental Council (IGC) and also of the IPDC Bureau. India has played a leading role in its activities over the years. Being one of the founding members of IPDC, this Ministry has been a representative at the meetings of the General Conference of UNESCO and Bureau Session of IPDC. India participated in the First South Asian Association for Regional Cooperation (SAARC) Information Ministers Meeting held in Dhaka (Bangladesh) in 1998. The Meeting discussed the need for greater cooperation among media personnel, cooperation among news agencies, improving the programs under SAARC Audio Visual Exchange, and taking steps to project SAARC outside the region.

More indications of India's support of international cooperation is its participation in the meeting of Asia-Pacific Regional Experts on the Legal Framework for Cyberspace from 8 to 10 September 1998 and the Third Regulatory Round Table for the Asia and the Pacific at Seoul from 14 to 16 September 1998 for finalizing the report on Trans-border Satellite Broadcasting.

NEWS AGENCIES

News agencies provide regularity and authenticity to news. K.C. Roy is credited with establishing the first Indian news agency, which became The Associated Press of India (API). However, it soon became a British-controlled agency unwilling to report about the national freedom movement. The Free Press of India News Agency came into existence under the management of S. Sadanand who had served Reuters. The United Press of India, The Orient Press, The Globe News Agency, The NAFEN News Agency, The United News of India and a number of syndicates later came to serve the news business.

The Non-aligned News Agencies Pool (NANAP), formally constituted in 1976 for the purpose of correcting imbalances in the global flow of information, is an arrangement for exchange of news and information among the national news agencies of non-aligned countries, including Asia, Africa, Europe and Latin America. Its affairs are managed by a coordinating committee elected for a term of three years. India is at present a member of the coordinating committee. The cost of running the pool is met by the participating members.

The Press Trust (PTI) continued to operate the India News Pool Desk (INDP) of the NANAP on behalf of the government of India. India continued to contribute substantially to the daily news file of the Pool Network. The reception of news into the Pool Desk during the year 1998-99 has been in the range of 20,000 words per day. INDP's own contribution to the Pool partners during the year has averaged 7,000 words per day. The organization and structure of Indian news agencies has been undergoing a controversial transformation for quite sometime.

This represents a mutual mistrust between privately owned news agencies and governmental structures. Their autonomy, believed to be crucial for objectivity and fairness, is based on their role as cooperatives and non-profit groups. News agencies in general are discouraged from taking any governmental favors. There is nothing in the Indian constitution, however, that can prevent government to nationalize its news agencies. There are four dominant news agencies in India: The Press Trust of India (PTI); the United News of India (UNI); the Hindustan Samachar (HS); and Samachar Bhatia (SB).

BROADCAST MEDIA

The Ministry of Information & Broadcasting, through the mass communication media of radio, television, films, the press, publications, advertising and traditional modes of dance and drama, plays a significant part in helping the people to have access to information. It fosters the dissemination of knowledge and entertainment in all sectors of society, striking a careful balance between public interest and commercial needs in its delivery of services. The Ministry of Information & Broadcasting is the highest body for formulation and administration of the rules, regulations and laws relating to information, broadcasting, the press and films. The ministry is responsible for international cooperation in the field of mass media, films and broadcasting, and interacts with its foreign counterparts on behalf of Government of India.

The mandate of the Ministry of Information & Broadcasting is to provide:

* News Services through All India Radio (AIR) and Doordarshan (DD) for the people
* Development of broadcasting and television
* Import and export of films
* Development and promotion of film industry
* Organization of film festivals and cultural exchanges India
* Advertisement and visual publicity on behalf of the Government of India
* Handling of press relations to present the policies of Government of India and to seek feedback on government policies
* Administration of the Press and Registration of Books Act of 1867 in respect of newspapers
* Dissemination of information about India within and outside the country through publications on matters of national importance
* Research, reference, and training to assist the media units of the Ministry to meet their responsibilities

* Use of interpersonal communication and traditional folk art forms for information/publicity campaigns on public interest issues
* International co-operation in the field of information and mass media

The main Secretariat of the Ministry is divided into three wings: the information wing, the broadcasting wing, and the film wing. The media units engaged in press and publicity activities include:

* Press: 1) Press Information Bureau; 2) Photo Division; 3) Research Reference & Training Division; 4) Publications Division
* Publicity: 5) Directorate of Advertising and Visual Publicity; 6) Directorate of Field Publicity; 7) Song and Drama Division
* Regulation of the Press: 8) Registrar of Newspapers for India; 9) Press Council of India
* Training: 10) Indian Institute of Mass Communication (Government of India, 2002).

MASS MEDIA AND COMMUNICATION

At the beginning of the third millennium, it hardly needs any emphasis that journalism and mass media or simply the "press" plays a central rolc in modern society. Even in the early 18th century, the press was recognised as a powerful entity. Thomas Carlyle (1795-1881) wrote that the British statesman Edmund Burke (1729-97) called the reporters' gallery in the British Parliament "a Fourth Estate more important by far" than the other three estates of Parliament-the peers, bishops, and commons. A Similar statement, however, is attributed to the English historian, Thomas Babington Macaulay (1800-1859) who in his Essay On Hallam's Constitutional History Published in Edinburgh Review (September 1828), observed with reference to the press gallery of the House of Commons, "The gallery in which the reporters sit has become a fourth estate of the realm". And over time, newspapers, news magazines, radio, television, cable video, video Cassettes and movies have been demanding more and more of our attention and leisure time. The mass media now markedly affect our politics, our recreation, our education in general and profoundly our culture, our perception and our understanding of the world around us. However, Prof. (Herbert) Marshall Mcluhan (1911-1980), whose theories on mass communication caused widespread debate, argued that each major period of history is characterised, not by the mass media per se, but by the nature of the medium of communication (print or electronic) used most widely at the time. In this Chapter will be discussed educational opportunities in four interrelated areas of studies, viz., Journalism and Mass Communication, Communication Studies, Public Relations, and Advertising. However, it would be in order to present first an overview of the media world, the role of the government, and to explain several terminologies.

MEDIA TERMINOLOGIES

First, a few words about the various terms used in this field because many such terms occur in admission advertisements. The term "journalism" often referred to as "news business" involves the gathering, processing, and delivery of important information relating to current affairs by the print media (news papers and new magazines), and electronic media (radio and TV). This integrated entity is also simply called "media". News and entertainment are communicated in a number of different ways using different media. The world "media" is often used to refer to the communication of news, and in this context means the same as news media. Media and mass media are often used when discussing the power of modern communication.

If there is a term that has appeared in more diverse publications than any other over the last few years, it is "multimedia". The number of definitions for it is as numerous as the number of companies that are involved in multimedia business. In essence, multimedia is the use or presentation of information in two or more forms. The combination of audio and video in film and television was probably the first multimedia application. It is the advent of the PC, with its ability to manipulate data from different sources and offer this directly to the consumers or subscribers that has sparked the current interest. In the context of mass media and communication, multimedia is an effective tool for the profession. Still journalism, which has long history beginning almost with the invention of printing, continues to be the core concept of the entire process of communication. The newer communication technologies, in fact, have been strengthening the cause of journalism and newspapers, the latest to appear on the scene being the Internet. However, education in multimedia is mainly offered by private IT institutes (e.g., Arena Multimedia).

THE MEDIA WORLD

The media world consists of a wide variety of agencies and organisations which are involved in media related activities. At its core are the mass media organisations per se and the users of mass media. The first category consists of:

(i) the print media (newspapers and magazines),

(ii) the electronic media (radio and television channels), and

(iii) the news agencies.

The electronic media now includes the World Wide Web (WWW) which hosts Internet versions of most of the well-known newspapers and news magazines and is also emerging as a potential advertisement medium.

In the second category are:

(i) the advertisers and advertising agencies, and

(ii) the public relations agencies. Advertising provide the financial sustenance to the mass media and their survival depends upon advertisements. Public relation agencies interact with the mass media to put across their messages.

They also have their own mechanisms to reach their target audience groups. Besides, there are other institutions and organisations associated with media related activities. They include:

(1) audit agencies which vouch for the circulation figures of the print media;

(2) agencies conducting readership surveys;

(3) schools of journalism and mass communication;

(4) statutory and non-statutory organisations dealing with regulatory and ethical issues; and

(5) organisations representing various interest groups in the media world.

Last but not the least, there are facilitators, such as the chain of distributors of the print media and the TV cable operators, who provide the vital link between the products of media organisations and their consumers.

However, apart from functional relationships among mass media, advertising, and public relations, from academic point of view what is necessary to appreciate is that at the heart of these three activities is the art and science of communication. The practitioners is these areas strive to communicate with their respective target audience groups, adopting the most effective communication strategies. The term communication, however, has a much wider connotation encompassing many fields of studies, the major areas being sociology and psychology, linguistics, cybernetics and information theory, and the study of non-verbal communication. Sociology and psychology produced the first academic studies in mass communication during the 1930s. Thereafter, many scholars studied the effects of mass communication on individuals and society. As will be discussed later, the theory and process of communication indeed has profoundly influenced the study of journalism and mass communication.

JOURNALISM AND MASS COMMUNICATION

Journalism education in the narrow sense prepares students for careers in newspapers, news magazines, broadcast news, and news services. Now it encompasses a much wider area under the broad label "mass communication ". By what ever name it may be called, journalism and mass communication study is not a discipline in the sense that sociology, economics, political science or history is, but a rather loose interdisciplinary field covering a wide range of issues somehow related to public concerns. As such, the field reflects in general, the growth of mass communication itself.

JOURNALISM EDUCATION IN THE USA

A brief account of the development of journalism education in the USA will be helpful in understanding the current trend in journalism and mass communication education in India. Journalism education which has a beginning in English Departments in America universities focussed more on techniques, such as, reporting, news writing, editing, design, photography. Often they were taught by former journalists. Willard G Bleyer, a professor of English in the University of Wisconsin may be called the father of journalism education. He was instrumental in introducing the first journalism course in the University in 1905 and his scholarly interests later greatly influenced the field.

However, the country's first school of Journalism came into existence in 1908 at the University of Missouri. This was followed by the establishment of the Graduate School of Journalism in 1911 at the Columbia University backed with a $2 million gift from Joseph Pulitzer (1846-1911), publisher of the New York World, Pulitzer is also remembered for the Pulitzer Prizes, also funded by him, and annually awarded for excellence in journalism, letters and music. The School, still rated as one of the best journalism schools in the USA, is the publisher of the scholarly journal Columbia Journalism Review published since 1961. Now there are 427 colleges and universities which offer programmes in journalism and mass communication.

The focus on newspapers continued to dominate journalism education throughout the 1940s at leading Schools of Journalism in the USA. With the emergence of radio and television as major news and entertainment media, the journalism schools incorporated such topics as radio news, television news and broadcasting production techniques in their programmes. Even the Speech Departments, offshoots of English Departments, became involved in the preparation of students for careers in broadcasting. In some universities, the speech of communication arts department were merged with the journalism programmes.

Around the same time, more and more journalism schools started offering courses in advertising and public relations, giving rise to the term "mass communication" to describe this amalgam of courses on newspapers, radio, television, news magazines, and an increasing involvement with the study of communication itself. Communication study as an academic discipline has long been a part of social sciences in the American higher education. It involves the study of mass media and other social institutions devoted, among other, to persuasion, communication processes and their effects, audience studies, contents analysis, and interpersonal communication.

Wilbur Schramm, a leading scholar of communication studies, who taught at University of Iowa, Illinois and Stanford, is credited with popularising communication studies in journalism departments. Increasingly, graduate programmes became more concerned with communication theory while undergraduate courses stressed pre-professional training for careers in news media, advertising, and public relations. However, such emphasis on communication has its share of criticism too. It has been argued that communication and media studies hardly have anything to do with the practice of journalism.

The increased emphasis on communication theory at the expense of basic reporting and writing skill has also led to the scrapping of exclusive journalism courses in some universities. The shifting of focus from conventional journalism to communication is reflected in the rechristening the Schools and Departments of Journalism as School of Journalism and Mass Communication, Department of Communication, or Schools of Communication. Some of the well-known schools, however, did not change their names. At Missouri and at Columbia they continue to be the School of Journalism and Graduate Department of Journalism, respectively.

GOVERNMENT OF MASS MEDIA

Governments and press are widely perceived as mutual adversaries. Freedom of the Press-the right of the press to report and to criticise the wrong doings of the powerful without retaliation or threat of retaliation-is the cornerstone of democracy. Freedom of the Press in the United States is more than a legal concept-almost a religious tenet. The First

Amendment to the US Constitution states clearly and unequivocally that the "Congress Shall Make No Law. Abridging Freedom of Speech or of the Press". The Indian Constitution does not have similar provision, but Art 19 (1) (a) protects the right to freedom of speech and expression subject to reasonable restrictions as mentioned in Art 19 (2) Though many governments vouch for protecting the freedom of the press, there are instances galore of throttling the press. There are several agencies in various countries which fight for the cause of press freedom. Be that as it may, governments themselves are also major users of mass media for putting across their messages.

The Ministry of Information and Broadcasting which was set up during the Second World War to mobilise support for war efforts, is now a very large mass media organisation of the Government of India. It performs its tasks through a number of specialised media units and other organisation. One of its most important units, the Directorate of Advertising and Visual Publicity (DAVP), is the primary multimedia advertising agency of the Central Government which uses about 6,240 newspapers for press advertisement. The Ministry, besides its own mass media activities performs several statutory functions, the most important of which is the registration of newspapers and periodicals. The Office of the Registrar of Newspapers in India (RNI), commonly known as Press Registrar, was created in 1956 in accordance with the Section 19A of the Press and Registration of regulation of titles of newspapers and periodicals, followed by their registration and allocation of registration numbers.

It is also responsible for the verification of circulation claims, receiving Annual Statements of registered newspapers and periodicals, and compiling and publishing the annual report titled `Press in India' containing detailed information about the print media, a valuable media reference tool. Another important statutory quasi-judicial authority, under the umbrella of the Ministry, is the Press Council of India (PCI). The objectives of the PCI established under the Indian Press Council Act 1978, are to preserve the freedom of the press and to maintain and improvement of standards of newspapers and news agencies.

The Ministry of Labour, on the other hand, is responsible for the operation of the provisions of two Acts relating to the employees of newspaper establishments: (1) The Working Journalists and Other Newspaper Employees (Conditions of Service) and Miscellaneous Provisions Act, 1955, and (2) The Working Journalists Act, 1958. The first Act provides for the constitution of two separate Wage Boards for fixing or revising rates of wages of working journalists (including those working in news agencies) and non-journalist newspaper employees.

So far five Wage Boards had been set up. The fifth one (Manisana Wage Board) set up in 1994, has submitted its tentative proposals on December 12, 1999. Besides, there are a number of Acts which directly or indirectly affect the mass media. Annexure 5 gives a list of some important ones. In December, 1999, the Government has introduced in the Parliament the Freedom of Information Bill. When enacted, it is likely to have a far reaching favourable effect on mass media. So far five States viz., Goa, Karnataka, Maharashtra, Rajasthan, and Tamil Nadu also have enacted similar laws.

MEDIA EDUCATION IN INDIA

In India, the very notion of journalism education in universities was looked at with askance. A write-up published in the Times of India (November 27, 1934) shares the most commonly held view of the time that "journalists are born and not made". It observed, "A faculty for criticism, a flair for essentials and a sense of news values can be developed by experience only if these qualities are innate from the beginning... The actual basis of journalism is its various departments can be only be acquired by direct contact and often bitter experience". Almost all the famous journalists of yesteryears learnt journalism on the job starting as "cub" reporters. Even many of the celebrated editors and columnists did not undergo any formal training in journalism. The credit for making journalism as a subject of study goes to Dr. Annie Besant, the distinguished theosophist and freedom fighter. The course in the National University (Adyar) introduced by her, however, did not survive. There were several other abortive attempts also. The oldest surviving Department of Journalism in the Indian sub-continent was established at Punjab University in Lahore (now in Pakistan) in 1914. After partition, the Department continued to function at the New Delhi campus of the Indian part of the divided Punjab University till July 1962. At present, it offers a two-year integrated Master of Mass Communication (MMC) programme. From 1947 to 1954, there were only five university departments of journalism:

(1) University of Madras (1947),

(2) University of Calcutta (1950),

(3) University of Mysore (1951),

(4) Nagpur University (1952) and

(5) Osmania University (1954),

Both the First (1952-54) and the Second (1980-82) Press Commissions emphasised the need for expanding the scope of journalism education. The Second Press Commission recommended the establishment of a National Council for Journalism and Communication Research. It also highlighted the need for inter-disciplinary approach in journalism education and recommended that admission should be based on the performance in aptitude tests. It was in 1963, that the Ford Foundation Mass Communication Study Team headed by Wilbur Schramm, who, as stated earlier greatly influenced journalism education in the USA, recommended the expansion of the scope of journalism education by broadening the curriculum to include mass communication, advertising, public relations and Radio and TV journalism, to fall in line with the American system. The Ford Foundation report set the trend of journalism and mass communication education in India.

It also led to the establishment in 1965, of the Indian Institute of Mass Communication at New Delhi, by the Ministry of Information and Broadcasting which over a period, has introduced separate courses in these areas. In 1981, the University Grants Commission published the Report on the Status of Journalism and Communication Education in India, which recommended various measures for the strengthening the University Departments of Journalism and improvement in the quality of education. In another document, English Plan Perspective on Journalism/Communication Education in India published in 1990-91, the UGC unveiled a proposal for strengthening of selected universities departments.

With the broadening of curriculum to include the various dimensions of mass communication, the Indian Universities followed the examples of their US counterparts and started incorporating the terms "communication" and "mass communication" in their names. Many new Departments do not even include the term "journalism" in their names. The nomenclature of both the degrees, Bachelor of Journalism (BJ), and Master of Journalism (MJ), accordingly were changed by some universities to incorporate the terms "communication", "mass communication", such as, Bachelor of Communication and Journalism (BCJ), Bachelor of Journalism and Mass Communication (BJMC), Master of Communication and Journalism (MCJ), and Master of Journalism and Mass Communication (MJMC).

In some other universities the nomenclature of the Master's degree courses in MA (Journalism), or MA (Communication and Journalism). Yet in some universities the term "Journalism" does not occur at all, for example, MA, MS or M.Sc (Communication, or Mass Communication), Master of Communication Studies (MCS), Master of Mass Communication (MMC), The choice of nomenclature often reflects the incorporation, in varying degrees, the components of the "journalism", "mass communication" and "communication" in the course curricula.

In the programmes with such labels as "Journalism" or "Journalism and Mass Communication", while topics such as communication theory and broadcast journalism (TV and Radio) are covered, the focus of graduate programmes is more on the basics of print journalism methods and techniques. In the latter category, apart from the preponderance of communication theory and process along with such issued as development communication, rural communication, educational communication, media research, the trust of many programmes is shifting towards TV and video production, web reporting and publishing, and Internet journalism. However, course contents vary from university to university. Advertising and public relations are covered in almost all the courses. The application of Information Technology (IT) of late is demanding more attention in many programmes.

EDUCATIONAL OPPORTUNITIES

There has been now a proliferation of university courses in journalism in packages of different combinations of topics. The number of universities offering journalism and related courses now exceeds 75. An exclusive journalism university, Makhanlal Chaturvedi Rashtriya Patrakarita Vishwavidyalaya, was established in Bhopal in 1990. The objective of the university is to develop itself into a national centre for teaching, training and research of journalism and mass communication through the medium of Hindi. It however, received considerable flak for its greater involvement in franchising out its BCA course to all and sundry throughout the country, rather then striving to achieve excellence in Hindi journalism. At present it offers nine journalism related courses. Several institutions outside the university system also offer these courses, which include, as stated, earlier, the Indian Institution of Mass Communication. Some of these institutions have been sponsored by newspaper establishments, such as, Eenadu School of Journalism, Times Journalism (Indian Express Group). Some members of the Indian Newspaper Society took the initiative to promote the Press Foundation of India to provide opportunities for training and retraining of journalists.

It may be mentioned that the Film and Television Institute of India (FTTI) (Pune) is the first institution to introduce courses in TV Production. Besides FTTI, its counterpart in Calcutta, Satyajit Ray Film & Television Institute, and several other institutions offer programmes in Television. The National Institute of Design (Ahmedabad) has courses in the area of Communication Design which include Print Media, Audiovisuals and Video Film. Levels of Education: Education in journalism and mass communication is offered at the first degree (three-year BA degree), postgraduate Bachelor's degree (BJ/BCJ/BJMC, etc.,) Master's degree (MJ/MCJ/MJMC, etc.,) and pre-doctoral and doctoral levels. Besides, some universities offer the subject as one of the combinations at the first degree levels. Three-year BA degree courses, open to candidates who have passed 10+2 examination, are available only in the affiliated colleges of University of Delhi and Bangalore University. There are also diploma and certificate courses in a number of universities. M.Phil and Doctoral programmes are also available in some universities.

The Bachelor's degree course is of one year duration and open to degree holders in any discipline. Master's degree, also of one year duration, is open to Bachelor's degree holders in journalism. The MA course in the subject, which is of two-year duration, is open to Bachelor's degree holders in any discipline. A number of universities have started introducing two year integrated programmes, instead of separate one year programmes leading successively to Bachelor and Master degrees. The diploma courses are of one-year duration and the entry requirement is mostly a degree in any discipline. The certificate courses are open to undergraduates.

Distance Learning Courses

About 18 universities offer journalism and mass communication courses at different levels through distance learning mode which include five open universities, viz., Indira Gandhi National Open University, Kota Open University, Karnataka State Open University, Nalanda Open University, and Yashwantrao Chavan Maharashtra Open University.

Specialised Courses

There are stray instances of journalism courses in specific areas e.g.,

Language Journalism

Although, both in terms of the number and circulation, Indian language newspapers far outnumber those in English, only a small number of universities offer courses in language journalism. As of now, there are courses only in Hindi, Urdu and Telugu journalism. Two universities offer courses in Hindi journalism: (1) Avinashilingam Institute for Home Science of Higher Education for Women-MA in Hindi Journalism, (2) Banaras Hindu University-MA (Functional Hindi) in Journalism, and PG Diploma in Hindi Journalism of two-year duration (after MA). As stated earlier, the Makhanlal Chaturvedi Rashtriya Patrakarita Vishwavidyalaya was established to promote journalism and mass communication through the medium of Hindi. Indian Institute of Mass Communication has a postgraduate Diploma course in Hindi Journalism.

Urdu journalism is taught only in Jawaharlal Nehru University. It offers an Advance Diploma in Mass Media course with Urdu as one of the subjects. Potti Sreeramulu Telugu University and Eenadu School of Journalism offer Journalism courses in Telugu. While the former offer BJ and MJ programmes, the latter has introduced a Diploma course. The Eenadu Journalism School established by Eenadu, the largest circulated Telugu daily, deserves special mention. Eenadu is the first newspaper in the country to establish a school of journalism. It offers a Diploma course in Journalism of six months duration.

Candidates who successfully complete the course with merit would undergo further TV channels. Candidates are paid a fellowship of Rs.2,000 per month during the course and Rs.3,400 per month while undergoing advanced training. After successful completion of the advances training, candidates will be put on probation. Eligibility requirements are: (a) graduate degree, (b) proficiency in English and Telugu, (c) flair for writing in Telugu, (d) age not more than 25 years. Admissions are made on the basis of reporting and editing, and an orientation in political, economic, geographical, and legal aspects relevant to print and visual media.

Public Relations

Public Relations (PR), one of the newest management disciplines, means different things to different people. It is widely perceived as the profession of corporate image making, a "lobbying" mechanism or "fixing things", and also as a face-saving device employed by organisations who find themselves in deep trouble. Yet others equated PR with publicity and propaganda. A PR professional once wryly described PR as "the art of making friends you don't need". Be that as it may, PR is a reality and is practised world over by organisations which have something to do with their publics. It has now attained the status of specialised profession of communication management. However, the definitions of PR are legion. There are as many definitions as there are PR "gurus". Dr R F Harlow, a PR practitioner, culled out 472 definitions from various sources. Analysing them, he put forward a sort of working definition thus: "Public relations is a distinctive management function which helps establish and maintain mutual lines of communication. Understanding, acceptance and cooperation between an organisation and its publics; involves the management of problems or issues; help management to keep informed on and responsive to public opinion; defines and emphasizes the responsibility of management to serve the public interest; helps management keep abreast of effectively utilising change, serving as an early warning system to help anticipate trends; and uses research and sound and ethical communication as its principle tools".

The concept of PR as a distinct branch of communication is comparatively a recent one, though it is an ancient practice. Perhaps, it was the American Telephone and Telegraph Company (now AT & T) which coined the term "public relations" and used it in its annual report for 1908. It is the Second World War that brought about new opportunities to the PR work. The International Public Relations Association was formed in 1955 and simultaneously many countries including India established national professional for a. In India it was the Tatas which first set up a PR Department in 1942.

In a sense, in India the first PR exercise on a very large scale was undertaken by the Government of India with the creation of a new Ministry of Information and Broadcasting in the 1940s. Its main function was to mobilise public opinion in favour of the war efforts in a situation where the Indian National Congress and national sentiment generally were against the war efforts. The professionalism in PR may be said to have emerged with the establishment in 1958 of the Public Relations Society of India (PRSI). It was not until 1968 when the first national level conference of PRSI which adopted Code of Ethics and defined the parameters of the PR profession that it earned a sort of professional respectability.

With 28 regional chapters, the PRSI is now a national organisation involved in promoting PR along ethical lines and develop human resources through seminars, conferences and training programmes. It also publishes a professional journal `Public Relations'. As stated earlier PR has a symbiotic relationship with mass media and advertising. Though public relations, and advertising are different professions yet they are interdependent. Often, the two have similar goals, a shared audience and the same media vehicles. As such, PR practitioners need the same level of communication skills and the knowledge of communications techniques as that of journalism and advertising professionals.

Public Relations Departments, often known as Corporate Communication Departments, exist in major business and industrial organisations. All the government agencies at different levels, both at the Centre and the States, have PR Departments. The international organisations of the Un family and even large non-governmental organisations (NGOs) fell the need for PR units. Besides, there are a large number of PR organisations, often set up by the advertising agencies, which provide PR service to a large number organisations although some of them have their own PR outfits. There are also a large number of individual PR consultants. Among the PR tools are press releases, press conferences, seminars, annual reports of the organisations, house magazines and newsletters, films, charitable donations, sponsorship of events (such as, sports and games, music recitals), community relations and last but not the least PR advertising, as distinct aimed at building a positive corporate image of an organisation in the context of its community on subjects of welfare or seeking to educate or inform the community on subjects of public interest, such as, road safety, immunisation; AIDS, family welfare.

Educational Opportunities

It has been mentioned earlier that PR is one of the essential components of almost all the courses in journalism and mass communication. The number of stand-alone courses in PR, however, is limited. Often the courses cover both PR and advertising. Most of the courses are at the diploma level offered by both universities and non-universities institutions. The courses generally cover such subjects as communication tools media of PR, media planning, editing and proof reading, advertising writing press releases, media production techniques. Annexure 12 gives a list of institutions which offer the courses at different levels.

Advertising

Way back in 1759, Samuel Johnson (1709-84) the English poet, critic and lexicographer observed "Promise, large promise, is the soul of an advertisement" (The Idler No.40, 20 January 1759). Stephen Leacock (1869-1944), a Canadian humourist described advertising "as the science of arresting human intelligence long enough to get money from it" (Garden of Folly (1924)-"The Perfect Salesman"). Leacock's dig at advertising perhaps signifies its enormous power. Though many TV watchers curse advertisers and their advertising agencies for the number of commercial breaks to show advertisements in between TV programmes, consciously and often willingly or unwillingly, they listen to their message and more often than not succumb to the allurements. In fact, we now live in an "advertisement-laden" society. Advertisements stare at us from the pages of newspapers and glossy magazines, TV screen and the huge outdoor billboards, often illuminated ones in the night. We cannot escape online advertisements while surfing the Internet. And now advertising via wireless devices carrying messages to the cell phone is in the offing!

Advertisements, a Marketing Management function, has been defined by the American Marketing Association as "any paid form of non-personal presentation and promotion of ideas, goals or services by an identified sponsor". In other words, advertisements involve purchasing time or space in such mass media as television, radio newspapers or magazines to explain, or to urge or to persuade the use or adoption of a product, service or an idea. The field of advertisement management is made up of a system of interacting organisations and institutions, all of which play a role in the advertising process.

At the core of the system are advertisers, the organisations that provide financial resources that support advertising. Advertisers are private and public sector organisations, that use mass media to achieve their respective organisational objectives. Increasingly, political parties are using advertising as a major tool for election campaign. The two other components of the system are: (i) advertising agencies, and (ii) the media that carry the advertisements. Another important adjunct of the advertising industry is the advertising models. Many celebrated women models went on to win laurels in beauty contests, both national and international, and made their marks in films. The expenditure incurred by advertisers provides the basis for estimates of the size of the burgeoning advertising industry.

According to the Eleventh A&M Agency Report prepared by the prestigious A&M magazines (15 September 2000), the total advertisement expenditure of 200 top spenders in 1998-99 was Rs.3,914.7 crore representing 2.3% of their sales. The top 200 spenders account for 90% of the total expenditure. However, the report is based on the data provided by advertising agencies and thus excludes expenditures incurred by small and private organisations which buy media space or time directly, the Central Governments and State Governments which release advertisements through the Directorate of Audio-Visual Publicity (DAVP), and Departments of Information and Public Relations, respectively.

Though the advertisers provide the nutrients, it is advertising agencies which are the backbone of the advertising industry and make things happen. The importance of advertising agencies has increased because the era of brand loyalty is almost a thing of the past. It is the agencies which now create brand images for new products and resurrect those of the fading ones. The agencies vary in size, organisation structure and services they offer. Large agencies have networks of branch offices in major cities. According to the A&M Agency Report, during 1999-2000, of the top 89 agencies, the first 15 garnered more than 65% of the gross income. Advertisement agencies do the planning for their clients, create advertisements, and select the appropriate media for placing them. Advertisement planning involves market research. Most of the big agencies, therefore, have in-house market research facilities, e.g., Indian Market Research Bureau, (IMRB), a Division of the Hindustan Thompson Associate. Besides, there are also independent agencies, such as, MARG Marketing and Research Group, and Operations Research Group (ORG). The Advertisers' Handbook (1999-2000), listed more than 690 accredited agencies.

Two of the oldest agencies are Hindustan Thompson Associates (1929) and Ogilvy & Mather (1928). Incidentally, David M Ogilvy (1911-1999), the most revered, albeit controversial, advertisement "guru" is the founder of Ogilvy & Mather. Besides, about 660 non-accredited agencies are also listed in it. As stated elsewhere, the Indian Newspaper Society (INS) operates the system of accreditation of advertising agencies. One of the conditions for accreditation is that the agency should be completely independent without control or ownership of the media or clients. The INS also has framed conditions for accepting advertisements from accredited advertising agencies by INS member publications. The income of advertising agencies comes mostly from commissions received not from the clients but from the advertising media. As stated earlier, the Directorate of Advertisement and Visual Publicity (DAVP) is the advertising agency of the Government of India. The Advertisement policy of the Government of India says that in "pursuance of broad social objectives of the Government and in order to achieve parity of rate between various categories of newspapers, appropriate weightage/consideration may be given to:

(1) small and medium newspapers and journals,
(2) specialised scientific and technical journals,
(3) language newspapers and journals, and
(4) newspapers and journals published especially in backward, remote, and border areas.

Many big advertisers and the print an electronic media have their own advertising departments which generally liaise with advertising agencies.

Advertising agencies have three different associations, to look after the business interest, viz., the Advertising Agencies Association of India (1948) (Mumbai), the National Council of Advertising Agencies (1967) (New Delhi), and the Indian Society of Advertisers (Mumbai). Besides, the Advertising Standards Council of India (1985) (Mumbai) comprising advertisers, advertising agencies, newspapers, magazines and others involved in advertising has prepared a Code for Self-Regulation in Advertising to create a sense of responsibility for its observance amongst advertisers, advertising agencies and others connected with the creation of advertising, and the media.

Educational Opportunities

Educational opportunities in advertising are very limited, although advertising along with relations are included in the journalism and mass communication courses. Advertisement Management is also component of marketing management in management programmes. As the courses in the topic are mostly available at the diploma level and often combined with public relations. The programmes offered by the Mudra Institute of Communications (MICA) set up by Mudra Communications, the third largest advertisement agency, deserves mention.

It offers three programmes:

(1) Postgraduate Programme in Communication,

(2) Programme in Creating Advertising, and

(3) Faculty Induction Programme.

The postgraduate programme open to graduates, offers specialisation in Brand Stewardship and Account Management, Marketing Research, Direct Marketing, Corporate Communication, and Media Planning and Marketing. Admission is based on the CAT score. The second programme of three-month duration is offered in collaboration with the National Institute of Design. The specialisation offered copywriting and

Art Direction. Eligibility requirement is a Bachelor's degree for the Art direction course. Computer literacy is an essential requirement. The third programme of two-year duration is aimed at developing teachers to be absorbed in MICA itself, Eligibility requirement is a Master's degree with experience in research, teaching, marketing, journalism, media and advertising. The selected candidates are given a stipend of Rs.10,000 per month during the first year and Rs.12,000 per month in the second year.

Indian Newspaper Society (INS): INS brings out a comprehensive annual reference publication titled the INS Press Handbook (both print and CD version) which contains detailed particulars of member newspapers and magazines, accredited advertising agencies, important newspapers and media organisations, accredited press correspondents, etc. Course on Online Journalism and Internet: Career Launcher, a Delhi-based preparatory education outfit had set up a journalism school called School of Contemporary Media to offer a programme on online journalism and web writing.

Career Opportunities

Journalism and Mass Communication: Career opportunities in journalism and mass communication exist in newspapers, news magazines, news agencies, TV Channels as well as in advertising and PR agencies. However, the bulk of journalists are employed in newspapers, news magazines and news agencies. Newspapers differ in language, size, circulation and as such the number and the category of staff vary widely. As stated earlier, the wage structure of journalists (rather working journalists) is governed by the recommendations of the Wage Boards for Working Journalists set up by the Ministry of Labour from time to time. The wage structure of various categories of working journalists is in turn determined by the size of the gross revenue of newspapers.

The Bachawar Wage Board (1984) classified the newspaper establishments into ten classes. At the top is Class IA with a gross revenue of Rs.100 crore followed by Class I (Rs.50 crore and above, but less than Rs.100 crore) and at the lowest level is the Class IX (less than Rs.25 lakh). The Manisana Wage Board (1994) reportedly has introduced a new classification with ten classes, introducing a new class IB at the top and merging Class IX with VIII. The Bachawat Wage Board grouped the working journalists into eight categories for newspaper establishments belonging to Class IA to VII. Annexure 14 gives the designations included in each category. However, the designations may vary. A perusal of such news magazines, as India Today, The Week, Outlook will give an idea about the positions obtaining in the increasing crop of news magazines.

Generally, fresh entrants to the profession being as sub-editors or junior reporters, often as trainees. Merely passing out of journalism school does not make one a good journalist. Four most important qualities of a prospective journalist are: (i) possession of what is called a "nose for news", (ii) general acquaintance with socio-economic, and political environment; (iii) knowledge of authoritative sources of background information about issues handled; (iv) skills for gathering sifting and analysing information and present it as lucidly as possible. The last one needs command over the language of the newspaper and a flair for writing. In addition, computer literacy is a must in modern day journalism. All these skills can be developed only through hard painstaking work.

This is now the age of specialisation. More and more specialised features and supplements relating to science, technology, education, environment, women, fashion are now being added to newspapers. The number of news magazines in the areas of business and industry, finance, economics are also growing. A formal educational qualification in these subjects would go a long way for making a mark in specialised areas of the profession. Whether electronic newspapers will be economically viable enough to replace the print media is still a matter of conjecture. However, the stunning possibility of Internet for journalism and the news business are somewhat obvious. The Internet multimedia information retrieval system on the WWW is on the verge of becoming a mass medium itself. The journalists of today and tomorrow must take note of the ongoing information revolution and prepare themselves for the future. The schools of Journalism in the country, therefore, should catch up with the revolutionary developments that are taking place in the field of information technology. Students should be taught how to navigate the www to get most out of the cast information resources now available online. Besides, they need to be exposed to some of the techniques involved in the creation of web pages, reporting and writing for electronic newspapers, cyber laws and ethics.

Public Relations: As has been states earlier, hardly there are any institution and organisations, which do not need PR professionals. However, job profiles differ from organisation to organisation. For new entrants. PR is a job that literally keeps them on their toes where only sheer hard work leads to a successful career. At this stage, they are often little more than errand boys doing different kinds of work. This is particularly true in the PR units of an organisation. As they go up the career ladder they enter into specialised functional areas. It is in the large PR agencies that the job prospects are bright.

Advertising: Though the advertisers and advertising departments of mass media organisations offer opportunities in advertising, it is the advertising agencies which provides really challenging professionals responsibilities. The types of tasks in advertising agencies vary from department to department and as such each task needs different type of training requirement and skills. A mid-size agency has typically four core departments, viz., client servicing, creative, media, and art production departments, besides other support services, such as, finance and accounts. The client servicing department provided the link between the agency and the client on the one hand, and with other departments in the agency, on the other. It is basically, a management function. Larger agencies, therefore, prefer persons with a management degree or advertising qualification.

The Creative Department, which actually creates the advertisement, is perceived as the most glamorous one in an advertising agency. It engages two types of people-visualisers and copywriters. Visualisers are artists who are responsible for the layout and visual aspects of the advertisement. Copywriters, on the other hand, prepare the copy, i.e., the written part of the advertisement or scripts for TV commercials. A visualiser should have a formal qualification in art or design. With increasing use of computers in designing work, familiarity with its use is a desirable requirement. A short-term course in multimedia designing would help in the profession. Though for copywriters, no specific formal qualification is necessary, they should have a good command over the language used for the copy, and have the ability to get across the message most effectively. By and large, the copy is written in English and thereafter translated into the language of the medium. Proficiency in English and a regional language (mother tongue) is the desirable requirement.

NEWS MEDIA

The news media refers to the section of the mass media that focuses on presenting current news to the public. These include print media (newspapers, magazines); broadcast media (radio stations, television stations, television networks), and increasingly Internet-based media.

Usually the term includes all working journalists and is often used by those who would make generalizations about the product of "most" journalists, for example that journalists who work for large media corporations, or who are based in New York City or Washington, D.C, harbor a liberal or conservative bias. The term news trade refers to the concept of the news media as a business separate from, but integrally connected to, the profession of journalism.

Etymology

A medium (plural media) is a carrier of something. Common things carried by media include information, art, or physical objects. A medium may provide transmission or storage of information or both. The industries which produce news and entertainment content for the mass media are often called "the media" (in much the same way the newspaper industry is called "the press"). In the late 20th century it became commonplace for this usage to be construed as singular ("The media is...") rather than as the traditional plural.

Broadcasting

Broadcasting is the distribution of audio and video signals (programs) to a number of recipients ("listeners" or "viewers") that belong to a large group. This group may be the public in general, or a relatively large audience within the public. Thus, an Internet channel may distribute text or music world-wide, while a public address system in (for example) a workplace may broadcast very limited ad hoc soundbites to a small population within its range.

The sequencing of content in a broadcast is called a schedule. Television and radio programs are distributed through radio broadcasting or cable, often both simultaneously. By coding signals and having decoding equipment in homes, the latter also enables subscription-based channels and pay-per-view services.

A broadcasting organisation may broadcast several programs at the same time, through several channels (frequencies), for example BBC One and Two. On the other hand, two or more organisations may share a channel and each use it during a fixed part of the day. Digital radio and digital television may also transmit multiplexed programming, with several channels compressed into one ensemble. When broadcasting is done via the Internet the term webcasting is often used. Broadcasting forms a very large segment of the mass media. Broadcasting to a very narrow range of audience is called narrowcasting.

Newsmagazines

A newsmagazine, sometimes called news magazine, is a usually weekly magazine featuring articles on current events. News magazines generally go a little more in-depth into stories than newspapers, trying to give the reader an understanding of the context surrounding important events, rather than just the facts. Major news magazines include:

- o Der Spiegel (Germany)
- o La Repubblica (Italy)
- o Le Nouvel Observateur (France)
- o Maclean's Magazine (Canada)

- o New African (Africa)
- o Newsweek (United States)
- o Frontline (India)
- o The Bulletin (Australia)
- o The Economist (United Kingdom)
- o The Nation (United States)
- o The Week (United Kingdom/United States)
- o TIME (United States)
- o U.S. News & World Report (United States)
- o Veja (Brazil)
- o WORLD (United States).

Newspapers

A newspaper is a lightweight and disposable publication (more specifically, a periodical), usually printed on low-cost paper called newsprint. It may be general or special interest, and may be published daily, weekly, biweekly, monthly, bimonthly, or quarterly. General-interest newspapers are usually journals of current news on a variety of topics. Those can include political events, crime, business, sports, and opinions (either editorials, columns, or political cartoons). Many also include weather news and forecasts. Newspapers increasingly use photographs to illustrate stories; they also often include comic strips and other entertainment, such as crosswords.

Newsreels

A newsreel is a documentary film that is regularly released in a public presentation place containing filmed news stories. Created by Pathé Frères of France in 1908, this form of film was a staple of the typical North American, British, and Commonwealth countries (especially Canada, Australia and New Zealand), and throughout European cinema programming schedule from the silent era until the 1960s when television news broadcasting completely supplanted its role. Pathé would eventually merge with RKO... An example of a newsreel story is in the film Citizen Kane (which was prepared by RKO's actual newsreel staff), which includes a fictional newsreel that summarizes the life of the title character.

Online Journalism

Online journalism is reporting and other journalism produced or distributed via the Internet. An early leader was The News & Observer in Raleigh, North Carolina, USA. Many news organizations based in other media also distribute news online. How much they take advantage of the medium varies. Some news organizations, such as the Gongwer News Service, use the Web only or primarily.

The Internet challenges traditional news organizations in several ways. They may be losing classified ads to Web sites, which are often targeted by interest instead of geography. The advertising on news Web sites is sometimes insufficient to support the investment. Even before the Internet, technology and perhaps other factors were dividing people's attention, leading to more but narrower media outlets. Online journalism also leads to the spread of independent online media such as open Democracy and the UK, Wikinews as well as allowing smaller news organizations to publish to a broad audience, such as mediastrike.

News Coverage

By covering news, politics, weather, sports, entertainment, and vital events, the daily media shape the dominant cultural, social and political picture of society. Beyond the media networks, independent news sources have evolved to report on events which escape attention or underlie the major stories. In recent years, the blogosphere has taken reporting a step further, mining down to the experiences and perceptions of individual citizens. An exponentially growing phenomenon, the blogosphere can be abuzz with news that is overlooked by the press and TV networks. Apropos of this was Robert F. Kennedy Jr.'s 11,000-word Rolling Stone article apropos of the 2004 United States presidential election, published June 1, 2006. By June 8, there had been no mainstream coverage of the documented allegations by President John F. Kennedy's nephew. On June 9, this sub-story was covered by a Seattle Post-Intelligencer article.

Visibility in the News Media

Visibility: Many groups attempt to gain the attention of the news media by performing violent and dramatic acts. One often repeated act is the suicide bombing. The critical paradox that underlines the actions of the suicide bomber relates to the problem of visibility. The suicide bomber takes a dramatic action on a global stage in order to attract attention to some critical problem. But the very process of self-immolation renders the producer of evidence absent. Of course the effects themselves are visible in the suffering of the wounded, dead, and other environmental destruction, but the visibility is generally achieved by making oneself "invisible". Critical here is the body itself, which can only come to represent through its substitution with discourse. The body must give itself up or trade itself with representation. The most mediated suicide bombings of all time were the attacks on the World Trade Center. Other suicide bombings, such as those performed by Palestinians on Israel, are largely absent from Western media for a variety of reasons (foremost among them--the issue of taste--but also important, the problem of cameras proximity). The failures of such an event, on the other hand, become quite visible as popular content in news and on the internet.

2

Movement of Modern Mass Media

During the recent years mass media has invaded the life of a common man in a big way. Upto seventies, mass media mainly remained confined to cinema, newspaper and radio. It was in the early eighties that audio-visual electronic medium in the form of television invaded the Indian scenario in a big way. The Government created huge infrastructure for spread of television network in the country. During this decade itself, advent of computers and Video Cassette Recorders (VCR) also supplemented the audio-visual media, putting well established medium of cinema to shade. During the early nineties, satellite television revolutionised the audio-visual media by reaching most of the households in the urban areas.

The latest invasion of audio-visual electronic media has suddenly increased the demand for professionals in journalism, technicians and other service individuals. These careers not only offer excellent opportunities, salaries, challenge and satisfaction of work, but also provide an opportunity for self-employment in various fields.

ROLE OF MASS MEDIA TODAY

A basic issue in the discussion of the role of the mass media in today's society is whether they do reflect social reality in a broad sense, or whether, instead, the elites which control them filter out the view of reality which they see fit to be made public.

To my mind, the answer to this question is that the media do both, depending on the way we define reality. To take, first, political reality, mass media, in one sense, do not provide a faked view of it. Taking into account what is considered as politics today, i.e. the activity of professional politicians 'representing' the people, one may argue that it is politics itself, which is faked, and mass media simply reproduce this reality. In this sense, the issue is not whether the mass media manipulate democracy, since it is democracy itself, which is faked, and not its mass media picture, which simply reflects the reality of present 'democracy'.

But, at the same time, if we give a different definition to political reality, mass media do provide, in general, a distorted picture of it. In other words, if we define as real politics the political activity of people themselves (for instance, the collective struggles of various sectors of the population around political, economic or social issues) rather than that of professional politicians, then, the mass media do distort the picture they present about political reality. They do so, by minimising the significance of this type of activity, by distorting its meaning, by marginalising it, or by simply ignoring it completely.

Furthermore, mass media do provide a distorted picture of political reality when they come to report the causes of crises, or of the conflicts involving various sections of the elites. In such cases they faithfully reflect the picture that the sections of the elites controlling them wish to reproduce. The latest example of this was the way in which the Anglo-American media, in particular, distorted the real meaning of the criminal bombardment of the Iraqi people at the end of 1998. Thus, exactly, as in their reporting during the war in the Gulf, the real cause of the conflict, (i.e. who controls the world's oil, irrespective of where the oil stocks are located—the elites of the North versus those in the South), was distorted as a conflict between the peace loving regimes in the North versus the rogue regimes in the South, or, in more sophisticated versions supported by socialdemocrat intellectuals, as a conflict between the 'democracies' in the North versus the 'despotic regimes' in the South over the control of oil.

Under these circumstances, it is obvious that the mass media usually offer a true glimpse of reality only when the elites are divided with respect to their conception of a particular aspect of political reality. From this point of view, concentration in the mass media industry is significant and whether the media are owned by 100 or 10 owners does indeed matter in the struggle for social change. It is for instance such divisions among the European elites over the issue of joining the European Monetary Union which have allowed a relatively wide media discussion on the true meaning of European integration, particularly in countries like Britain where the elites were split.

It was also similar divisions between the Anglo-American and the European elites over the latest war crime in the Gulf which made a bit clearer the directly criminal role of the former (support for the bombardments), as well as the indirectly criminal role of the latter (support for the embargo). It is not accidental that in the USA and UK, where the media played a particularly despicable role in distorting the truth and misinforming the public, the polls showed consistently vast majorities in favour of the criminal activities of their elites. Of course, this does not mean that decentralisation of power in the mass media industry (or anywhere else) represents by itself, even potentially, a radical social change leading to an authentic democracy. Still, the significance of decentralisation in the media industry with respect to raising consciousness should not be ignored.

THE ECONOMIC REALITY

As regards economic reality, mass media, in one sense again, do provide a relatively accurate picture of what counts as economic reality today. This is when the media, taking for granted the system of the market economy, end up with a partial picture of economic reality where what matters is not whether the basic needs of the population are covered adequately but whether prices (in commodity and stock markets), interest rates, exchange rates and consequently profit rates are going up or down. Still, in another sense, the very fact that mass media take for granted the system of the market economy means that they cannot 'see' the 'systemic' nature of most of the real economic problems (unemployment, poverty and so on) and therefore inevitably end up with a faked image of economic reality. This way of seeing economic reality is not imposed on the media by their owners, important as their influence may otherwise be, or by their internal hierarchical structure etc. The media simply reflect the views of orthodox economists, bankers, businessmen and professional politicians, i.e. of all those who express the dominant social paradigm. But if the picture of political and economic reality offered by the media is mixed this is not the case with respect to ecological reality. As no meaningful reporting of the ecological crisis is possible unless it refers to the systemic causes of it, which by definition are excluded by the discourse in the mainstream media, the result is a complete misinformation, or just straightforward description of the symptoms of the crisis. The mass media are flooded by the 'realist' Greens who fill the various ecological parties and who blame technology, consumerist values, legislation etc—anything but the real cause of the crisis, i.e. the very system of the market economy.

Similarly, the reporting of the present social crisis never links the explosion of crime and drug abuse, for instance, with their root cause, i.e. the increasing concentration of political, economic and social power in the hands of various elites. Instead, the symptoms of the social crisis are distortedly reported as its causes and the media blame, following the advice of the establishment 'experts', the breaking of the traditional family, or of the school, as the causes of crime. Similarly, various 'progressive' intellectuals (like the lamentable ex 'revolutionary' and now well promoted by the mainstream media Euro-parliamentarian Con Bendit) blame the prohibitive legislation on drugs for the massive explosion of drug abuse! However, there is another approach being promoted recently by system theorists, according to which mass media do not just either reflect or distort reality but also manufacture it. This is not said in the usual sense of manufacturing consent described by Chomsky and Herman or, alternatively, by Bourdieu, which is basically a one-way process whereby the elites controlling the mass media filter out the information, through various control mechanisms, in order to create consent around their agenda. Instead, system theorists talk about a two-way process whereby social reality and mass media are seen as two interdependent levels, the one intruding into the other. This is based on the valid hypothesis that reality is not just something external to the way it is conceived. TV watching is a constituent moment of reality since our information about reality consists of conceptions that constitute reality itself. At the same time, the conception of reality is conditioned by the media functioning, which is differentiated in relation to the other social systems (political, economic etc).

In the systems analysis problematique, it is not the economic, or the political systems, which control the media functioning. What determines their functioning, as well as their communicative capability, is their ability to generate irritation-a fact that could go a long way to explain the high ratings of exciting or irritating TV programs.

The diversified functioning of mass media creates, in turn, the conditions for a social dynamic which, in a self-reflective and communicative way, reproduces, as well as institutes, society. Thus, whereas the early modern society is instituted through a transcendental subjectivity and a material mode of production, the present post-modern society's reproduction depends on the processes of communicative rationality. The mass media are an integral and functional part of the communicative processes of post-modern society.

However, one may point out here that although it is true that social reality and mass media are interacting, i.e. that our conception of TV news is a constituent element of reality and at the same time our conception of reality is conditioned by TV functioning, this does not imply that the diversified functioning of mass media creates the conditions for a social dynamic which acts for the institution of society, although it does play this role as far as its reproduction is concerned. The meaning we assign to TV reporting is not determined exogenously but by our world view, our own paradigm, which in turn, as we have seen above, is the result of a process of socialisation that is conditioned by the dominant social paradigm.

Furthermore, TV functioning plays a crucial role in the reproduction of the dominant social paradigm and the socialisation process generally. So, the diversified functioning of TV does indeed create the conditions for a social dynamic leading to the reproduction of the status quo, but in no way could be considered as doing the same for instituting society.

AIMS AND ACHIEVEMENTS

The goals of the mass media are determined by those owning and controlling them, who, usually, are members of the economic elites that control the market economy itself. Given the crucial role that the media could play in the internalisation of the dominant social paradigm and therefore the reproduction of the institutional framework which secures the concentration of power in the hands of the elites, it is obvious that those owning and controlling the mass media have broader ideological goals than the usual goals pursued by those owning and controlling other economic institutions, i.e. profit maximising.

Therefore, an analysis that would attempt to draw conclusions on the nature and significance of media institutions on the basis of the profit dimension alone, (i.e. that they share a common goal and consequently a similar internal hierarchical structure with all other economic institutions and that they just sell a product, the only difference with other economic institutions being that the product is the audience,) is bound to be one-dimensional. Profit maximising is only one parameter, often not even the crucial one, which conditions the role of mass media in a market economy. In fact, one could mention several instances where capitalist owners chose even to incur significant losses (which they usually cover from other profitable activities) in order to maintain the social influence (and prestige), which ownership of an influential daily offers to them (Murdoch and The Times of London is an obvious recent example).

Given the ultimate ideological goal of mass media, the main ways in which they try to achieve it are:

- first, by assisting in the internalisation of the dominant social paradigm and,

- second, by marginalising, if not excluding altogether, conceptions of reality which do not conform with the dominant social paradigm.

But, what are the mechanisms through which the media can achieve their goals? To give an answer to this question we have to examine a series of mechanisms, most of them 'automatic' built-in mechanisms, which ensure effective achievement of these goals. It will be useful here to distinguish between 'internal' and 'external' control mechanisms, which function respectively as internal and external constraints on the freedom of media workers to reproduce reality.

Both internal and external mechanisms work mainly through competition which secures homogenisation with respect to the media's main goals. Competition is of course the fundamental organisational principle of a market economy; but, it plays a special role with respect to the media. As Bourdieu points out, competition 'rather than automatically generating originality and diversity tends to favour uniformity'. Still, competition is not the only force securing homogenisation. In a similar way as with the market economy itself, competition provides only the dynamic mechanism of homogenisation. It is the fact that owners of mass media, as well as managers and the highest paid journalists, share the same interest in the reproduction of the existing institutional framework which constitutes the 'base', on which this competition is developed.

But, let us consider briefly the significance of the various control mechanisms. The main 'internal control' mechanisms are ownership and the internal hierarchical structure, which are, both, crucial in the creation of the conditions for internal competition among journalists, whereas the 'ratings' mechanism plays a similar role in the creation of the conditions for external competition among media. Starting with ownership, it matters little, as regards the media's overall goals defined above, whether they are owned and controlled by the state and/or the state-controlled institutions or whether, instead, they are owned and controlled by private capital. However, there are certain secondary differences arising from the different ownership structures which may be mentioned. These secondary differences have significant implications, particularly with respect to the structure of the elites controlling the media, their own organisational structure and their 'image' with respect to their supposedly 'objective' role in the presentation of information.

As regards the elite structure, whereas under a system of state ownership and control the mass media are under the direct control of the political elite and the indirect control of the economic elites, under a system of private ownership and control, the media are just under the direct control of the economic elites.

This fact, in turn, has some implications on whether filtering out of information takes place directly through state control, or indirectly through various economic mechanisms (e.g. ratings).As regards the media organisational structure, whereas state-owned media are characterised by bureaucratic rigidity and inefficiency, privately owned media are usually characterised by more flexibility and economic efficiency. Finally, the 'objective' image of mass media suffers less in case of private ownership compared to the case of state ownership. This is because in the latter case control of information is more direct and therefore more obvious than in the former.

Another important internal control mechanism is the hierarchical structure which characterises all media institutions (as it does all economic institutions in a market economy) and which implies that all-important decisions are taken by a small managerial group within them, who are usually directly responsible to the owners.

The hierarchical structure creates a constant internal competition among journalists as to who will be more agreeable to the managerial group (on which their career and salary prospects depend). Similarly, people in the managerial group are in constant competition as to who will be more agreeable to the owners (on which their highly paid position depends). So, everybody in this hierarchical structure knows well (or soon learns) what is agreeable and what is not and acts accordingly. Therefore, the filtering of information works through self-censorship rather than through any kind of 'orders from above'.

The effect of the internal hierarchical structure is to impose, through the internal competition that it creates, a kind of homogenisation in the journalists' performance.

But, does this exclude the possibility that some media workers may have incentives other those determined by career ambitions? Of course, not. But, such people, as Chomsky points out, will never find a place in the corridors of media power and, one way or another, will be marginalised:

They (journalists) say, quite correctly, "nobody ever tells me what to write. I write anything I like. All this business about pressures and constraints is nonsense because I'm never under any pressure." Which is completely true, but the point is that they wouldn't be there unless they had already demonstrated that nobody has to tell them what to write because they are going to say the right thing... it is not purposeful censorship. It is just that you don't make it to those positions. That includes the left (what is called the left), as well as the right. Unless you have been adequately socialised and trained so that there are some thoughts you just don't have, because if you did have them, you wouldn't be there.

But, how is it determined what is agreeable? Here it is where the 'external' control mechanisms come into play. It is competition among the various media organisations, which homogenises journalists' behaviour. This competition takes the form of a struggle to improve ratings (as regards TV channels) or circulation (as regards newspapers, magazines etc). Ratings or circulation are important not per se but because the advertising income of privately owned mass media (which is the extra income determining their survival or death) depends on them. The result is, as Pierre Bourdieu points out that: Ratings have become the journalist's Last Judgement... Wherever you look, people are thinking in terms of market success.

Only thirty years ago, and since the middle of the nineteenth century—since Baudelaire and Flaubert and others in avant-garde milieux of writers' writers, writers acknowledged by other writers or even artists acknowledged by other artists—immediate market success was suspect. It was taken as a sign of compromise with the times, with money... Today, on the contrary, the market is accepted more and more as a legitimate means of Iegitimation. The pressures created by the ratings mechanism, as Bourdieu points out, have nothing to do with the democratic expression of enlightened collective opinion or public rationality, despite what media ideologues assert. In fact, as the same author points out, the ratings mechanism is the sanction of the market and the economy, that is, of an external and purely market law. I would only add to this that given how 'public opinion' is formed within the process of socialisation and internalisation of the dominant social paradigm, it is indeed preposterous to characterise the ratings mechanism as somehow expressing the democratic will of the people. Ratings, as well as polls generally, is the 'democracy of the uninformed'. They simply reflect the ignorance, the half-truths, or the straightforward distortions of the truth which have been assimilated by an uninformed public and which, through the ratings mechanism, reinforce the role of the mass media in the reproduction of the dominant social paradigm. One may therefore conclude that the role of the media today is not to make the system more democratic. In fact, one basic function of the media is, as Chomsky stresses, to help in keeping the general population out of the public arena because 'if they get involved they will just make trouble.

Their job is to be "spectators," not "participants". Furthermore, the media can play a crucial role in offsetting the democratic rights and freedoms won after long struggles. This has almost always been the case when there was a clash between the elites and trade unions, or popular movements generally. Walter Lippmann, the revered American journalist was explicit about it, as Chomsky points out. For Lippmann, there is a new art in the method of democracy, called "manufacture of consent." By manufacturing consent, you can overcome the fact that formally a lot of people have the right to vote. We can make it irrelevant because we can manufacture consent and make sure that their choices and attitudes will be structured in such a way that they will always do what we tell them, even if they have a formal way to participate. So we'll have a real democracy. It will work properly. That's applying the lessons of the propaganda agency. Within this analytical framework we may explore fruitfully the particular ways through which the filtering of information is achieved, as, for instance, is described by Chomsky and Herman in their 'propaganda model'. Similarly Bourdieu shows in a graphic way how the filtering of information takes place in television, through the structuring of TV debates, the time limits, the methods of hiding by showing etc. Particularly important is the way in which the media, particularly television, control not just the information flow, but also the production of culture, by controlling the access of academics as well as of cultural producers, who in turn, as a result of being recognised a public figures, gain recognition in their own fields.

Thus, at the end, the journalistic field, which is structurally very strongly subordinated to market pressures and as such is a very heteronomous field, applies pressure, in turn, to all other fields. An illustrative application of the above analytical framework is the crucial contribution of the mass media in the creation of the subjective conditions for the neoliberal consensus. Thus, the mass media have played a double ideological role with respect to the neoliberal consensus. On the one hand, they have promoted directly the neoliberal agenda:

- by degrading the economic role of the state,
- by attacking the 'dependence' on the state which the welfare state supposedly creates,
- by identifying freedom with the freedom of choice, which is supposedly achieved through the liberation of markets etc. (talk radio and similar TV shows play a particularly significant role in this respect).

On the other hand, the media have also attempted to divert attention from the consequences of the neoliberal consensus (in terms of growing inequality and poverty, the explosion of crime and drug abuse and so on):

- by promoting irrational beliefs of all sorts (religion, mystical beliefs, astrology etc). The film and video explosion on the themes of exorcism, supernatural powers etc (induced mainly by Hollywood) has played a significant role in diverting attention from the evils of neoliberalism.

- by manufacturing irrelevant and/or insignificant 'news stories' (e.g. Monica Lewinsky affair), which are then taken over by opposition politicians who are eager to find fictitious ways (because of the lack of real political differences within the neoliberal consensus) to differentiate themselves from those in power.
- by creating a pseudo 'general interest' (for instance around a nationalist or chauvinist cause) in order to unite the population around a 'cause' and make it forget the utterly dividing aspects of neoliberalism.

At the same time, the creation of the neoliberal conditions at the institutional level had generated the objective conditions for the mass media to play the aforementioned role. This was because the deregulation and liberalisation of markets and the privatisation of state TV in many European countries had created the conditions for homogenisation through the internal and external competition, which I mentioned above. It is not accidental anyway that major media tycoons like Murdoch in the Anglo-Saxon world, Kirsch in Germany, or Berlusconi in Italy have also been among the main exponents of the neoliberal consensus agenda.

PRINT MEDIA

An old saying goes "pen is mightier than sword". The saying is not just a rhetoric. It reflects the power of print media. Being the most important media, print media pertains to broad activity of publication of newspapers, magazines and books and all persons connected with this activity have their contribution in successful running of this medium. While writing of books and contributing to magazines is largely a self-employment occupation, publication of newspapers and magazines involves a huge work force such as editors, technicians, printing technicians, composers, etc. In all these jobs the options of either working on desk or working in the field are available to the candidates. Reporters and correspondents generally operate in the field and submit their reports or stories on local, national or international issues pertaining to politics, trade, commerce, defence, sports, etc. One special category of reporters and correspondents operates in the field of investigative journalism.

This category of reporting pertains to investigation on the issues of public importance. This type of journalism and reporting attracts public attention instantaneously. Special attention in such reporting is required in the authenticity of information, selection of issues of public interest and succinct reporting in interesting and convincing language. In case of magazine reporting, many a times the reports, stories and features are contributed by free-lance reporters and part-time amateur writers. To pursue the career as a reporter one may attain bachelor's degree or post-graduate diploma in journalism. Some of the universities offer post graduate diplomas of 9-month duration while others offer post-graduate one-year diploma in Public Relations or post graduate degree in mass-communication.

Latest trend in this regard is that big groups of newspapers advertise the posts of trainees in any of the above categories for which all graduates are eligible. After conducting the entrance examination, suitable graduate trainees, with flair for writing are selected and employed. In other words, now the formal academic qualification for being a reporter, copy writer or correspondent is not an essential qualification. Similarly, for writing features or analytical articles in magazines, one need not have any formal and professional academic qualification.

What is required is in-depth knowledge, command over the language concerned and outstanding analytical capability. Broadly speaking, anyone keen to pursue this career in any capacity must have outstanding general awareness, good perception, an eye for details and very keen observation. In turn, the career offers challenge, immense job satisfaction and fairly good compensation. For acquiring general awareness regular reading of newspapers, magazines and books on variety of topics is a must. Discussions on current topics also go a long way in widening the horizons of knowledge. For the beginners, it is better to consult a good book on the background to current affairs so that further knowledge is strengthened after acquiring fundamental knowledge. Latest edition of "Current Affairs and Backgrounders" published by M/s Khanna Brothers (Publishers) Pvt Ltd is an ideal book for this purpose. Command over the concerned language is not a capability which can be acquired overnight. Regular and intensive reading as well as regular writing practice not only improves the command over the language, but also improves the flair for writing.

Candidates seriously pursuing this career should also go in for academic degree/diploma in Journalism/Public Relations/ Mass Communication from a good university or institute to have an edge over others.

AUDIO-VISUAL MEDIA

The requirement of personnel for the audio and audio-visual media is a little different than that for the print media. Traditionally, Radio has been the audio media having farthest reach. It was only with effect from the early eighties that Radio started getting replaced by Television. In most of the cases TV just supplemented the Radio. Despite the recent invasion by Doordarshan channels and Satellite and Cable TV, importance of Radio has not been undermined. The percentage of population covered by Radio is much more than the TV, mainly due to better technical infrastructure, longer range of short wave radio and cheaper cost and running cost of radio and transistors. Hence, Radio still remains very important medium.

Radio needs various types of personnel which includes announcers, news-readers, news-composers, writers, producers, commentators, and various categories of radio artists like singers, musicians, drama artists, narrators, etc. There is also a growing demand for good programmes and producers of such programmes. Audio-visual media is the strongest form of medium, but has limited reach. The earliest form of audio-visual medium was cinema which had very limited reach and people had to spend some money to have an access to it. Cinema, however, still enjoys the most glamorous place in the entire media. In this feature, Cinema as career in audio-visual media has been left out and will be covered later in a separate feature on careers. Television, satellite and cable TV offer varied opportunities for career seekers. This medium offers excellent opportunities for newsreaders, composers, announcers, technicians, commentators, producers, models, actors, cameramen, script writers, etc. In addition to the Government-run Doordarshan, all other companies in the field of television, be it in production, direction, acting, cable operation and satellite TV operation, are handled by the individuals or private companies.

The choice of career is available in a variety of fields, not only with Doordarshan but with commercially-run media companies also. Candidates seeking any type of career in audio-visual electronic media must have characteristics like artistic inclination, expertise in own field of activity, pleasing personality, adaptability, general awareness, quick reflexes, flexibility and imagination. All these qualities must be coupled with the required technical and academic qualifications and professional competence. In case of announcers and newsreaders the qualities of good voice and presentable and photogenic face are additional requirements.

Good flow of spoken language and command over the language concerned are also pre-requisites in these cases. Capabilities to compare and compose become added qualifications. In addition to programmes and news, three other aspects of advertisement, engineering and management are also of paramount importance in TV and other electronic media. Technical and professional staff provide engineering services and act from behind the screen. These personnel are responsible for providing support services so essential for good quality of transmission, colour combinations, creation of support infrastructure for transmission, day-to-day management of video recording, time-management and other related aspects.

JOURNALISM

Journalism fascinates many young people who have a keen desire of seeing their name in print. Anyone who has written something for the college paper believes a career in journalism can be pursued. This feature points out that a career in journalism means more than merely writing well. As we receive a number of queries from our readers who want to become famous journalists and editors, we decided to describe in detail the requirements of newspapers and television channels today. This feature describes the skills required, as also the upside and the downside of the field. It also gives information about how one can become a journalist, the qualities that are required to be a successful one and addresses of some of the well known institutes. To an outsider, journalism is an exciting field in which fame and fortune can be achieved if one is able to write well. The names of some famous journalists come easily to mind. Khushwant Singh, who writes columns in several newspapers; M.J. Akbar, the editor of The Asian Age; and Shobha De, former editor of Stardust and now a celebrated writer. Opportunities in the field have also multiplied with the boom in magazines and television channels.

Each of these requires people who can report and interpret events in a coherent and interesting manner. To assess whether you can be a famous journalist, you have to first know the skills that are required. The first is a good command over language. You must be able to express yourself well. A course in journalism will help sharpen these skills. But this is not all. What is required is the ability to collect information and report events quickly. If you are in a television channel, it may mean going on camera as the event is happening, often a difficult task. In newspapers one has to write out the story before the deadline and it must contain all the correct information and the drama. Even a small error can destroy the credibility of the journalist. So journalism is just not about being able to write well alone.

The nature of a journalist's job is also changing. With news becoming competitive and personality-oriented, the job of a TV journalist often means waiting outside the offices or homes of politicians for hours and trying to catch a "sound byte" as the leader comes out. The pursuit of truth does not extend beyond getting a small segment in the news programme. In this race, there is no room for being creative or following stories that one may like to. Threats of law-suits have made news channels and newspapers increasingly wary about publishing scoops and many of the investigative stories are just killed. There is little room for creativity in today's news organisations.

Increasing Scope

Once you accept these limitations, a career in journalism may be a good option. Some years back there was a boom in television channels which led to an increase in opportunities for aspiring journalists. Many print journalists shifted to television. Salaries had jumped. Today, there is a shakeout among the channels, which has led to the opportunities being reduced drastically. Newspapers and magazines continue to employ journalists, but with circulations and profitability under stress, three has been a decrease in opportunities somewhat. However, this situation may be linked to the economic slowdown and things may become better once the economy picks up. It may be mentioned that there are over 4,000 newspapers in 100 languages registered in India and the scope for employment will always exist, despite difficulties.

Avenues in journalism have multiplied because of unexpected growth in two new areas: (a) Niche publications; and (b) Web editing. We explain these below: Niche Publications: This means special purpose publications catering to particular industries, for example, travel and tourism, hotels, textiles or computers. Many such publications have been started in the past few years. These "niche" publications may not have the mass circulations of newspapers but are highly profitable. However, to work in them one needs to have journalistic skills as well as industry knowledge. Hence, MBAs are employed in business publications while computer experts find jobs in information technology magazines. The idea is to develop a specialisation and build on it. In the future, journalists with specialised skills in an industry may be more in demand than those with mere writing skills.

CULTURE AND DEMOCRACY

A fruitful way to start the discussion of the significance of culture and its relationship to the mass media would be to define carefully our terms. This would help to avoid the confusion, which is not rare in discussions on the matter. Culture is frequently defined as the integrated pattern of human knowledge, belief, and behaviour. This is a definition broad enough to include all major aspects of culture: language, ideas, beliefs, customs, taboos, codes, institutions, tools, techniques, works of art, rituals, ceremonies and so on. However, in what follows, I am not going to deal with all these aspects of culture unless they are related to what I call the dominant social paradigm. By this I mean the system of beliefs, ideas and the corresponding values which are dominant in a particular society at a particular moment of its history. It is clear that there is a significant degree of overlapping between these two terms although the meaning of culture is obviously broader than that of the social paradigm.

But, let us see first the elements shared by both terms. Both culture and the social paradigm are time-and space-dependent, i.e. they refer to a specific type of society at a specific time. Therefore, they both change from place to place and from one historical period to another. This implies that there can be no 'general theory' of History, which could determine the relationship between the cultural with the political or economic elements in society. In other words, our starting point is the rejection not only of the crude economistic versions of Marxism (the economic base determines the cultural superstructure) but also of the more sophisticated versions of it (the economic base determines 'in the last instance' which element is to be dominant in each social formation). In my view, which I expanded elsewhere, the dominant element in each social formation is not determined, for all time, by the economic base, or any other base. The dominant element is always determined by a creative act, i.e. it is the outcome of social praxis, of the activity of social individuals. Thus, the dominant element in theocratic societies was cultural, in the societies of 'actually existing socialism' political and so on.

Similarly, the dominant element in market economies is economic, as a result of the fact that the introduction of new systems of production during the Industrial Revolution in a commercial society, where the means of production were under private ownership and control, inevitably led to the transformation of the socially-controlled economies of the past (in which the market played a marginal role in the economic process) into the present market economies (defined as the self-regulating systems in which the fundamental economic problems—what, how, and for whom to produce—are solved 'automatically', through the price mechanism, rather than through conscious social decisions).

Still, the existence of a dominant element in a social formation does not mean that the relationship between this element and the other elements in it is one of heteronomy and dependence. Each element is autonomous and the relationship between the various elements is better described as one of interdependence. So, although it is the economic element which is the dominant one in the system of the market economy, this does not mean that culture is determined, even 'in the last instance' by this element. But, there are also some important differences between culture and the dominant social paradigm. Culture, exactly because of its greater scope, may express values and ideas, which are not necessarily consistent with the dominant institutions. In fact, this is usually the case characterising the arts and literature of a market economy, where, (unlike the case of 'actually existing socialism', or the case of feudal societies before), artists and writers have been given a significant degree of freedom to express their own views. But this is not the case with respect to the dominant social paradigm. In other words, the beliefs, ideas and the corresponding values which are dominant in a market economy and the corresponding market society have to be consistent with the economic element in it, i.e. with the economic institutions which, in turn, determine that the dominant elites in this society are the economic elites (those owning and controlling the means of production).

This has always been the case in History and will also be the case in the future. No particular type of society can reproduce itself unless the dominant beliefs, ideas and values are consistent with the existing institutional framework. For instance, in the societies of 'actually existing socialism' the dominant social paradigm had to be consistent with the dominant element in them, (which was the political), and the corresponding political institutions, which determined that the dominant elites in this society were the political elites (party bureaucracy). Similarly, in the democratic society of the future, the dominant social paradigm had to be consistent with the dominant element in them, which would be the political, and the corresponding democratic institutions, which would secure that there would be no formal elites in this kind of society (although, of course, if democracy does not function properly the emergence of informal elites could not be ruled out).

So, culture and, in particular, the social dominant paradigm play a crucial role in the determination of individual and collective values. As long as individuals live in a society, they are not just individuals but social individuals, subject to a process, which socialises them and induces them to internalise the existing institutional framework as well as the dominant social paradigm. In this sense, people are not completely free to create their world but are conditioned by History, tradition and culture. Still, this socialisation process is broken, at almost all times-as far as a minority of the population is concerned-and in exceptional historical circumstances even with respect to the majority itself.

In the latter case, a process is set in motion that usually ends with a change of the institutional structure of society and of the corresponding social paradigm. Societies therefore are not just "collections of individuals" but consist of social individuals, who are both free to create their world, (in the sense that they can give birth to a new set of institutions and a corresponding social paradigm), and are created by the world, (in the sense that they have to break with the dominant social paradigm in order to recreate the world).

VALUES OF THE MARKET ECONOMY

As the dominant economic institutions in a market economy are those of markets and private ownership of the means of production, as well as the corresponding hierarchical structures, the dominant social paradigm promoted by the mainstream mass media and other cultural institutions, (e.g. universities) has to consist of ideas, beliefs and values which are consistent with them. Thus, the kind of social 'sciences' which are taught at universities and the kind of articles which fill academic journals, explicitly, or usually implicitly, take for granted the existing economic institutions. Therefore, their search for 'truth' in the analysis of major economic or social problems is crucially conditioned by this fundamental characteristic. The causes of world-wide unemployment, for instance, or of massive inequality and concentration of economic power, will not be related to the system of the market economy itself; instead, the malfunctioning of the system or bad policies will be blamed, which supposedly can be tackled by the appropriate improvement of the system's functioning, or the 'right' economic policies.

In economics, in particular, the dominant theory/ideology since the emergence of the market economy has been economic liberalism, in its various versions: from the old classical and neo-classical schools up to the modern versions of it in the form of supply-side economics, new classical macro-economics etc. But, from Adam Smith to Milton Friedman, the values adopted are the same: competition and individualism, which, supposedly, are the only values that could secure freedom. Thus, for Adam Smith, the individual pursuit of self-interest in a market economy will guarantee social harmony and, therefore, the main task of government is the defence of the rich against the poor. So, in Smith's system, as Canterbery puts it, 'individual self-interest is the motivating force, and the built-in regulator that keeps the economy from flying apart is competition'. Similarly, for Milton Friedman, the Nobel-prize winner in economics (note: the Nobel Prize in economics was never awarded to an economist who challenged the very system of the market economy) the capitalist market economy is identified with freedom:

The kind of economic organisation that provides freedom directly, namely, competitive capitalism, also promotes political freedom because it separates economic power from political power and in this way enables the one to offset the other...The two ideas of human freedom and economic freedom working together came to their greatest fruition in the United States

It is obvious that in this ideology, which passes as the 'science' of economics, the values of individualism and competition are preferred over the values of collectivism and solidarity/co-operation, since freedom itself is identified with the former values as against the latter. But, it 'happens' also that the same values are the only ones, which could secure the production and reproduction of the market economy. No market economy can function properly unless those in control of it, (i.e., the economic elites), at least, and as many of the rest as possible, are motivated by individualism and competition.

This is because the dynamic of a market economy crucially depends on competition and individual greed. Furthermore, the fact that often the economic elites resort to state protection against foreign competition, if the latter threatens their own position, does not in the least negate the fact that competition is the fundamental organising principle of the market economy. It is therefore no historical accident that, as Polanyi has persuasively shown, the establishment of the market economy implied sweeping aside traditional cultures and values and replacing the values of solidarity, altruism, sharing and co-operation (which usually marked community life) with the values of individualism and competition as the dominant values. As Ray Canterbery stresses:

The capitalistic ethic leans toward the extreme of selfishness (fierce individualism) rather than toward altruism. There is little room for collective decision making in an ethic that argues that every individual should go his or her own way. As we have seen, the idea that capitalism protects 'individual rights' would have been rejected during the early Middle Ages. 'Individual rights' were set in advance by the structure of feudalism, governed by the pull of tradition and the push of authority. Economics was based upon mutual needs and obligations. A good example of the enthusiastic support for these values today is, again, the Nobel-prize winner in economics Milton Friedman. According to him:

Few trends could so thoroughly undermine the very foundations of our free society as the acceptance by corporate officials of a social responsibility other than to make as much money for their stockholders as possible. This (social responsibility) is a fundamentally subversive doctrine. Indeed, it is not Friedman who supports values which are inconsistent with the market economy system but the various social democrats and Green economists, who, taking for granted the market economy system, proceed to argue in favour of utopian economic institutions incorporating values which are inconsistent with this system (*e.g.*'stakeholding' capitalism, 'social investment' etc).

As I attempted to show elsewhere, the basic cause of the failure of both the 'actually existing socialism' in the East and social democracy in the West was exactly that they attempted to merge two fundamentally incompatible elements: the 'growth' element, (which implies the concentration of economic power and expresses the logic of the market economy), with the social justice element (which is inherently linked to equality and expresses socialist ethics).

Chomsky's Views

However, quite apart from social democrats and reformist Greens, there is an alternative view about the values of the market economy proposed by Noam Chomsky, which, however, ends up with similar conclusions about the feasibility and desirability of state action with respect to controlling today's market economy. Thus, for Chomsky, the values which motivate today's elites in advanced capitalist countries are not individualism and competition; instead, these elites simply use such values as propaganda in their attempt to 'persuade' their own public and the countries in the periphery and semi-periphery to implement them whereas they themselves demand and enjoy the protection of their own states:

For the general public, individualism and competition are the prescribed values. Not for elites, however. They demand and obtain the protection of a powerful state, and insist on arrangements that safeguard them from unfettered competition or the destructive consequences of individualism. The process of corporatization is a standard illustration, as is the reliance in every economy—crucially, the US—on socialisation of risk and cost. The need to undermine the threat of competition constantly takes new forms: today, one major form, beyond corporatization, is the development of a rich network of "strategic alliances" among alleged competitors: IBM-Toshiba-Siemens, for example, or throughout the automotive industry. This has reached such extremes that prominent analysts of the business world now speak of a new form of "alliance capitalism" that is replacing the managerial/corporate capitalism that had largely displaced proprietary capitalism a century ago in advanced sectors of the economy.

Chomsky has recently expanded on the same theme in a New Left Review article in which it is made clear that his views above about the values of the market economy are perfectly consistent with his views on the nature of today's capitalism. In this article he first states that the word 'capitalist' does not mean capitalist but rather it refers to state subsidised and protected private power centres, or 'collectivist legal entities,' which embody today's corporatization of the market economy. He then goes on to describe corporatization and the role of the state as follows:

The corporatization process was largely a reaction to great market failures of the late nineteenth century, and it was a shift from something you might call proprietary capitalism to the administration of markets by collectivist legal entities-mergers, cartels, corporate alliances-in association with powerful states...the primary task of the states-and bear in mind that, with all the talk about minimising the state, in the OECD countries the state continues to grow relative to GNP, notably in the 1980s and 1990s-is essentially to socialise risk and cost, and to privatise power and profit.

Furthermore, Chomsky's views about the market economy's values and the nature of present capitalism are, in turn, entirely consistent with his present views on the potential role of the state in controlling today's market economy. Thus, as Chomsky stresses in the aforementioned article: The long-term goal of such initiatives (like the Multilateral Agreement on Investment-MAI) is clear enough to anyone with open eyes; an international political economy which is organised by powerful states and secret bureaucracies whose primary function is to serve the concentrations of private power which administer markers through their own internal operations, through networks of corporate alliances, including the intra-firm transactions that are mislabelled 'trade'. They rely on the public for subsidy, research and development, for innovation and for bailouts when things go wrong. They rely on the powerful states for protection from dangerous 'democracy openings'. In such ways, they seek to ensure that the 'prime beneficiaries' of the world's wealth are the right people: the smug and prosperous 'Americans'; the 'domestic constituencies and their counterparts elsewhere. The scale of all of this is nowhere near as great or, for that matter, as novel as claimed; in many ways it's a return to the early twentieth century. And there's no reason to doubt that it can be controlled even within existing formal institutions of parliamentary democracy.

One, however, could object on several grounds this stand, as portrayed by the above extracts. First, the argument about the values of the economic elites, as I attempted to show above, is contestable; second, the nature of today's market economy could be seen in a very different analytical framework than the one suggested by Chomsky and, finally, it could be shown that the way out of the present multi-dimensional crisis and the related huge concentration of power can not be found in fragmented and usually 'monothematic' defensive battles with the elites. Such battles, even if sometimes victorious, are never going to win the war, as long as they are not an integral part of a new popular movement's fight against the system of the market economy itself, which is the ultimate cause of the concentration of economic power. Shift from proprietary (or entrepreneurial) capitalism to the present internationalised market economy, where a few giant corporations control the world economy, did not happen, as Chomsky presents it, as the outcome of 'a reaction to great market failures of the late nineteenth century.' What Chomsky omits is that it was competition, which led from simple entrepreneurial firms to the present giant corporations.

The market failures he mentions are not a God-given calamity. Excepting the case of monopolies, almost all market failures in history have been directly or indirectly related to competition. It is competition, which creates the need for expansion, so that the best (from the profit of view of profits) technologies and methods of organising production (economies of scale etc) are used. It is the same competition, which has led to the present explosion of mergers and take-overs in the advanced capitalist countries, as well as the various 'strategic alliances'. For instance, the recently announced merger of giant oil companies, in a sense, is the result of a 'market failure' because of the fall in their profits. But, in a deeper sense, this merger, as well as the take-overs, strategic alliances etc going on at the moment, are simply the result of self-protective action taken by giant corporations, in order to survive the cut-throat competition launched by the present internationalisation of the market economy. Therefore, it is competition, which has led to the present corporate (or 'alliance') capitalism, not 'market failures' and/or the associated state activity, which just represent the effects of competition.

Similarly, the present internationalisation of the market economy is not just the result of state action to liberalise financial and commodity markets. In fact, the states were following the de facto internationalisation of the market economy, which was intensified by the activities of multi-nationals, when, (in the late seventies), under pressure from the latter, started the process of liberalising the financial markets and further deregulating the commodity markets (through the GATT rounds). Therefore, the present inter-nationalisation is in fact the outcome of the grow-or-die dynamics, which characterises the market economy, a dynamics that is initiated by competition, the crucial fact neglected by Chomsky.

It is also the same internationalisation of the market economy, which became incompatible with the degree of state control of the economy achieved by the mid seventies, that made necessary the present neoliberal consensus. The latter, therefore, is not just a policy change, as socialdemocrats and their fellow travellers suggest, but represents an important structural change. So, minimising the state is not just 'talk', as Chomsky assumes basing his argument on the assumption that 'the state continues to grow relative to GNP, notably in the 1980s and 1990s'. However, not only the fall in the growth rate of government spending in OECD countries was higher than that of the other parts of aggregate demand in the period 1980-93 but, in fact, the (weighted average) general government consumption of high income economies was lower in 1995, at 15% of GNP, than in 1980 (17%). All this, not taking into account the drastic reduction in the overall public sectors in the last twenty years, as a result of the massive privatisation of state industries. Therefore, minimising the state, far from being 'talk' is a basic element of the present neoliberal consensus.

Also, strategic alliances, mergers and take-overs do not represent a movement away from the market economy but a movement towards a new form of it. Away from a market economy, which was geared by the internal market and towards a market economy, which is geared by the world market. This means further and further concentration of economic power not only in terms of incomes and wealth but also in terms of concentration of the power to control world output, trade and investment in fewer and fewer hands. However, the oligopolisation of competition does not mean lack of competition. Furthermore, it will be wrong to assume that the main characteristic of the present period is an 'assault against the markets', as the purist neoliberal argument goes, which Chomsky accepts. The present period of neoliberal consensus can be characterised instead, as an assault against social controls on markets, particularly those aiming at the protection of humans and nature against the effects of marketization, (the historical process that has transformed the socially controlled economies of the past into the market economy of the present). Such controls have been introduced as a result of social struggles undertaken by those who are adversely affected by the market economy's effects on them (social security legislation, welfare benefits, macro-economic controls to secure full employment etc).

What is still debated within the economic elites is the fate of what I call social controls in the broad sense, i.e. those primarily aiming at the protection of those controlling the market economy against foreign competition (tariffs, import controls, exchange controls—in the past, and non-tariff barriers, massive public subsidy for R&D, risk-protection (bailouts), administration of markets etc—at present). Thus, pure neoliberal economists, bankers, some politicians and others are against any kind of social controls over markets (in the narrow or broad sense above). On the other hand, the more pragmatic governments of the neoliberal consensus, from Reagan to Clinton and from Thatcher to Blair, under the pressure of the most vulnerable to competition sections of their own economic elites, have kept many social controls in the broad sense and sometimes even expanded them (not hesitating to go to war to secure their energy supplies) giving rise to the pure neoliberal argument (adopted by Chomsky) about an assault on markets.

In this context, one should not confuse liberalism/ neoliberalism with laissez-faire. As I tried to show elsewhere, it was the state itself that created the system of self-regulating markets. Furthermore, some form of state intervention has always been necessary for the smooth functioning of the market economy system. The state, since the collapse of the socialdemocratic consensus, has seen a drastic reduction in its economic role as it is no longer involved in a process of directly intervening in the determination of income and employment through fiscal and monetary policies. However, even today, the state still plays an important role in securing, through its monopoly of violence, the stability of the market economy framework and in maintaining the infrastructure for the smooth functioning of it.

It is within this role of maintaining the infrastructure that we may see the activities of the state in socialising risk and cost and in maintaining a safety net in place of the old welfare state. Furthermore, the state is called today to play a crucial role with respect to the supply-side of the economy and, in particular, to take measures to improve competitiveness and to train the working force to the requirements of the new technology, in supporting research and development and even in subsidising export industries wherever required. Therefore, the type of state intervention which is compatible with the marketization process not only is not discouraged but, instead, is actively promoted by most of the professional politicians of the neoliberal consensus. It is true that the economic elites do not like the kind of competition which, as a result of the uneven development of the world market economy, threatens their own interests and this is why they have always attempted (and mostly succeeded) to protect themselves against it.

But, it is equally true that it was the force of competition which has always fuelled the expansion of the market economy and that it was the values of competition and self-interest which have always characterised the value system of the elites which control the market economy. Chomsky, however, sometimes gives the impression that, barring some 'accidents' like the market failures he mentions, as well as the aggressive state support that economic elites have always enjoyed, the 'corporatization' of the market economy might have been avoided.

But, of course, neither proprietary capitalism (or any other type of it) is desirable—since it cannot secure covering the basic needs of all people—nor can we deny all radical analysis of the past hundred and fifty years or so, from Marx to Bookchin, and all historical experience since then, which leads to one conclusion: the market economy is geared by a grow-or-die dynamic fuelled by competition, which is bound to lead to further and further concentration of economic power.

Therefore, the problem is not the corporatization of the market economy which, supposedly, represents 'an attack on markets and democracy', and which was unavoidable anyway within the dynamic of the market economy. In other words, the problem is not corporate market economy/capitalism, as if some other kind of market economy/capitalism was feasible or desirable, but the market economy/capitalism itself. Otherwise, one may easily end up blaming the elites for violating the rules of the game, rather than blaming the rotten game itself!

If the above analytical framework is valid then obviously it is not possible, within the existing institutional framework of parliamentary democracy and the market economy to check the process of increasing concentration of economic power. This is a process that is going since the emergence of the market economy system, some two centuries ago, and no social-democratic governments or grassroots movements were ever able to stop it, or even to retard it, apart from brief periods of time. In fact, even the grass root 'victory' hailed by Chomsky against the MAI proposals is doubtful whether it would have been achieved had there been no serious divisions among the economic elites about it.

Furthermore, the 'victory' itself has already started showing signs that it was hollow, as it is now clear that the MAI agreement was not, in fact, set aside, but it is simply implemented 'by installments', through the 'back door' of the IMF at present, and possibly the World Trade Organisation in the future. The basic reason why such battles are doomed is that they are not an integral part of a comprehensive political program to replace the institutional framework of the market economy itself and, as such, they can easily be marginalised or lead to simple (easily reversible) reforms.

The inevitable conclusion is that only the struggle for the building of a new massive movement aiming at fighting 'from without' for the creation of a new institutional framework, and the development of the corresponding culture and social paradigm, might have any chances to lead to a new society characterised by the equal distribution of power.

CULTURAL HOMOGENISATION

The establishment of the market economy implied sweeping aside traditional cultures and values. This process was accelerated in the twentieth century with the spreading all over the world of the market economy and its offspring the growth economy. As a result, today, there is an intensive process of culture homogenisation at work, which not only rules out any directionality towards more complexity, but in effect is making culture simpler, with cities becoming more and more alike, people all over the world listening to the same music, watching the same soap operas on TV, buying the same brands of consumer goods, etc. The establishment of the neoliberal consensus in the last twenty years or so, following the collapse of the socialdemocratic consensus, has further enhanced this process of cultural homogenisation. This is the inevitable outcome of the liberalisation and de-regulation of markets and the consequent intensification of commercialisation of culture.

As a result, traditional communities and their cultures are disappearing all over the world and people are converted to consumers of a mass culture produced in the advanced capitalist countries and particularly the USA. In the film industry, for instance, even European countries with a strong cultural background and developed economies have to effectively give up their own film industries, unable to compete with the much more competitive US industry. Thus, in the early 1990s, US films' share amounted to 73% of the European market. Also, indicative of the degree of concentration of cultural power in the hands of a few US corporations is the fact that, in 1991, a handful of US distributors controlled 66% of total cinema box office and 70% of the total number of video rentals in Britain.

Thus, the recent emergence of a sort of "cultural" nationalism in many parts of the world expresses a desperate attempt to keep a cultural identity in the face of market homogenisation. But, cultural nationalism is devoid of any real meaning in an electronic environment, where 75 percent of the international communications flow is controlled by a small number of multinationals. In other words, cultural imperialism today does not need, as in the past, a gunboat diplomacy to integrate and absorb diverse cultures. The marketization of the communications flow has already established the preconditions for the downgrading of cultural diversity into a kind of superficial differentiation akin to a folklorist type. Furthermore, it is indicative that today's 'identity movements', like those in Western Europe (from the Flemish to the Lombard and from the Scots to the Catalans) which demand autonomy as the best way to preserve their cultural identity, in fact, express their demand for individual and social autonomy in a distorted way.

The distortion arises from the fact that the marketization of society has undermined the community values of reciprocity, solidarity and co-operation in favour of the market values of competition and individualism. As a result, the demand for cultural autonomy is not founded today on community values which enhance co-operation with other cultural communities but, instead, on market values which encourage tensions and conflicts with them. In this connection, the current neoracist explosion in Europe is directly relevant to the effectual undermining of community values by neoliberalism, as well as to the growing inequality and poverty following the rise of the neoliberal consensus.

Finally, one should not underestimate the political implications of the commercialisation and homogenisation of culture. The escapist role traditionally played by Hollywood films has now acquired a universal dimension, through the massive expansion of TV culture and its almost full monopolisation by Hollywood subculture. Every single TV viewer in Nigeria, India, China or Russia now dreams of the American way of life, as seen on TV serials (which, being relatively inexpensive and glamorous, fill the TV programmes of most TV channels all over the world) and thinks in terms of the competitive values imbued by them. The collapse of existing socialism has perhaps more to do with this cultural phenomenon, as anecdotal evidence indicates, than one could imagine.

As various TV documentaries have shown, people in Eastern European countries, in particular, thought of themselves as some kind of 'abnormal' compared with what western TV has established as the 'normal'. In fact, many of the people participating in the demonstrations to bring down those regimes frequently referred to this 'abnormality', as their main incentive for their political action. In this problematique, one may criticise the kind of cultural relativism supported by some in the Left, according to which almost all cultural preferences could be declared as rational (on the basis of some sort of rationality criteria), and therefore all cultural choices deserve respect, if not admiration, given the constraints under which they are made.

But, obviously, the issue is not whether our cultural choices are rational or not. Nor the issue is to assess 'objectively' our cultural preferences as right or wrong. The real issue is how to make a choice of values which we think is compatible with the kind of society we wish to live in and then make the cultural choices which are compatible with these values. This is because the transition to a future society based on alternative values presupposes that the effort to create an alternative culture should start now, in parallel with the effort to establish the new institutions compatible with the new values. On the basis of the criterion of consistency between our cultural choices and the values of a truly democratic society, one could delineate a way beyond post-modern relativism and distinguish between 'preferable' and 'non-preferable' cultural choices.

So, all those cultural choices involving films, videos, theatrical plays etc, which promote the values of the market economy and particularly competition for money, individualism, consumerist greed, as well as violence, racism, sexism etc should be shown to be non-preferable and people should be encouraged to avoid them. On the other hand, all those cultural choices, which involve the promotion of the community values of mutual aid, solidarity, sharing and equality for all (irrespective of race, sex, ethnicity) should be promoted as preferable.

3

Role of Media in a Democracy

Democracy means 'A system of government in which all the people of a country can vote to elect their representatives'. Media came into existence in 1780 with the introduction of a newspaper namely 'The Bengal Gazette' and since then it has matured leaps and bounds. It has been playing a very important role in shaping human minds.

ROLE OF MEDIA

Media plays a crucial role in shaping a healthy democracy. It is the backbone of a democracy. Media makes us aware of various social, political and economical activities happening around the world. It is like a mirror, which shows us or strives to show us the bare truth and harsh realities of life. The media has undoubtedly evolved and become more active over the years. It is the media only who reminds politicians about their unfulfilled promises at the time of elections. T.V news channels' excessive coverage during elections helps people, especially illiterates, in electing the right person to the power. This reminder compels politicians to be upto their promises in order to remain in power.

Television and radio have made a significant achievement in educating rural illiterate masses in making them aware of all the events in their language. Coverage of exploitative malpractices of village heads and moneylenders has helped in taking stringent actions against them by attracting government's attention. The media also exposes loopholes in the democratic system, which ultimately helps government in filling the vacuums of loopholes and making a system more accountable, responsive and citizen-friendly. A democracy without media is like a vehicle without wheels. In the age of information technology we are bombarded with information. We get the pulse of the world events with just a click of a mouse. The flow of information has increased manifolds. The perfect blend of technology and human resources (journalist) has not left a single stone unturned in unearthing rampant corruption in politics and society. We all are well aware of what tehelka did. Thanks to technology that has brought a kind of revolution in journalism.

IMPACT OF MEDIA

The impact of media is really noteworthy. Excessive coverage or hype of sensitive news has led to communal riots at times. The illiterates are more prone to provocations than the literates. Constant repetition of the news, especially sensational news, breeds apathy and insensitivity. For instance, In Dhananjoy Chatterjee case, the overloaded hype led to death of quite a few children who imitated the hanging procedure which was repeatedly shown in most of the T.V. news channels. There is a plethora of such negative impacts. Media should take utmost care in airing or publishing such sensational news. Commercialization has created a stiff competition in media. In order to outdo each other print media has often gone one step further in publishing articles, cover stories, etc. on sex. Media experts say this is one of the means of attracting readers who are glued to T.V. news channels, which have cropped up swiftly in a recent past and they believe this is a cheap form of journalism.

CITIZENS AND THE MEDIA

Is there any reason why citizens must be informed about and participate in debates about media policy and regulation? Consider the facts. First, the news media are supposed to play a vital role in democratic societies as the

Fourth Estate, one of the four pillars of democracy alongside the Legislature, the Executive and the Judiciary. It stands to reason that the watchdog of the other three Estates, and of society as a whole, must also, ultimately, be accountable to the public. Secondly, few would deny that the mass media wield enormous power in today's world. They are increasingly playing the role once played by family, community, religion and formal education: not only disseminating information and knowledge, but also shaping values and norms, moulding attitudes and behaviour, and influencing the very process of living.

Thirdly, the media set the public agenda in a number of ways: for example, they more or less determine which wars and conflicts citizens should know about and what they should know about them, which disasters and diseases are worthy of public attention, which scams and scandals people must get hot and bothered about, what issues and developments they should be informed and concerned about, which events in a city residents need to be aware of, and so on.

The media are also in a position to pressurise the State to act; and they enjoy this privilege because they are supposed to represent the public interest. The news media in particular have traditionally played a key role in democracy by creating what is known as the "public sphere", where information essential to citizen participation in national and community life is supposed to be presented and where issues of importance to the public are meant to be discussed and debated. Such a public sphere is indispensable to democratic society because democracy critically depends upon an informed populace making political choices.

So citizens of a democracy do have a stake in the media and, consequently, they have the right to be heard on media-related matters– not only issues relating to media content but also those concerning media policy. Indeed, the democratisation of the media is one of the important challenges of the future.

A growing number of people in different parts of the world are becoming aware of the need for citizens to be critically aware of the media, not just in terms of programming, but also with regard to various determinants of policy, such as institutional structure, funding and regulation. Broadcast audiences, long presumed to be passive consumers, are beginning to turn active, and increasingly seeking recognition as stakeholders who have a right to be heard on all issues relating to the media.

Unfortunately, in India, even sections of civil society that are vigorous and vocal on a wide range of important issues have yet to intervene actively in media matters. Yet, as P V Satheesh of the Deccan Development Society, Andhra Pradesh, says, media sovereignty is as critical as sovereignty in food, natural resources, seeds and markets-for all citizens, and especially for the poor.

A landmark judgment of the Supreme Court of India in 1995 provides legitimacy to the notion that the primary purpose of all broadcasting is to serve the public interest. The apex court has made it clear that "the airwaves or frequencies are a public property" (belonging neither to the State nor to private entities) and that "their use has to be controlled and regulated by a public authority in the interests of the public and to prevent the invasion of their rights". This is a potentially powerful tool that has, so far, not been sufficiently highlighted, let alone effectively used. In the resulting vacuum, the judgment has been narrowly interpreted to promote private participation in broadcasting. Only a small group of media advocates have used the judgment to press home the imperative of community media – thanks to their efforts community radio is slowly but surely becoming a reality in different parts of the country at long last.

While the entry of private players has certainly broadened the field and provided citizens with more choice, and while the long-awaited dawn of community media is certainly to be welcomed, what is equally significant about the judgment is that it represents a sound basis for citizens to get involved in matters concerning broadcasting. Such involvement is necessary to secure people's right to diverse as well as independent media, which are essential if the public sphere so vital for democracy is to be truly public.

Despite the judgment, however, media policy – with far-reaching implications – is still being formulated without the knowledge, let alone the participation, of even the cognoscenti among media professionals and users, not to mention the ever-growing number of citizens who are consumers in the burgeoning media market. In the absence of people's participation it is hardly surprising that it is, primarily, the broadcast industry that engages with the government on the wide range of issues relating to the electronic media. This is so despite the lip service paid to public consultation in the form of postings on official websites, "open house" meetings in a couple of cities, etc.

CHAOS AND CONFUSION

One reason why it is difficult even for those who wish to engage in media matters to do so is the confusion that prevails in the realm of media policy and legislation, especially with respect to the broadcast sector. This situation is aided and abetted by the paucity and fragmented nature of information in this area. Media regulation in India is currently a maze, with multiple agencies involved in formulating and implementing policy, drafting and enforcing legislation. To make matters worse, they often appear to be unaware of each other's interventions and seem to work at cross purposes. Among the official organisations-currently involved in media regulation are the following:

Union Ministry of Information & Broadcasting, which functions as policy-maker and content regulator. Telecom Regulatory Authority of India, at one point given responsibility for regulation of the broadcast sector (in addition to the telecommunications sector) but involved primarily with issues of technology, such as carriage regulation and pricing. Telecom Disputes Settlement & Appellate Tribunal which, as the name implies, is the body to which appeals can be made for problems relating to broadcast regulation.

Ministry of Communications & Information Technology, which has responsibility for licensing transmission equipment (eg, radio through the Wireless Planning & Coordination or

WPC wing), satellites, Internet Protocol Television (IPTV) and, potentially, Mobile TV.

The courts – in the absence of an independent regulator, the courts are often called upon to adjudicate on broadcast-related issues and they are playing an increasingly proactive role in matters of media regulation. Head post offices in various cities, given responsibility for registering cable TV networks. State/District level Monitoring Committees and Authorised Officers, entrusted under the Cable Television Act with the responsibility to prevent the transmission of "certain programmes in public interest" (NB: The Authorised Officer is empowered to seize broadcast equipment).

The Inter-Ministerial Committee constituted by the Ministry of Information & Broadcasting to look into complaints regarding violations of the programme and advertisement codes connected to the Cable Television Act and Rules. There may well be others. In addition, other semi-official players also occasionally enter the field. For example, in mid-2008 the National Commission for Women recommended amendments to the Indecent Representation of Women Act (relating to the depiction of women in the media) aimed at expanding the scope of the Act to include electronic and digital media, besides broadening the definition of 'indecent representation,' and making punishment for infringements more stringent.

In a parallel development, the National Commission for the Protection of Child Rights sought clarifications from the Ministry of Labour in an effort to determine whether or not children's participation in TV programmes, including reality shows, should be viewed as child labour and thereby violative of laws against the economic exploitation of children.

Around the same time the Union Ministry for Women & Child Development also weighed in, criticising the media – especially some television channels – for their handling of the murder of 14-year-old Aarushi Talwar in May 2008.

In mid-December 2008 the Committee on Petitions of the upper house of Parliament (Rajya Sabha) focused its 132nd report on a petition regarding the alleged misuse of the right to freedom of speech and expression by both print and electronic media and the need to restrict this under Article 19 [2] of the Constitution. Giving its opinion on a variety of media issues the Committee came out in favour of statutory regulations to cover the media – both print and electronic – in the larger interests of society.

According to the Committee, "Self-regulation is an ideal situation but it may not be effective to regulate the media, particularly in the scenario of growing competition amongst the channels for supremacy in the business of ratings. The Committee is, therefore, in favour of having statutory regulations in place covering the print and electronic media, in the larger interest of the society, on the model of the Press Council of India vested with more powers. The Committee understands that the Government has proposed to put in place the Broadcasting Regulatory Authority of India (BRAI) under an Act of Parliament and a new Content Code to be issued thereunder. The Committee expects the Government to address all the issues raised by it, while going ahead with the proposed legislation. The Committee hopes that the proposed Broadcasting Services Regulation Bill will incorporate the views of all concerned and the same introduced in Parliament without further delay."

IN SEARCH OF A REGULATOR

The need for a body to oversee India's burgeoning broadcast media is debated every now and then, with discussions usually triggered off by controversial media coverage and/or official announcements or initiatives, including draft legislation pertaining to the broadcast sector. A common proposal made at such times is that the entity be modelled on the Press Council of India (PCI) whose jurisdiction – such as it is – is currently restricted to the print media.

The idea of a broader Media Council or Commission has been floating around for several years. For example, in 2004, both the Prime Minister, Manmohan Singh, and the then Minister for Information and Broadcasting, S Jaipal Reddy, made statements highlighting the need to review existing media policies in the context of current realities. This sparked off some discussion on the possible nature and structure of such an organisation. But over the years the concept remained in the realm of general, intermittent discussion, even though the broadcast scenario in the country has been transformed in recent years and is continuing to expand and evolve at a rapid pace, overtaking policy and regulation.

The controversial draft Broadcasting Services Regulation Bill, 2007, floated by the Union Ministry of Information and Broadcasting in July that year, finally gave legislative form to a regulatory body meant to oversee the broadcasting industry. However, the Broadcasting Regulatory Authority of India (BRAI), as described in the Bill, had little resemblance to an independent and autonomous public authority, in view of the overarching influence of the government over almost every aspect of it – from its constitution and composition to its powers and functions.

The prescribed process of selecting and appointing the chairperson and members of BRAI also did not inspire confidence. The fact that, both, the chief executive officer of the Authority, and the regional directors of its satellite offices across the country were to be government officers drawn from the civil services contradicted the claim that BRAI was to be an independent institution. With "Licensing Authorities" as well as "Authorised Officers" also likely to be drawn from the bureaucracy, the proposed regulatory infrastructure appeared indistinguishable from the government.

In addition, a number of sections in the Bill listing the powers and functions of the central government reinforced the perception that BRAI would be neither independent nor autonomous. Other provisions suggested that it was meant to merely implement policy determined by the government. The fact that it was empowered to make recommendations to the central government made little sense as long as the latter was not committed to even considering the recommendations, let alone accepting them. Similar weaknesses afflicted the Public Service Broadcasting Council (PSBC) as envisaged in the draft Bill. There was also undue confusion about the division of responsibility and labour between the various players listed in the draft Bill. Critics pointed out that the lack of clarity and focus in the terms of reference for each would, in all probability, result in wasteful, fruitless overlap.

Most importantly, the draft Bill did not make any provision for public involvement in the regulatory framework. Media regulators in several democratic across the world have established transparent procedures for public consultation on matters relating to media policy and legislation. So this was clearly a serious omission. In the final analysis, the Broadcast Bill 2007 perpetuated a problem that has dogged all efforts in the direction of a Media Council/Commission in India: the virtual absence of public consultation and discussion.

With neither the media nor citizens involved in the process of determining the purpose and nature of such an organisation, let alone its frame of reference, composition, powers, and so on, the government has repeatedly laid itself open to the suggestion that its intention is to control or even muzzle the media. Lack of transparency and dialogue is clearly a fundamental flaw, especially since media regulatory authorities are meant to be public institutions, accountable above all to citizens. In a democracy the need for media regulation cannot be used as a fig leaf to mask the promotion of state control over media. The first step towards media regulation in the public interest in a democratic society must necessarily be the setting up of a properly constituted, independent public authority empowered with a clear mandate and guaranteed autonomy, as envisioned by the Supreme Court of India.

IN SEARCH OF MODELS

There are at least two aspects to media regulation within what was once known as the broadcast sector. One relates primarily to organisational structures and technological systems (including ownership, licensing, spectrum allocation, etc.), while the other has to do with content and includes facilities for receiving and addressing complaints from the public. Although many regulatory organisations deal with both functions it is useful to acknowledge and understand the difference. Take, for example, the situation in Sweden, where the two facets of regulation are dealt with by separate organisations. The Swedish Radio and TV Authority, the national authority for the media sector, grants licences for digital terrestrial television, local and community radio broadcasting, and issues publishing licences for databases. It also issues regulations on television standards and exercises a supervisory role in this area. In addition, the Authority monitors developments in the field of media and publishes statistics and other relevant information on the subject.

On the other hand, the Swedish Broadcasting Commission– also a national body – oversees the content of radio and television broadcasts. While viewers or listeners can file complaints about programmes before the Commission, the SBC can also review programmes on its own initiative. In both instances the Commission evaluates the programmes *vis a vis* their compliance with the provisions of the Radio and Television Act and the terms of the licence agreement between the broadcaster and the government. Internationally, however, the trend seems to be towards convergence. In several countries existing, parallel regulatory institutions have been merged over the past few years to form a single one dealing with a broad spectrum of media and communications technologies as well as both components of regulation.

For example, the Australian Communication and Media Authority, established in 2005, is a statutory authority within the federal government portfolio dealing with Broadband, Communications and the Digital Economy. It is responsible for the regulation of broadcasting, the Internet, radio communications and telecommunications. Created by merging the Australian Broadcasting Authority and the Australian Communications Authority, the ACMA aims "to enable the communications needs of the Australian community to be met by supporting and encouraging an innovative and vibrant communications sector". Its goal is "to manage an effective regulatory environment that supports a dynamic communications sector and enables industry to meet the communications needs of the community". The ACMA's mandate includes regulation of media content and advertising. Working closely with relevant industries to promote active self-regulation, the Authority oversees industry compliance with licence conditions, codes and standards. It also monitors the effect of regulations in order to ensure that they are responsive to the community's needs.

Among the ACMA's responsibilities, as listed on its website, are the following: promoting self-regulation and competition in the communications industry, while protecting consumers and other users fostering an environment in which electronic media respect community standards and respond to audience and user needs managing access to the radiofrequency spectrum representing Australia 's communications interests internationally The ACMA regulates broadcasting services in Australia in a number of ways: planning the radiofrequency spectrum used by radio and television services use issuing and renewing licences to broadcasters administering commercial ownership and control rules to maintain media diversity, regulating broadcasting content, developing programme standards or licence conditions on specific issues supporting the development of codes of practice for the industry to ensure community safeguards.

The key word in all this is, clearly, "community". The *raison d'etre* of regulation is, obviously, the public good. In fact, the home page of the ACMA website places the public above licensees and industry: information meant for the former on how regulation works, together with advice for consumers and communities, is literally in the top spot, before details meant for the latter. The Broadcasting Bill 2008 announced by the government of Ireland in May 2008 also follows the trend of convergence and is expected to significantly change the broadcasting landscape in the country. The proposed legislation provides for the establishment of a single content regulator, the Broadcasting Authority of Ireland, which will assume the roles currently held by the Broadcasting Commission of Ireland (BCI) and the Broadcasting Complaints Commission (BCC). It will also have a range of new functions, including oversight of the public service broadcasters. A detailed and comprehensive legislative proposal, the Bill seeks to deal with virtually all aspects of regulation and provision of broadcasting. It represents a consolidation of almost 50 years of Irish broadcasting legislation, repealing key Acts dating from 1960. Significantly, the Bill also amends legislation concerning public service broadcasters and the allocation of public funding for broadcast services.

The draft law was reportedly approved by the Irish government following a wide-ranging and informed debate, much of which was carried out through an e-consultation process. It is believed to be the first such legislation in the country to undergo such widespread consultation and rigorous scrutiny prior to its introduction.

The Bill includes a number of proposals meant to protect the interests of viewers and listeners. This includes a 'right of reply' mechanism whereby individuals who feel their reputations have been damaged by the media may seek to have the wrong corrected in a further broadcast. The proposed legislation also contains a provision for the establishment of Audience Councils to represent the views of listeners and viewers. In addition it puts forward some new approaches to codes and rules for broadcasting in Ireland, particularly in relation to food advertising aimed at children.

According to the Irish communications minister, the primary focus in the drafting of the Bill has been to ensure that the broadcasting sector delivers on the needs and wants of the viewer and listener. In his view, this can be achieved only through an appropriate and fair regulatory structure, which mandates the Authority to work with everyone in the sector.

The Office of Communications of the United Kingdom was established in 2002 as the independent regulator and competition authority for the country's communications industries. A statutory corporation accountable to Parliament but independent of Government, Ofcom's jurisdiction extends across television, radio, telecommunications and wireless communications services; and its responsibilities cover both content and infrastructure in the communications sector. The new institution took over the functions of the Radio Authority and the Independent

Television Commission, which consequently ceased to exist in 2003. Ofcom's statutory duties under the Communications Act, 2003, are "to further the interests of citizens in relation to communications matters, and to further the interests of consumers in relevant markets, where appropriate by promoting competition". Ofcom's specific responsibilities, listed on its website, include the following:

ENSURING THE OPTIMAL USE OF THE ELECTRO-MAGNETIC SPECTRUM

Ensuring that a wide range of electronic communications services-including high speed data services-is available throughout the UK.

Ensuring a wide range of TV and radio services of high quality and wide appeal.

Maintaining plurality in the provision of broadcasting.

Applying adequate protection for audiences against offensive or harmful material.

Applying adequate protection for audiences against unfairness or the infringement of privacy.

Significantly, the home page of the Ofcom website highlights advice for consumers as prominently as information on licensing, etc., meant for the industry. The Finnish Communications Regulatory Authority also places consumers side by side with industry, providing information on FICORA's services for the public.

The clearly stated regulatory principles that are meant to guide Ofcom's actions leave little room for arbitrary action and sufficient basis for public scrutiny of its initiatives and questions about its sins of omission and commission, if any:

It will regulate with a clearly articulated and publicly reviewed annual plan, with stated policy objectives.

It will intervene where there is a specific statutory duty to work towards a public policy goal which markets alone cannot achieve.

It will operate with a bias against intervention, but with

a willingness to intervene firmly, promptly and effectively where required.

It will strive to ensure its interventions will be evidence-based, proportionate, consistent, accountable and transparent in both deliberation and outcome.

It will always seek the least intrusive regulatory mechanisms to achieve its policy objectives.

It will research markets constantly and will aim to remain at the forefront of technological understanding.

It will consult widely with all relevant stakeholders and assess the impact of regulatory action before imposing regulation upon a market.

Also on the Ofcom website are detailed guidelines on the process of consultation on matters of media policy. The following excerpts from Ofcom's Consultation Guidelines, issued in November 2007, make it clear that the regulator's ultimate responsibility and accountability is to citizens (certain sections have been underlined here for emphasis):

During the controversy over the Broadcast Bill 2007, the Indian Ministry of Information & Broadcasting claimed that it had studied media regulation systems in different parts of the world. Unfortunately the draft made public in July 2007 did not reflect any of the positive trends in media regulation in the public interest across the globe. There is no dearth of international examples and models of media regulatory bodies accountable to the public that can be used to create democratic institutions and systems of media regulation in India.

This review of the media regulation debate in India in recent times, together with the accompanying documents (an overview of broadcast-related legislation in India and summaries of some recent recommendations from the Telecom Regulatory Authority of India and the Supreme Court judgment on the airwaves, as well as case law dealing with sting operations, obscenity and political advertisements) are intended to facilitate more informed and active public debate on issues relating to media regulation in the country.

MEDIA RESPONSIBILITY AND REGULATION

Having reflected on media and democracy, let us now focus on the mechanisms of media responsibility and accountability. As well shown by people such as McQuail (1997), all media under all circumstances are responsible and accountable either in the sense of liability or answerability. Christians & al. (1998) lead us further by asking who media professionals are responsible and accountable to. To whom is moral duty owed? Five parties are singled out:

1. themselves
2. their clients (subscribers, supporters, etc.)
3. their organization (company, etc.)
4. their colleagues (workplace, association, etc.)
5. the society at large.

In the European tradition, the legacy of Enlightenment and human rights demands that the media should be free – free from coercion by the power holders and free for the pursuit of truth and creativity. However, no social institution can be absolutely free, and even the freest media are always tied to some social forces, serving some political objectives – often indirectly and even unintentionally so but still, sociologically speaking, far from absolutely free. The question then is not whether the media are free but how they are controlled and held accountable.

Three main mechanisms of media control can be distinguished (Bertrand 1998):

1. Law promulgated by Parliament and other state bodies and executed by courts
2. Market based on private property, commercial advertising, etc.
3. Media themselves through various means of maintaining "ethics".

In most countries today (certainly in Europe), these categories are mutually dependent. They coexist. Thus, self-regulation is always accompanied by some degree of legal regulation to ensure than minimum standards of democratic order and human rights are respected. This form of self-regulation is a preferred alternative to more heavy-handed legislation Similarly, as media concentration and tabloidization increase, it is natural for society and the public to prefer this form of self-regulation over commercial markets. Media ethics as another way of highlighting self-regulation is today one of the booming areas of communication studies and literature.

Accordingly, while self-regulation is mostly accompanied by legal and market regulation, we should take it as a most valuable form of regulating the media in society. It is one aspect of a mega trend in contemporary thinking, whereby established political institutions, including nation states, lose their importance – at least in terms of their intellectual potential-and are gradually replaced by more flexible structures, such as grassroots approaches and networking. Part and parcel of this trend is a new emphasis on (ordinary) people as the main subject in communication – as consumers, citizens and 'owners' of the right to freedom of information– instead of journalists and media proprietors.

In fact, citizens and civil society could be added to Bertrand's list of regulatory mechanisms. Yet, in reality regulation on the part of civil society is possible only in small vehicles of communication owned by members of associations and in information networks formed by restricted interest groups. Citizens can bring influence to bear on the main media only marginally, by their own consumer behaviour (i.e. as a market force) and by participating in the activities of pressure groups. Likewise, we must remember that citizens constitute the electorate which ultimately determines, in theory at least, what Parliament and the government – the whole state apparatus – is doing with the media.

The idea that the media are responsible to the general public made up of citizens is widely accepted, not least among journalists (as will be documented below). Journalists see themselves as using freedom of speech as the representatives of the citizens, and the professional ideal of the journalist typically embodies the roles of both a watchdog and an educator.

On the other hand journalists, not to mention media owners, are anxious to remain independent, at least regarding the state, and therefore they are reluctant to accept laws to concretize their abstract responsibility. Accordingly, while media professionals speak warmly about responsibility, they remain lukewarm about accountability. Upon closer examination the media present a constitutional dilemma. On the one hand, some countries have freedom of speech and a ban on advance censorship written into their Constitution (e.g., the US First Amendment and corresponding provisions in many countries such as Finland). On the other hand the media, like any institution in society, including free enterprise, are to a certain extent accountable to a democratic society.

The responsibility of communication has been specified in international agreements on human rights, which both guarantee freedom of opinion and expression and set limitations on the dissemination of things like racist and warmongering propaganda. In general, human rights instruments set clear boundary conditions for the media, just as there are boundary conditions on other aspects of life. It is thus impossible for the media to use freedom of speech to justify their setting themselves above social norms and institutions. They have, on the contrary, a special responsibility, for in a democratic society both constitutional protection for freedom of speech and human rights agreements place the media in the position of a tool in the service of citizens.

PUBLIC SPHERE AND DEMOCRACY

Most directly, "the public sphere is paradigmatically associated with discussions on democracy and its shortcomings". In this respect, the public sphere is viewed as a resource for growth of democracy, promoting discussions of civil society and public life. The concept of the public sphere appeals to the nature of civil society as it attempts to explain the social foundations of democracy and to introduce a discussion of the specific organization of social and cultural bases within civil society for the development of an effective rational-critical discourse. Habermas (1992) saw the public sphere as a domain of social life in which public opinion could be formed out of rational public debate. Ultimately, informed and logical discussion, could lead to public agreement and decision making, thus representing the best of the democratic tradition.

Blumler and Gurevitch (2001) argue that the new interactive media have a "vulnerable potential" to enhance public communications and enrich democracy. Scholars of political sciences also ask if it is possible to foster democratic development with the help of communication technology. Hagen states that research on the relationship between communication technologies and democracy has turned up ample evidence illustrating that concepts of electronic democracy contribute both to democratic theory and our understanding of the working of a democratic political system in the information age (Newhagen, 2000).

Accordingly, it is the condition of the public sphere that differentiates democratic political systems from non-democratic ones. In the absence of the public sphere, people are deprived from a space through which they can govern themselves by themselves for themselves. "The importance of the public sphere to democratic theory and democratic movements cannot be underestimated. For a functioning and purposeful citizenry to develop, it is argued that they must have a space in which to engage debate and make decisions. This space is thought to exist outside of the governmental sphere and the private sphere. The public sphere is seen to lie between these two other parts of social life in order to develop solutions to social problems. Citizens in the public sphere are meant to leave their personal concerns behind, and transcend their limited subjectivities in pursuit of 'the common good'" (Franko, 2005).

Engagement in the public sphere defines the public, and it is best to envision the public sphere not necessarily as a public space, but as a purposeful interaction towards discussion and democratic decision-making. Habermas tells us that, "a public sphere comes into being in every conversation in which private individuals assemble to form a public body" (Franko, 2005). To better understand the nature of the public space we need to differentiate it from other types of spaces. A space is private when given individuals are recognized by others as having the right to establish criteria that must be met for anyone else to enter it. Thus, we speak of a private room, a private meeting, and private parts. Such a space is belongs to someone that has the right to establish criteria by which access is allowed or denied. Sacred space is different and similar. Such a space is neither made by human action nor can it be owned. It is the God. The sacred space as identified here reflects the European view which is completely different from that of Islam, as there is no separation between private and public spaces from the Islamic point of view. At the other extreme, a space may be common to human beings. There are no criteria for common space. It is not owned or controlled and is open to everyone. Thus, the sea or forests are (or can be) common space. This is not a space to which one goes to speak with others and therefore, it is not a public realm, and its boundaries are not contestable per se. Public space is a space created by and for humans that is always contestable, and it is open to those who meet the criteria, but it is not owned in the sense of being controlled.

In the tradition of Western thought, the very idea of democracy is inseparable from that of public space. It is perceived as a disposition to open and contradictory debate with the aim of making possible a reasoned understanding between citizens with regard to the matter of the definition of institutions, the formulation of laws, and their enforcement. From this point of view, public means simultaneously: open to all, well known to all, and acknowledged by all. Public space stands in opposition to private space, because it is civic space and it belongs to the citizens. Historically, the public sphere has been associated with revolution. The public gathering of individuals, to make decisions and garner support is critical to most reform movements. Thus, Habermas defines the public sphere as "the scene of a psychological emancipation that corresponded to a political economic one".

The public sphere and democracy should not be considered as inseparable from one another, because the democratic political systems are based on the voice of the people and the rule of the majority that is likely formed through a liberal public sphere in which people freely discuss the critical public issues. In Egypt, the situation is different from that of Western countries, as the separation between public sphere and democracy is the most likely dominant principle in the Egyptian milieu. The government is obliged to allow a partly-free public sphere. However, it restricts the formation of real public opinion and establishes the types of laws and legislations that perpetuate the dominance of the ruling party. Simply speaking, it seems that the government allows people to say whatever they want, while allowing itself to act whatever it wants. In this political atmosphere, it is difficult to find a link between public sphere and democratic transformations. However, a free or partly-free public sphere may eventually lead to formation of public opinion that will govern.

Habermas (1989) first conceived of the public sphere as a physical space that first emerged in coffee houses in England and salons in France in the 17th and 18th centuries with the rise of capitalism and the state. He describes the public sphere as a physical place where propertied, educated men who were members of the bourgeois joined together to engage in rational-critical discourse on public matters and other issues of the day. Even in the early public sphere, newspapers and journals were an enabling technology that helped create a network bringing the forums of the coffee houses and salons together to create the larger public sphere. For Habermas and Alexis de Tocqueville, the public sphere was a place where men gathered to rationally discuss issues of the day. Newspapers played a key role in the public sphere by supplying information, creating interest, and helping set the agenda for participants in the public sphere.

Conversation and action oriented around discussion define what the public sphere should be, according to classic theorists. John Keane describes the public sphere as "a particular type of spatial relationship between two or more people, usually connected by a certain means of communication...in which nonviolent controversies erupt, for a brief or more extended period of time, concerning the power relations operating within their given milieu of interaction and/or with the wider milieus of social and political structures within which the disputants are situated" (Rajagopal, 2004). The linkage between people via means of communication is critical here, whether this communication exists via conversation, in the press or on satellite television. Communication is essential for the public sphere, and in many ways, it is the only constitutive element of that space (Franko, 2005).

At a general level, the concept of the public sphere is defined by many scholars as designating a realm related to democratic political discourse. Here, the notion of "public" as in "public opinion" refers to a collection of politically significant shared common interests impacting ideologically upon the exercise of state of power. Of course not all politics (democratic or otherwise) take place through discussion (public or not). The public sphere, however, is a concept applicable to voluntary and violence-free political behaviour. For this reason, Habermas argues that the public sphere needs institutional guarantees of a constitutional state on the one hand, and on the other, a political culture in the broader society of populace accustomed to freedom. This perception helps explain the importance of a democratic constitution and the rule of law as contextual conditions of media's optimum democratic role.

When Alexis de Tocqueville, a French nobleman and political scientist, visited the United States in 1831, he was so impressed with what he termed the "voluntary associations" of men in the United States; he devoted much study and later description of these associations in his treatise on American life, democracy in America. Although Tocqueville utilizes the term "associations" rather than "public sphere," a thorough reading of both men's writings leaves little doubt that they are talking about the same thing. There are obviously some differences between the European and American public spheres. These differences are both political and cultural, but the similarities are more numerous and profound than are the differences. Tocqueville even surmised that the notion of associations in America was imported from England and that the differences can be attributed to Americans' incorporation of their manners and customs.

There are numerous and profound similarities between the American public sphere of the 19th century as described by Tocqueville and the European public sphere of the 17th and 18th centuries as described by Habermas. Nonetheless, there are also discernible differences between the spheres with the greatest difference resting in the relationships between the spheres and their governments. The American public sphere did not clearly reside in the private realm; it was often tied to government. The stronger relationship between government and the American public sphere is logical when one remembers that the Americans were members of a self-governing democracy who believed they had a duty to take an active role in the official governance of their communities. The public spheres of Europe occurred at times and within countries where political power was still very much vested in monarchs and church leaders.

Another difference between the two public spheres is that within the American associations, people pursuing public interests coexisted with people pursuing private interests (Tocqueville, 1956 in Newhagen, 2004) Habermas believed that the pursuit of private interests displaced the pursuit of public interests in the European public spheres (Habermas, 1989in Newhagen, 2004) In Habermas' conceptualization of the public sphere he privileges face-to-face communication, believing the most valuable role for the media is to provide information for intimate exchanges. He accepts that the printed word played a significant role in the development of the bourgeois public sphere, but he did not fully conceive of the key role for media in the public sphere. In his writings he also expresses a distrust for mediated communication, seeing it as an obstacle to "discursive rationality and communicative authenticity".

Taking the aforementioned discussion into account, it is safe to state that public sphere depends to a large extent on the nature of the political system in which it exists. In Europe, the public sphere-which was achieved despite opposition from the state powers, is at odds with what transpired in the United States. Habermas' suggestion that the European public sphere was regulated by its individual members is contradicted by the U.S.'s case, where the media emerge instead as the first and foremost project of nation-building. Starr considers three extended and overlapping "constitutive moments" when political choices and technological developments shaped the media's growth. "America's first information revolution" was the first constitutive" moment," extending from the colonial period to the onset of the civil war" (Rajagopal, 2006). Its distinctive trait was the deliberate development of inexpensive postage, schools, and newspapers through direct and indirect subsidies. The intent was to enable the people of the nascent and geographically dispersed republic to communicate with each other and thereby strengthen their internal ties. The result was a population that actively participated in public and political life. Thus, while European countries discouraged communication by placing taxes on the postal service, the early Post Office in the U.S. saw its goal as promoting intercourse, and reducing the mental distance between town and country. At one point, America's ratio of post offices to people was four times that of England or France.

Starr also notes the government's early realization of the importance of public education, although it was public schools of the North, not the South, that regularly increased enrollment. Starr explains at length the policies that made books and newspapers far less expensive in the United States than in Europe (among these was a disregard for European copyright laws that made windfall profits possible for U.S. publishers). Contemporary observers noted the effects of the early development of the press in the US. The private realm did not arise from a struggle against state absolutism, as in Europe, but as an effect of state formation. Not surprisingly, the constitution and the government are frequently granted cultural sanction to restrict the scope of these customs (Starr, 2004).

On the other hand, Arab political systems have created a politically repressive atmosphere to control the public sphere. The development of media and state in the Arab world confirm the fact that all Arab states controlled the media, especially radio and television, to prevent the establishment of a free public sphere, to restrict the formation of public opinion and to hinder any democratic transformation in the region. "There are several reasons for the predominance of government–owned broadcasting system in the Arab World. However, the most important factor is the intense government interest in the media as political instruments, media reach beyond borders and literary barriers; the government has a much greater interest in controlling them or at least keeping them out of hostile hands" (Rugh, 2004).

In his research on "Arab media and communication systems in the information age", Hamada concludes that democratizing the media and communication system represents a real threat to any undemocratic regime. The majority of Arab governments have never been interested in creating a democratic communication environment in which the citizens can have a voice regarding public issues. Government operated media agencies provide most of the information, and much of the content it supplies is politically biased, incomplete, and of poor quality.

Most Arab governments claim that the issues of development must take priority and that the time is not right for democracy. Therefore, democracy is not a part of most Arab leaders' political agenda.. Although democracy and development represent two distinctly different human endeavours, they are both required, to ensure success, sustainability, adequate levels of information and popular participation. The more objective and the wider the scope of information conveyed, the more likely it will be to sustain democracy and development. Modern communication technology is essential in the speed and efficiency with which data and news are processed and disseminated among different citizens of the society. Another common and related requirement for both democracy and development is an active and public participation (Attiga, 2001).

The bulk of the discussion on media pluralism as a political value continues to be based on the conceptual framework of the public sphere. As a general normative concept against which to assess the media, much of the debate draws upon Habermas's early work (1989) but also, more broadly, the public sphere is understood as a general context of interaction in which deliberation and discussion take place and citizens in general inform and form themselves into the public (Karppinen, 2004).

Lippman conceives of public opinion as the aggregate opinion of persons whose individual opinions are pieced together from what they hear, read, see and are able to imagine. He also believes that their exposure to information is manipulated to create a certain opinion that meets the needs of elites. Lippman's idea of public opinion is quite different from Habermas' conception. Habermas believes public opinion is what develops in the public sphere as the result of rational discourse. He views public opinion as the culmination of sharing of information among enlightened individuals operating in the public interest.

The author completely agrees with Hbermas's notion of the priority of public interests as a condition for the public sphere. First, in order for the public sphere to exist, priority has to be given to social issues. If people left public issues behind and concentrate on their private interests, there will never be a space for the common good, common grounds for members of the public to exchange experience, but personal interests that work against the collective mind. In Egypt, the overwhelming majority are poor, illiterate, and unemployed people who spend much of their time trying to save their food. Hence, the majority is handicapped by illiteracy, poverty, ills and unemployment to such a great extent that they lack motivation to engage in the "public sphere". Also complicating the problem is the government's intolerance with the activities of the opposing parties and political movements. Due to this atmosphere, the role of new communication technologies, especially the Internet, in enhancing public sphere is limited.

MEDIA DIVERSITY: A CORE ELEMENT OF TRUE DEMOCRACY"

Governments often complain about the mass media in their own country; they feel that their messages are distorted and unfairly criticized. True, there are media outlets which are not very serious and professional. However, this problem should not be exaggerated and is not a good excuse for draconian interventions or state control. Instead governments should promote a media policy which encourages voluntary self-discipline and allows for a wide variety of media voices. This is what democracy requires; it also enhances further democratization.

Editors and other media representatives should take careful note of criticism levelled against the quality of some their reporting. Improved training of journalists and a developed system of self-regulation, including codes of ethics and press councils, is of paramount importance. However, the main media problems are these: too little meaningful information is circulated and too few voices are heard. Though the internet has created new possibilities for a more democratic dialogue on political matters, the mass media will surely continue to function as the main messenger of common interest news and as the key arena for public debate.

All over the world, governments and strong business interests dominate media production, not least on the television side. This is to some extent inevitable in view of heavy investment costs. However, this makes it even more essential to encourage competition and take steps to democratize media structures. A minimum requirement is that there is transparency about who is behind the various media outlets. It is sometimes said that the consumers act as a corrective. Media outlets which are too propagandistic tend not to be read, viewed or listened to. However, when there are no or very few alternatives, the problem largely remains. The increased possibility to tune into foreign radio transmissions or satellite television does help but it is still not a realistic option for many because of language and other barriers. Some principles are particularly essential in democratic media policies: that governments and parliaments encourage genuine competition; that the official public service media act impartially and in the interest of all people in society; and that governments are transparent and allow access to their own information.

First: Competition

There are governments and parliaments in Europe which have actively subsidized smaller media, often those run by minorities, in order to secure a broader output. Other governments, however, have actively undermined media they have felt negative about and thereby sabotaged free competition. The way wave lengths for television and radio are allocated is a test which some governments have failed. State agencies deciding on this should work according to agreed, objective criteria and not discriminate against more independent applicants. Another problem in some countries is that the government buys advertisement space only in the "loyal" media, signalling to business companies to follow their lead, with the consequence that independent media in reality are boycotted.

A number of other discriminatory measures have been taken against independent media; some of them obviously intended to push these into bankruptcy. Repeated defamation charges in court and obstacles to buying print paper, printing or distributing the papers are some examples. Such actions must be seen as violations of freedom of expression. It is important that there are real alternatives. A person asked the Ombudsman in one of the former Soviet states what reform he would consider as the most important for human rights protection in the country. His answer was: a truly independent TV channel! This, in his opinion, would be the most efficient way of promoting an open, free debate and an honest monitoring of problems in society.

Second: The Role of "Official" Media

They should operate in an impartial manner in the interest of the population at large. They could indeed be an essential counter weight to the business driven entertainment media. The "public service" media – often financed from tax money or other common resources – should of course not be used as propaganda instruments for certain politicians. Their independence and impartiality are of paramount importance and ought to be protected through agreed guidelines and an appropriate procedure of appointing directors.

Third: The Transparency of the Public Authorities

Media culture is considerably affected by the attitude of the authorities towards journalists asking for data, also on sensitive matters. The media have a legitimate interest in requesting information about government decisions and actions. They can serve as representatives of citizens who have the right to know how their elected leaders act on their behalf. Open access to government information is therefore a democratic principle of high priority. It is not enough that ministers are generous in giving interviews. There should be legal affirmation of the right of citizens, including journalists, to obtain written documents and other information from the authorities. Exceptions from this transparency rule should be regulated strictly and allowed only for the protection of legitimate state secrets. These problems are still more acute in transition countries where news and political information previously were firmly controlled by those in power. However, there is a need to discuss these questions all over Europe: Do we have a genuine competition in the media market? Do the public service media play the role it should? Are governments genuinely transparent?

4

Theory and Practices of Mass Media

"Cultivation analysis concentrates on the enduring and common consequences of growing up and living with television. Theories of the cultivation process attempt to understand and explain the dynamics of television as the distinctive and dominant cultural force of our age. Cultivation analysis uses a survey instrument, administered to representative samples of respondents.

The responses are analyzed by a number of demographic variables including gender, age, race, education, income, and political self-designation (liberal, moderate, conservative). Where applicable, other controls, such as urban-rural residence, newspaper reading, and party affiliation are also used.

Cultivation analysis is a part of the Cultural Indicators (CI) research project. CI is a data base and a series of reports relating recurrent features of the world of television to viewer conceptions of reality. Its cumulative content data archive contains observations on over 4,500 programmes and 40,000 characters coded according to many thematic, demographic and action categories." "...specifies that repeated, intense exposure to deviant definitions of 'reality' in the mass media leads to perception of the 'reality' as normal. The result is a social legitimisation of the 'reality' depicted in the mass media, which can influence behavior. Gerbner first introduced cultivation theory in 1969 with his work Toward "Cultural Indicators": The

Analysis of Mass Mediated Public Message Systems. Gerbner begins developing cultivation as a structural piece for the long-term examination of public messages in media influence and understanding. He notes in the introduction that "the approach is based on conception of these message systems as the common culture through which communities cultivate shared and public notions about facts, values, and contingencies of human existence". Gerbner clarifies that his objectives are not with "information, education, persuasion, and the like, or with any kind of direct communication 'effects.'" More accurately, his concern remains with "the collective context within which, and in response to which, different individual and group selections and interpretations of messages take place". Nonetheless, Gerbner's works present a social psychology theory on communication effects, and consequently, on persuasion as related to mass media.

Gerbner speaks of the "cultivation of collective conscious" in relation to the rapid growth of media outlets (in particular, television) and the capacity of mass media to transcend traditional "barriers of time, space, and social grouping". Cultivation then describes the process in which entire publics are affected by content on television. Potter (1993) notes Gerbner's intentions for using "cultivation" as an academic term to define his interest in "the more diffuse effects on perceptions that are shaped over a long period of exposure to media messages". "Cultivation," rather than "long-term effects" indicates the emphasis on the constant nurturing, exposure, and consistent incorporation the viewing public experiences through mass media channels.

THE MEANING

The first concept most students learn about the meaning of meanings is the Semantic Triangle. This label refers to the three part connection among a referent, a reference, and a symbol. The referent is the thing, such as my cat Baxter. The reference is the thought I have of Baxter, a 12 year old grey tabby who loves to lounge on my computer keyboard. The symbol is the word "Baxter." Notice that if I am talking about Baxter I have selected the referent and have control over the reference and symbol. However, if I talk to you about Baxter lounging on my keyboard you will not understand my meaning until you understand the thing (the referent) I am speaking of and the thoughts (references) I have of that thing.

The Semantic Triangle allows for some ambiguity. After all, it is not possible for you to know exactly what my thoughts are. Still, there needs to be ways for people to help make sure they are understand by others, especially when referents, references, or symbols are new to one or more of the communicators. There are four ways in which we help each other understand what we mean:

1. Definitions--these tell others what is in our heads, or what we mean when we use a certain word;
2. Metaphors--metaphors allow us to talk about something unfamiliar in terms of something else that is familiar. Metaphors also allow us to merge two concepts whose result is a third concept. For example, I could speak of Baxter as a furry bundle of energy.
3. Feedforward--this is the process of providing feedback to ourselves before we even speak, so that we help ourselves choose the best way to communicate in a given situation to a given audience; and
4. Basic English--the set of 850 words out of which any person can effectively communicate ideas, simple or complex.

ATTRIBUTION THEORY

Attribution Theory assumes that people try to determine why people do what they do. This search for a reason behind behavior allows people to attribute causes to behavior. A behavioral cause could be situational, where a person had to do something because of the situation they were in. A behavioral cause could also result from something unique to person. Examples of those unique attributes include, but are not limited to:

1. the person's desire to perform the behavior (e.g., they did it because they wanted to do it),

2. the person's whim (e.g., they did it because they felt like doing it),
3. the person's ability (e.g., the person is capable of doing the behavior),
4. the person's sense of obligation (e.g., the person did it because they felt they had to or should do the behavior), and
5. the person's sense of belonging (e.g., the person did it to fit in with a group of people important to the person).

A person seeking to understand why another person did something may attribute one or more causes to that behavior. However, a three-stage process leads up to the final attribution:

1. the person must perceive or observe the behavior,
2. then the person must believe that the behavior was intentionally performed, and
3. then the person must determine if they believe the other person was forced to perform the behavior (in which case the cause is attributed to the situation) or not (in which case the cause is attributed to the other person).

CONSTRUCTIVISM

Constructivism makes three assumptions regarding communication:

1. all communication is intentional
2. communication is goal-driven
3. negotiation comes into play with shared interpretation (meaning)

Constructivism focuses on individuals rather than interactions. It tries to account for why people make the certain communicative choices. Constructs are the basis of constructivism. They are dimensions of judgment and can be thought of as filters, files, templates, or interpretive schemes. They are domain specific, almost exclusively focusing on interpersonal message variations. Constructs are assumed to change over time, following Werner's Orthogenetic Principle (impressions start globally, undifferentiated, and unorganized then get more complex, abstract, differentiated, and organized as people develop).

Constructivist research uses the Role Category Question to find constructs embedded in free response writing, often about a person the writer likes and a person the writer dislikes. The more constructs a person uses the more cognitively differentiated they are. Cognitive differentiation is a subset of cognitive complexity, which measures the organization, quantity, and level of abstractness of the constructs a person holds about another person. Cognitive differentiation measures only the quantity of constructs but still predicts the degree to which a communicator is person centered and other oriented. Constructivism claims that the more cognitively differentiated a person is the more likely they are to be a competent communicator (one who intentionally uses knowledge of shared interpretations to express meaning is such a way as to control another person's interpretations of some event, object, person, etc.).

Constructivist research shows moderately strong correlations between the organizational level of a person and cognitive differentiation, persuasive ability, and perspective taking. Smaller correlations have been found between organizational level and self monitoring.

ELABORATION LIKELIHOOD MODEL

The Elaboration Likelihood Model claims that there are two paths to persuasion: the central path and the peripheral path. The central path is most appropriately used when the receiver is motivated to think about the message and has the ability to think about the message. If the person cares about the issue and has access to the message with a minimum of distraction, then that person will elaborate on the message. Lasting persuasion is likely if the receiver thinks, or rehearses, favorable thoughts about the message. A boomerang effect (moving away from the advocated position) is likely to occur if the subject rehearses unfavorable thoughts about the message. If the message is ambiguous but pro-attitudinal (in line with the receiver's attitudes) then persuasion is likely. If the message is ambiguous but counter-attitudinal then a boomerang effect is likely.

If the message is ambiguous but attitudinally neutral (with respect to the receiver) or if the receiver is unable or not motivated to listen to the message then the receiver will look for a peripheral cue. Peripheral cues include such communication strategies as trying to associate the advocated position with things the receiver already thinks postively towards (e.g., food, money, sex), using an expert appeal, and attempting a contrast effect where the advocated position is presented after several other positions, which the receiver despises, have been presented. If the peripheral cue association is accepted then there may be a temporary attitude change and possibly future elaboration. If the peripheral cue association is not accepted, or if it is not present, then the person retains the attitude initially held.

If the receiver is motivated and able to elaborate on the message and if there are compelling arguments to use, then the central route to persuasion should be used. If the receiver is unlikely to elaborate the message, or if the available arguments are weak, then the peripheral route to persuasion should be used.

COMMUNICATION

Humans communicate with each other across time, space, and contexts. Those contexts are often thought of as the particular combinations of people comprising a communication situation. For example, theories of interpersonal communication address the communication between dyads (two people). Group communication deals with groups, organizational communication addresses organizations, mass communication encompasses messages broadcast, usually electronically, to mass audiences, intercultural communication looks at communication among people of different cultures, and gender communication focuses on communication issues of women and between the sexes. Newer contexts include health communication and computer-mediated communication.

Contexts of communication are best thought of as a way to focus on certain communication processes and effects. Communication context boundaries are fluid. Thus, we can see interpersonal and group communication in organizations. Gender communication occurs whenever people of different sexes communicate. We can have mass communications to individuals, group, and organizations. Using communication contexts as a means to help us study communication helps ùs out of problems some people associate with the intrapersonal context (some say the "so-called" intrapersonal context). Some people facetiously say intrapersonal communication exists when someone talks to themselves. It's more accurate to define intrapersonal communication as thinking. While thinking normally falls within the purview of psychology we can recognize that we often think, plan, contemplate, and strategize about communication past, present, and future. It is legitimate to study the cognitive aspects of communication processes. So, even if some people call those cognitive aspects of communication thinking, it can be helpful to allow the context of intrapersonal communication to exist, thereby legitimating an avenue of communication research.

COORDINATED MANAGEMENT OF MEANING

The Coordinated Management of Meaning theorizes communication as a process that allows us to create and manage social reality. As such, this theory describes how we as communicators make sense of our world, or create meaning. Méaning can be understood to exist in a hierarchy, depending on the sources of that meaning. Those sources include:

1. raw sensory data--the inputs to your eyes and ears, the visual and auditory stimuli you will interpret to see images and hear sounds;
2. content--interpreted stimuli, where the words spoken are understood by what they refer to;
3. speech acts--content takes on more meaning when it is further interpreted as belonging to a speaker who has specific communication styles, relationships with the listener, and intentions;

4. episodes--in common terms, you may think of this as the context of the conversation or discourse where when you understand the context you understand what the speaker thinks he or she is doing;
5. master contracts--these define the relationships the communicating participants, or what each can expect of the other in a specific episode;
6. life scripts--the set of episodes a person expects they will participate in; and
7. cultural patterns--culturally created set of rules that govern what we understand to be normal communication in a given episode.

Persons use two types of rules to coordinate the management of meaning among those seven levels of meaning. First, we use constitutive rules to help understand how meaning at one level determine meaning at another level. Second, we use regulative rules to help us regulate what we say so that we stay within what we consider to be normal communication in a given episode.

SOCIAL JUDGMENT THEORY

The key point of the Social Judgment Theory is that attitude change (persuasion) is mediated by judgmental processes and effects. Put differently, persuasion occurs at the end of the process where a person understands a message then compares the position it advocates to the person's position on that issue. A person's position on an issue is dependent on:

1. the person's most preferred position (their anchor point),
2. the person's judgment of the various alternatives (spread across their latitudes of acceptance, rejection, and noncommitment), and
3. the person's level of ego-involvement with the issue.

Consider the course choices available to you next term. For the sake of argument, let's say you have four required courses to finish but have one three credit hour elective remaining. What courses open to you would you definitely not enroll in, no matter what? Those courses fall in your Latitude of Rejection.

Do you think anyone could persuade you to take a class that falls in that latitude? Not likely. And, the more ego-involved you are in the decision to enroll in your course (the more you care about that decision) the larger your Latitude of Rejection will be. Persuasive messages that advocate positions in your Latitude of Rejection will be contrasted by you. That is, they will appear to be further away from your anchor point than they actually are. That's not good news for the would-be persuader.

Now consider the courses that you really don't have an opinion about, that you don't have positive or negative feelings toward. Those courses fall in your Latitude of Noncommitment. It's possible that someone could persuade you to enroll in one of those courses, but you'd have to learn more about the course first, at least enough until you an opinion, or judgment, about it. Now, consider all those courses you would consider enrolling in. Those courses fall in your Latitude of Acceptance. A person with good arguments might be able to persuade you to take one of those courses, especially if, in your judgment, the course is similar to your anchor point course. Persuasive messages that advocate positions in your Latitude of Acceptance will be assimilated by you. That is, they will appear to be closer to your anchor point than they actually are. That's good news for the would-be persuader.

If you are persuaded, then the further a message's position is away from your anchor point, the larger your attitude change will be. But remember that it is very unlikely that you will be persuaded out of your Latitude of Rejection. So, once a message enters that region and moves away from your anchor point, the amount of your attitude change decreases.

SOCIAL PENETRATION THEORY

Social Penetration Theory asserts that as relationships develop persons communication from superficial to deeply personal topics, slowing penetrating the communicators' public persona to reach their core personality or sense of self. First viewed as a direct, continuous penetration from public person to private person, social penetration is know considered to be a cyclical and dialectical. Relationships have normal ebbs and flows. They do not automatically get better and better where the participants learn more and more about each other. Instead, the participants have to work through the tensions of the relationship (the dialectic) while they learn and group themselves and a parties in a relationships. At times the relationships is very open and sharing. Other time, one or both parties to the relationship need their space, or have other concerns, and the relationship is less open. The theory posits that these cycles occur throughout the life of the relationship as the persons try to balance their needs for privacy and open relationship.

Persons allow other people to penetrate their public self when they disclose personal information. The decision to disclose is based on the perceived rewards the person will gain if he or she discloses information. If a person perceives that the cost of disclosing information is greater than the rewards for disclosing information then no information will be disclosed. The larger the reward-cost ratio the more disclosure takes place. If you think to the relationships you have been in you will probably find that in almost all of them more disclosure took place at the outset of the relationship than at any other place. That happens because people initially disclose superficial information that costs very little if another person finds it out. It matters little if you know that I enjoy all types of music but especially enjoy listening to blues, saxophone jazz, and straightforward rock-n-roll.

It gets a bit more personal when I start explaining why I like those types of music, so I, like most people, will wait until you reciprocate and tell me your favorite types of music before I allow you more visibility into who I am. The deeper I allow you to penetrate my self, the more affective information I will disclose to you. The closer you get to my core self the higher my perceived costs will be for disclosing that information. Thus, it is not likely that I will disclose very personal information to very many people.

UNCERTAINTY REDUCTION

The Uncertainty Reduction Theory asserts that people have a need to reduce uncertainty about others by gaining information about them. Information gained can then be used to predict the others' behavior.

Reducing uncertainty is particularly important in relationship development, so it is typical to find more uncertainty reduction behavior among people when they expect or want to develop a relationship than among people who expect or know they will not develop a relationship. Consider how you try to reduce uncertainty about someone you have just met and want to spend more time with. Now consider how you try to reduce uncertainty about people you meet on an elevator.

There are three basic ways people seek information about another person:

1. Passive strategies--we observe the person, either in situations where the other person is likely to be self-monitoring* (a reactivity search) as in a classroom, or where the other person is likely to act more naturally (a disinhibition search) as in the stands at a football game.
2. Active strategies--we ask others about the person we're interested in or try to set up a situation where we can observe that person (e.g., taking the same class, sitting a table away at dinner). Once the situation is set up we sometime observe (a passive strategy) or talk with the person (an interactive strategy).
3. Interactive strategies--we communicate directly with the person.

GROUPTHINK

Groupthink occurs when a homogenous highly cohesive group is so concerned with maintaining unanimity that they fail to evaluate all their alternatives and options. Groupthink members see themselves as part of an in-group working against an outgroup opposed to their goals. You can tell if a group suffers from groupthink if it:

1. overestimates its invulnerability or high moral stance,
2. collectively rationalizes the decisions it makes,
3. demonizes or stereotypes outgroups and their leaders,

4. has a culture of uniformity where individuals censor themselves and others so that the facade of group unanimty is maintained, and
5. contains members who take it upon themselves to protect the group leader by keeping information, theirs or other group members', from the leader.

Groups engaged in groupthink tend to make faulty decisions when compared to the decisions that could have been reached using a fair, open, and rational decision-making process. Groupthinking groups tend to:

1. fail to adequately determine their objectives and alternatives,
2. fail to adequately assess the risks associated with the group's decision,
3. fail to cycle through discarded alternatives to reexamine their worth after a majority of the group discarded the alternative,
4. not seek expert advice,
5. select and use only information that supports their position and conclusions, and
6. does not make contingency plans in case their decision and resulting actions fail.

Group leaders can prevent groupthink by:

1. encouraging members to raise objections and concerns;
2. refraining from stating their preferences at the onset of the group's activities;
3. allowing the group to be independently evaluated by a separate group with a different leader;
4. splitting the group into sub-groups, each with different chairpersons, to separately generate alternatives, then bringing the sub-groups together to hammer out differences;
5. allowing group members to get feedback on the group's decisions from their own constituents;
6. seeking input from experts outside the group;

7. assigning one or more members to play the role of the devil's advocate;
8. requiring the group to develop multiple scenarios of events upon which they are acting, and contingencies for each scenario; and
9. calling a meeting after a decision consensus is reached in which all group members are expected to critically review the decision before final approval is given.

ORGANIZING

Karl Weick writes of the process oriented organizing, rather than the structural oriented organization. Communication is key to the organizing process because it is a large factor in the sense-making process people use when they organize. The sense-making process is an attempt to reduce equivocality, or multiple meanings, in the information used by the people in the organization. When information is handled by the organizers they go through the stages of:

1. enactment--where they define the situation and begin the process of dealing with the information,
2. selection--where they narrow the equivocality by deciding what to deal with and what to leave along, ignore, or disregard, and
3. retention--where they decide what information, and its meaning, they will retain for future use.

In both the selection and retention stages there are additional processes. These processes depend on double interacts. An act occurs when you say something ("Can I have a popsicle?"). An interact occurs when you say something and I respond ("No, it will spoil you dinner."). A double interact occurs when you say something, I respond, then you respond to that, adjusting your first statement ("Well, how about half a popsicle?"). Double interacts works in:

1. assembly rules--the operating procedures (e.g., all requests for information from the media must be handled by the Corporate Communications Dept., requests for pay raises must be made through your immediate

supervisor, etc.) used by the company to choose what to do maximize the likelihood of achieving the goal at hand, and in the

2. behavior cycles--sets of double interacts the organization uses to facilitate the selection and retention process. Examples of behavior cycles include staff meetings, coffee-break rumoring, e-mail conversations, internal reports, etc.

Weick sees the the organization as a system taking in equivocal information from its environment, trying to make sense of that information, and using what was learned in the future. As such, organizations evolve as they make sense out of themselves and their environment.

MUTED GROUP THEORY

Muted Group Theory is a critical theory because it is concerned with power and how it is used against people. While critical theories can separate the powerful and the powerless any number of ways, this theory chooses to bifurcate the power spectrum into men and women. Muted Group Theory begins with the premise that language is culture bound, and because men have more power than women, men have more influence over the language, resulting in language with a male-bias. Men create the words and meaning for the culture, allowing expression of their ideas. Women, on the other hand, are left out of this meaning creation and left without a means to express that which is unique to them. That leaves women as a muted group.

The Muted Group Theory rests on three assumptions:

1. Men and women perceive the world differently because they have different perception shaping experiences. Those different experiences are a result of men and women performing different tasks in society.
2. Men enact their power politically, perpetuating their power and suppressing women's ideas and meanings from gaining public acceptance.
3. Women must convert their unique ideas, experiences, and meanings into male language in order to be heard.

The premise and assumptions leads to a number of hypotheses about women's communication:

1. Women have a more difficult time expressing themselves than do men.
2. Women understand what men mean more easily than men understand what women mean.
3. Women communicate with each other using media not accepted by the dominant male communicators.
4. Women are less satisfied with communication than are men.
5. Women are not likely to create new words, but sometimes do so to create meanings special and unique to women.

Muted Group Theory does not claim that these differences are based in biology. Instead, the theory claims that men risk losing their dominant position if they listen to women, incorporate their experiences in the language, and allow women to be equal partners in language use and creation. Language is about power, and men have it.

FACE

Erving Goffman wrote about face in conjunction with how people interact in daily life. He claims that everyone is concerned, to some extent, with how others perceive them. We act socially, striving to maintain the identity we create for others to see. This identity, or public self-image, is what we project when we interact socially. To lose face is to publicly suffer a diminished self-image. Maintaining face is accomplished by taking a line while interacting socially. A line is what the person says and does during that interaction showing how the person understands the situation at hand and the person's evaluation of the interactants. Social interaction is a process combining line and face, or face work. Brown and Levinson use the concept of face to explain politeness. To them, politeness is universal, resulting from people's face needs:

1. Positive face is the desire to be liked, appreciated, approved, etc.

2. Negative face is the desire not to be imposed upon, intruded, or otherwise put upon.

Positive politeness addresses positive face concerns, often by showing prosocial concern for the other's face. Negative politeness addresses negative face concerns, often by acknowledging the other's face is threatened. Anytime a person threatens another person's face, the first person commits a face-threatening act (FTA). Face-threatening acts come in four varieties, listed below in order from most to least face threatening:

1. Do an FTA baldly, with no politeness (e.g., "Close your mouth when you eat you swine.").
2. Do an FTA with positive politeness (e.g., "You have such beautiful teeth. I just wish I didn't see them when you eat.").
3. Do an FTA with negative politeness (e.g., "I know you're very hungry and that steak is a bit tough, but I would appreciate it if you would chew with your mouth closed.").
4. Do an FTA indirectly, or off-record (e.g., "I wonder how far a person's lips can stretch yet remain closed when eating?"). An indirect FTA is ambiguous so the receiver may "catch the drift" but the speaker can also deny a meaning if they wish.

Of course, a person can choose not to threaten another's face at all, but when a face must be threaten, a speaker can decide how threatening he or she will be.

THE SPIRAL OF SILENCE

The Spiral of Silence is a model of why people are unwilling to publicly express their opinions when they believe they are in the minority. The model is based on three premises:

1. people have a "quasi-statistical organ," a sixth-sense if you will, which allows them to know the prevailing public opinion, even without access to polls,
2. people have a fear of isolation and know what behaviors will increase their likelihood of being socially isolated, and

3. people are reticent to express their minority views, primarily out of fear of being isolated.

The closer a person believes the opinion held is similar to the prevailing public opinion, the more they are willing to openly disclose that opinion in public. Then, if public sentiment changes, the person will recognize that the opinion is less in favor and will be less willing to express that opinion publicly. As the perceived distance between public opinion and a person's personal opinion grows, the more unlikely the person is to express their opinion. Consider the case of Dennis Rodman, one of the stars of the Chicago Bulls basketball team. Mr. Rodman has consistently been an incredible competitor and rebounder for the Detroit Pistons, San Antonio Spurs, and Chicago Bulls. Over the years he attracted a large fan base, but watched it fall in recent years as he got "weirder" or more "individualistic" (depending on how you interpret his behavior). Fans in San Antonio welcomed Mr. Rodman when he first arrived, but vocal supporters were hard to find just before he was traded to Chicago. At the start of the 1996-1997 season Mr. Rodman's stock was high in Chicago, falling off somewhat after the "kick the cameraman" incident. I wish him well, but if the public becomes displeased with him the Spiral of Silence will strike his supporters once again.

STANDARD FORMAT FOR A SOCIAL SCIENTIFIC JOURNAL ARTICLE

Social scientific research reports and journal articles are designed to describe what researchers did, why they did it, how they did it, what they found, and what that means. While all journals have their specific requirements, all research reports and journal articles follow the same standard format. The format is standardized to make it easy for readers to study research presented in a variety of journals. The speed with which you read journal articles and the understanding you gain from those articles will increase once you become familiar with the standard format.

1. *Title:* The title should be brief but clearly describe the focus of the research described in the article.

2. *Author(s):* The names of all authors is given. The institutional affiliation is also given, sometimes with the authors' names, sometimes at the bottom of the first page, sometimes at the end of the article, and sometimes at the end of the journal.
3. *Abstract:* The abstract is a brief summary of the article designed to give the reader an overview of what the researchers did, how they did it, what they found, and what it means.
4. *Introduction:* This section describes all prior research and theories that all relevant to the study described in the article. That prior literature is integrated to form the basis of an argument(s) supporting why the present study was conducted. The introduction also introduces and argumentatively supports whatever research hypotheses and/or research questions are addresses in the study.
5. *Method:* This section describes what the researchers did. The section is written in sufficient detail and precision to allow a reader to replicate the study. There are exceptions to this principle of replication (e.g., lengthy surveys are not normally included, complex and detailed instructions to experimental subjects are often summarized, etc.). The method section contains as many of these five subsections as are appropriate for the study:

   Subjects: The demographics of the persons used in the study.

   Apparatus: Detailed description of special equipment used, if any, in the study.

   Procedures: Detailed description of what the researchers and subjects did.

   Design: Description of the type of experimental design used in the study.

   Materials or Measures: Description of which testing and measuring instruments were used, and how they were used if differently than their normal use.

6. *Results:* This section describes what the researchers found. You will often find this section to be a mixture of statistical reports, tables, and prose describing those numbers.
7. *Discussion:* This section provides the authors' the opportunity to tell what their research results mean, both to the study and to the world at large.
8. *References:* A list of all works (e.g., books, articles, personal communication, etc.) cited in the study. Most, and usually all, of the cited works will be cited and discussed in the introduction section of the article.

Readers familiar with statistical analyses and the theories, prior research, and methodologies used in field related to the article should have no problem understanding the article. Readers lacking familiarity with field related theories, research, and methodology usually have some difficulties grasping the big picture of the study, but if the article is well written the readers can understand enough to understand the gist of the study. Readers unfamiliar with statistical analyses fare worse. These readers often entirely skip the Method and Results section, relying solely on the Introduction and Discussion sections. When read alone, the Introduction and Discussion sections can work well to provide the reader with an overview of the study. However, these sections generally stay at a higher level, leaving the details for the Method and Results sections. Often, the prize is in the details.

Certainly, the Results section contains the basis for determining the validity of information in the Discussion section. Readers lacking statistical analyses expertise will be best served by taking a course on experimental design and statistical analysis, preferably in the same discipline as the journal articles they read (e.g., readers of communication articles benefit from an experimental design and statistical analysis course offered by the communication department, readers of psychology articles benefit from an experimental design and statistical analysis course offered by the psychology department, etc.). An abstract is presented to the reader before the beginning of an article.

The abstract briefly tells what the researchers did, how they did it, what they found, and what that means. More specifically, an abstract of an social scientific study will describe:

1. the problem being investigated or question being answer,
2. the subjects, along with key information about those subjects,
3. the experimental method(s) used,
4. the results of the study, including statistical significance levels; and
5. what the results mean, both in the study and with regard to prior research, theories, and the world outside the research lab.

A properly written abstract will convey all that information in about 100 to 120 words. There should be no reason to refer to the article to understand jargon, abbreviations, or other oddities in the abstract.

Use abstracts to gain a first glance into journal articles. When you are researching a particular topic you can usually tell if a journal article pertains to that topic just by reading the abstract. If you determine that the article is relevant then be sure to read the entire article. Be aware that when a journal article reports multiple significant findings only the most important four or five will be mentioned in the abstract. When writing about a journal article never rely solely on the abstract (unless you absolutely cannot find the journal article, then be sure to cite the abstract, not the article).

JARGON BUSTING

Typical of an emerging technology, the Semantic Web literature is veiled in a bewildering array of technical jargon. So much so that a time-pressed researcher might be forgiven for concluding that the Semantic Web is something for geeks and that it has no bearing on real work and real people; that it (unrealistically) requires everyone to create all online content in the RDF (Resource Description Framework)

Semantic Web language. This, of course, could not be further from the truth. Take the Weblogs (Blogs) phenomenon as an example. Few users of Weblogs are aware that they are publishing, syndicating and aggregating data onto the Semantic Web as well as the human-readable Web. Weblog technology revolves around the RSS (Rich Site Summary or RDF Site Summary) family of languages that vary in their human-readability but are united in their machine readability. This resultant machine processibility is exploited to connect even the most human-centric RSS vocabularies into the Semantic Web directly, or through automated transformation to RDF. Weblogs thus form a valuable (and vast) source of richly interconnected information that requires little or no knowledge of the Semantic Web in order to create and use it.

For the information researcher, the Semantic Web view of this data enables seamless fusion of Weblog data with data from completely different sources such as dictionaries, thesauri, catalogues, databases as well as the 'traditional' Web. Where all this will lead is uncertain but the jargon is no obstacle to its creation and use.

BOTTOM-UP REVOLUTION

What seems certain is that both evolution and revolution will occur, and that the latter is all too easily overlooked. For instance, given the proliferation of data about data (metadata) that underpins the Semantic Web, it is tempting to focus in on the obvious prospect of a better-than-Google search engine. Such a "semantic search" engine is able to determine whether the query "orange" refers to the colour, the fruit, the mobile phone company, or a chemical weapon used by the United States. As clever and useful as this may be, it is only an evolutionary enhancement of something that is already possible on the Web today. By looking in a little more detail at what is happening on the Semantic Web today, it is possible to gain a deeper insight into where revolution is starting to occur. In this article we will do just that; we will take a look at one of the most exciting new developments on the Semantic Web. Joined-up information about people, emanating not from some centralistic database but from individuals themselves. In many ways, the explosive growth of social networking software, sites and data is representative of the way the Semantic Web is emerging. Weblogs were the first wave of this evolution/ revolution; they allowed individuals to publish data in a sufficiently structured format for machine processing of that data to be relatively trivial.

Communities formed around weblogs in a bottom-up fashion, defined implicitly through syndication and through the lists of other weblogs ("blogrolls") that frequently accompanied weblogs. The next step, perhaps more revolutionary than evolutionary, is to explicitly define these (and other) communities in a way that is more easily machine processible. The Friend Of A Friend (FOAF) project is one such initiative that is making this possible and, like weblogs, it does this from the bottom up. One of the aims of the FOAF project is to improve the chances of happy accidents by describing the connections between people (and the things that they care about such as documents and places).

FOAF is a vocabulary for describing people, used analogously to Dublin Core metadata for documents. The idea is to use FOAF to describe the sorts of things you would put on your homepage-your friends, your interests, your pictures-in a structured fashion that machines find easy to process. What you get from this is a network of people instead of a network of web pages: the Web now contains descriptions of real things in the world-people-and because the Semantic Web is designed to be open and extensible, information about what these people do (their calendar), what they own (cars, houses, pets), what they create (documents, pictures, weblogs), can all be described as well.

Several million FOAF documents are out there on the Web already, created both by individuals and by various social software and networking sites. FOAF documents can be created by hand, but increasingly, FOAF is being created from existing databases or by mining the existing Web. When people need to know something and the area is outside their expertise, they need a way into the information landscape. They need to find out what the main topics of interest are; who is well thought of; what where the important issues and papers in the area. People often serve as conduits for this type of information, with personal contacts serving as a way into an area and the key individuals within a field serving as a way of finding the main issues. FOAF applications cannot replace the subtle social interactions which characterise personal information exchange, but they can help to make connections that might not otherwise have occurred: for example, by enabling certain sorts of information to be accurately processed by computers and therefore much easier to search.

Privacy and trust are clearly issues in FOAF as with all digital information on the Web or elsewhere. Organisations of various sorts already intensely mine the Web for information about individuals, email spammers being the most frequent example. FOAF includes protection against email spammers but in wider terms the very network of connections described in FOAF is likely to be its greatest asset in assessing reliability and quality of digital information on the Web.

MEDIA CONTROL

"The conditions associated with a particular class of conditions of existence produce habitus, systems of durable, transportable dispositions, structured structures predisposed to function as structuring structures, that is, as principles which generate and organize practices and representations that can be objectively adapted to their outcomes without presupposing a conscious aiming at ends or an express mastery of the operations necessary in order to attain them. Objectively 'regulated' and 'regular' without being in any way the product of obedience to rules, they can be collectively orchestrated without being the product of the organizing actions of a conductor" (Bourdieu, p. 53)

The above quote by Bourdieu, when viewed from the perspective of the society as the 'habitus', is quiet informing (in theory as well as in practice) of media's interplay with the social structures within which they are embedded. As we have seen throughout our course readings, media technologies-as important instruments at various levels of communication processes in the society, have encountered resistance by various cultural and social norms, and somewhat mixed response from economical and political forces because of their profit making potentials or power generation ability. More then any other type of technology, media and communication technologies have been the subject of public and scholarly debates because of their intrinsic characteristics to be able to convey (asynchronously) content across time and space (at distance), inscribed in form of data, information, images, knowledge, and wisdom, in mediums such as books, data tape drives, CD-ROMS, video and audio tapes, etc. Additionally, synchronous communication has enabled instantaneous communication among people (e.g. telephone, audio and video conferencing, online chat) enabling efficient, but not necessarily effective exchange of information, ideas, thoughts, and concepts.

The pervasive and widespread use of media technologies, often used ubiquitously for symbolic purposes, is also used by the governing elites to maintain the status quo and ensure stability. The necessity to reproduce and maintain a stable state, the habitus (to borrow from Bourdieu whose habitus concept is similar to the stable state produced and maintained by the hegemonic ideology), requires ways for disseminating cultural and political material of the dominant ideology. Similarly to how Bourdieu describes the functioning of the habitus, Gitlin defines the status quo as hegemony, "a ruling class's (or alliance's) domination of subordinate classes and groups through the elaboration and penetration of ideology (ideas and assumptions) into their common sense and everyday practice," and contends that it "is systematic (but not necessary or even usually deliberate) engineering of mass consent to established order" (Gitlin, 1980, pp. 253). Further, elaborating on the aspect of hegemony and clarifying the composition of the elite, mostly government, corporate establishment and those institutions that produce cultural artifacts, Schiller (1996) explains their economic reason for cooperation: "The American economy is now hostage to a relatively small number of giant private companies, with interlocking connections, that set the national agenda. This power is particularly characteristic of the communication and information sector where the national cultural-media agenda is provided by a very small (and declining) number of integrated private combines. This development has deeply eroded free individual expression, a vital element of a democratic society".

This paper will attempt to elaborate on the interplay between media and communication technologies, and social structures and forces (social, cultural, economical, political), whether institutionalized or not, emphasizing that both the content and the channels of communication through which the content is distributed are important factors in the production, maintenance and further reproduction of the artifacts of the dominant ideology. I will argue that the content that is being represented and recorded, when conveyed via open communication (such as the Internet), can show us the liberating potentials of various media technologies. As such, communication technologies are situated as important actors in the process to displacing or shifting the status quo.

Evident from Gitlin's and Schiller's arguments is their emphasis on the necessity of free and open communication among the masses if there is to be any deliverance from the 'claws' of the media. On the contrary, it is the one-way communication (radio, TV, cable) utilized by the elites to achieve the subordination and dissemination of the hegemonic ideology. Fiske (1996) further elaborates this in his argument that surveillance technology is also used as means to discern the norms and regulations necessary to maintain the hegemony ideology: "Norms are crucial to any surveillance system, for without them it cannot identify the abnormal. Norms are what enable it to decide what information should be turned into knowledge and what individuals need to be monitored". Fiske's technologised surveillance of the physical goes hand-in-hand with surveillance of the discourse (what issues are raised on TV, radio, etc.) "because unequal access to those technologies ensures their use in promoting similar power-block interests". The important point brought forth here, directly or indirectly, is the identification of the closed, unidirectional (with masses on the receiving end) and restricted access of communication technology.

These aspects are identified as necessary characteristics for the maintenance and reproduction of the hegemonic ideology, enabling the elites to set the form, format and content of the public discourse (broadcasting, TV, radio, press, etc.), and as importantly decide who can participate. Therefore, it can be argued that this manifestation of communication technologies, entangled in the web of one-way communication and used by the elites for power control and dissemination of material in support of the hegemonic ideology, has shaped the traditional scholarly and public discourse, as well as their practical use, to view communication technology as intrinsically embedded with features, characteristics and functionalities, for reinforcing and aiding the hegemonic ideology.

This biased view, that communication technologies are inherently suited to help media control, is troublesome and factually wrong. For example, the scholarly and public discourse on early cable technology shows that cable access was intended for use unlike it is being used today (for dissemination popular consumer culture through its various formats with the aims of making profit). Streeter (1997) argues that cable "had the potential to rehumanize a dehumanized society, to eliminate the existing bureaucratic restrictions of government regulation common to the industrial world, and to empower the currently powerless public". He further notes that the cable system had the potential to enable two-way communication and interactivity, but apparently failed to do so due to the social (un)response on the part of the audience: "Cable television was something that could have an important impact upon society, and it thus called for a response on the part of society; it was something to which society could respond and act upon, but that was itself outside society". And then adds that cable should not be viewed as an "autonomous entity that had simply appeared on the scene as the result of scientific and technical research". Here we see a distinction between the current social status of cable as profit making machinery and its potentials to have become socially responsible technology that would have empowered the audience with two-way open communication.

The above suggests that the communicative aspects of the production and reproduction of the dominant ideology, including the production of consent in the audience/consumer or citizen, are identified by media and communication technologies characterized by closed, one-way communication. This provides the elites with the ability to control the public discourse by selectively choosing the issues of discussion, and at the same time is able to control the access to the discourse: "But communication and information technology does not merely circulate discourse and make it available for analysts, it also produces knowledge and applies power". This process ensures conformity with the accepted cultural, social, economical, and political norms of the dominant ideology: "focus on communication technology both as ways of engaging in discourse struggles and, through their surveillance capability, as ways of producing a particular form of social knowledge and thus of exerting power"

That the various media and communication technology exhibit characteristics of closed systems with one-way communication can be hardly argued. However, the proper question to ask is: why is the communication technology so restrictive and a closed system that can be so easily controlled (deliberately or otherwise) by the elite? First, lets ask the following question regarding how does media fit in the economic system. Do the existing media/communication technologies exhibit characteristics that make them a better fit for the capitalistic free market (economy whose ultimate goal is the bottom-line, i.e. profit), rather than empowering the publics/ audiences with information to better participate in representative democracy? Second, are the exhibited characteristics intrinsic to a particular technology embedded in the technology itself, or they are a result of the features and functionalities which designers embellished a particular technology?

To answer the above questions, I first turn to Schiller (1996) who argues in favor of original purpose and design: "When military or commercial advantages are the motivating forces of research and development, it is to be expected that the laboratories will produce findings that are conducive to these objectives. If other motivations could be advanced, the common good, for instance, different technologies might be forthcoming" (Schiller, p.71). Schiller's idea of the original purpose is also supported by the adaptive structurations theory (AST) that differentiates between technology's spirit (the original intent as thought by the designers who might be operating 'outside' of the hegemonic control, relatively speaking) and its subsequent functionality due to the appropriation process as the technology becomes embedded in institutionalized social structures. As such, more then often the existing socially and politically brokered power structures reflect themselves in the structure of the technology: "Information technology is highly political, but politics are not directed by its technological features alone".

The AST might appear in contradiction to Schiller's argument that the social use of technology is determined by the original purpose: "What the evidence here demonstrates is the strong, if not determining, influence of the original purpose that fostered the development of each new technology. The social use to which the technology is put, more times that not, follows its originating purpose". The seemingly contradictory arguments need to be scrutinized in light of the social constructionist theory and technological determinism applied together. Neither one can explain the interplay of communication technology and society alone. The argument is that if a particular technology was designed to serve the corporate interest, most of its features will be driven to maximize the profits. In contrast, if a group of people designs technology for open communication and democratic access to information, the technology in question will have such features as to enable ease of access to information and make it hard for that technology to be used for restrictive purposes.

But again, it is not the technology per se; it is the social structures that tilt the design, development, and subsequent use of the technology for particular purposes. Unfortunately, most of the communication technology in use today has been built and appropriated for profit making activities and perhaps is unfit to support activities related to participatory democracy.

For example, the development of cable as medium of communication was relatively uneventful until the media corporations saw potentials for profits via advertising. As the fight of discourses got under way between government officials, media corporations and the liberal progressive forces, the elite elements appeared on the scene controlling and moderating the discourse: "The talk about cable ... was characterized by a systemic avoidance of central issues and assumptions, and by a pattern of unequal power in the discussion of its outcomes: the discourse of the new technology was shaped not so much by full fledged debate as by the lack of it". Thus, the future of the cable technology was affected by the social structures and institutions, striping away from its technological potential the ability to become a technology that could link the masses and bring them together.

The communication's technological determinism and social constructionism are interrelated in circular and iterative nature. It is hard to conceptualize isolated technology that is not being affected by the social structures, but constantly affects the same:

"As Raymond Williams has shown, this assumption of autonomous technology is characteristic of much though about television and society, and constitutes a false abstraction of technologies out of their social and cultural context" "Such speculations naively assumed that telecommunication could magically resolve the power relations among people that caused racist, poverty, and international strife".

Even when a particular communication technology changes the social structures, it does not necessarily mean that such changes will be progressive and liberating. Streeter argues that relations in social structures are created by people and can only be changed by the people themselves, suggesting that even if technology has changed some structures, the changes have been appropriated by the elite and incorporated in the production and reproduction of the dominant ideology: "The constrains were not caused by old technological limits, nor can they be eliminated by new technologies: they were caused by relationship between people and can be overcome only by changing relations between people". Or, as Fiske has put it very succinctly: "Technology may determine what is shown, but society determines what is seen".

If technology's role in the society is determined both by its own characteristics and by the moderating characteristics of its social surroundings, what might be there that causes a particular technology to become a closed system, one-way communication, disseminating content which is controlled by the stakeholders whose primary concern is to advertise to the consumers or in the case of the government control its citizen through selective and strategic communications?

Arguing that one way communication by media companies (TV, cable, radio, movies) is a very important ingredient in the process of reproduction of the dominant ideology, because it is able to control the discourse by controlling the content and restricting the access to the discourse, Gitlin suggests that the centrally controlled one way communication (one-to-many) must disappear and be replaces by many-to-many communications if we wish to empower the masses. He further contends that a possible "revolutionary movement must aim to transform mass media by liberating communications technology for popular use. Apparently, Gitlin believes and posits the open communication (many-to-many) as a possible antidote to the hegemonic ideology.

Therefore, it can be argued that the communication technology, which is constantly modified and affected by the social structures in which it is embedded, while at the same time influencing and modifying those same social structures, has the potential to shift or displace the center of gravity (i.e. the status quo, the habitus) through its characteristics of open communication, which can induce mass communication amongst the masses themselves empowering them with many-to-many communication relatively outside of elites' controls.

Constrained by the historical discourse and practicality of most of the communication technology used for one way communication and for profit making purposes, Schiller is skeptical that such technology can be of any benefit to the society: "The customary argument that commerce and profit seeking go hand-in-hand with social benefit, is still to be demonstrated after hundreds of years of contrary experience" (Schiller, p.71).

At this point I would like to argue that the newest media technology, the communication facet of the Internet, exhibits characteristics of open communication that could position it as potential antidote to hegemonic ideology. As it has been argued above, whoever controls the content can control the scope of the public discourse, and whoever controls the access to the mass communication technology can practically control the voices that can debate the already restricted content/discourse. Unfortunately, TV, radio and cable technologies have been socially (various social and institutional structures) constructed such that both content and access control are in the same hands.

However, the Internet, especially the website portion of it (ability to publish) and the email discussion lists exhibit characteristics contrary to those of earlier technologies (as shaped by the social structures). For example, almost anyone can publish anything on the Internet, relatively speaking, without the fear that the server hosting firms might block the website (apart from criminally related material). In addition, the masses, can freely organize into groups of citizens, consumers, special interests groups, hobbyists, etc., and advocate their causes openly. This is partially enabled by the ability to establish many-to-many communication via email discussion lists. These two examples show that the content is not necessarily controllable by corporate power, and that the access to that content is not restricted by any corporate power. As matters of fact, both are subject to the ability to pay for Internet access, however, many libraries provide free Internet access for interested individuals. From the traditional technologies, public cable access channels resemble the above cases. However, most communities seldom use public cable access channels. When used, they are marginalized by not being included in programming listings (e.g. TV Guide) with the rest of cable and broadcast channels.

What social conditions and circumstanced led to the development of the Internet technologies which seem to exhibits open content and open communication properties, unlike the TV, radio and cable that have remained one-way communication channels? Why haven't then the same social structures and forces restricted various Internet technologies to be used for one-way communication only?

The apparent power to reach the masses, as well as the ability to interact with them, could not have escaped the elite. All of a sudden, as the number of Internet users increased manifolds each year, previously uninterested media corporations (there were repeated public claims that profit cannot be made with this new technology) invaded the Internet landscape, using it not much different than the TV: "Whether deceptively labeled as 'entertainment,' 'news,' 'culture,' 'education,' or 'public affairs,' TV programs aim to narrow and flatten consciousness-to tailor everyman's world view to the consumer mentality, to placate political discontent, to manage what cannot be placated, to render social pathologies personal, to level class-consciousness" (Gitlin, 1972, pp.345). The obviousness of the above is that almost all commercial sites support their Internet presence by online advertising. Yes, one can choose to visit a web site only to be bombarded by advertising, similar to TV advertising. However, studies have shown that web site visitors are increasingly becoming aware and do not necessarily get influenced by advertisements. This is a bit different from the TV. A visitor can still view the page without wasting time, whereas on TV you either watch the commercials or need to switch the channel.

In other words, the Internet, fueled by the open content and open communication, in its infancy and during its development until mid 90s, before it become obvious that it can be used by corporation for making profit, was truly the liberating technology alluded by Gitlin.

To think that the elites were so naive to overlook Internet's potential as mass medium is at best naivety itself. They could not have also overlooked the potential for the masses to utilize the Internet to organize themselves outside elite's control, however, perhaps the elite thought that any such conflict should be domesticated as Gitlin suggests: "What permits it to absorb and domesticate criticism is not something accidental to the liberal capitalist ideology, but rather its core". Then, it seems that the inevitable happened, as many times before: "The hegemonic ideology changes in order to remain hegemonic; that is the peculiar nature of the dominant ideology of liberal capitalism".

The elite moved to utilize the open communication technology, taking control over various aspect of it. Internet users still have to access the Internet via commercial entities that use online advertising as a profit stream. Various mergers and acquisition have occurred between traditional media and online industry, successfully trapping the masses to a particular content. Yet, it is still easier to escape the online advertisers than those on TV.

Corporations find this very problematic, as it is hard to centrally control a technology that was build to be managed in distributed fashion. Therefore, they have turned more than ever before to manage the access to the Internet technology and control the Internet visiting habits (through content portals) of the masses.

Despite these attempts by corporations, if a group of people wants an Internet presence, with potential readership/viewership of all who have access to the Internet, it can do so with minimal cost. The same cannot be said for the TV, the radio or cable. Whether the possibility for inexpensive presence on the Internet and its potential mass viewership will remain so, only the future will tell.

What could change? The unimaginable could happen. Governments can for example restrict who publishes what in their country by requiring licenses to operate a website. Obviously, for it to be effective the entire world has to enact the same laws since it is easy to move website servers around the world. Next, imagine that by some 'strange' imagination a judge rules that a US firm that provides Internet access can be held responsible for the content published by its customers. If such ruling is to be enforced, it could require that a corporation first approve each websites' content.

This could potentially lead various Internet access and Internet hosting providers to utilize their central role to their advantage. Why was the Internet build with open communication in mind? Adherents of the theory of hegemony could argue that this is contrary to the theory. If the Internet contains such power that can be used as an antidote to hegemony, why did the elite allow it to be developed in the form it is? Did they intent it or is it an unintentional byproduct of government's action to create communication network that can sustains nuclear attack by creating a very distributed communication network? The Internet and its open communication and open content technologies and principles are still in the infancy. Whether the open concepts will remain part of the Internet in the future remains to be seen.

If previous communication technologies are any indication, we might expect the same with the Internet. However, as I have attempted to show in this paper, the Internet communication technologies have more or less embedded in their technology some characteristics that lend themselves to be used for open communication where the masses can communicate amongst themselves without the corporate media's oversight.

Claiming that there are embedded characteristics in a given technology sounds like technological determinism. That would be an oversight. One needs to look at the social, political, economical, and cultural factors that have helped construct those characteristics in the first place so they could be embedded in the underlying Internet technologies. Further, as time goes on, the social situatedness of the Internet technology could change and the social structures of the future might modify, change or even restricts the initially acquired and embedded open communication and open content characteristics of the Internet. Alternatively, if the open characteristics of the Internet take strong hold in society and overcomes the already entrenched hegemonic forces as they are embedded deeply in various social structures, it might empower the masses to shift and displace the status quo and thus bring forth more representative democracy.

5

Role of Print Media During Independence Movement

ROLE OF PRESS IN INDIA'S STRUGGLE FOR FREEDOM

At the time of the first war of independence, any number of papers were in operation in the country. Many of these like *Bangadoot* of Ram Mohan Roy, *Rastiguftar* of Dadabhai Naoroji and *Gyaneneshun* advocated social reforms and thus helped arouse national awakening. It was in 1857 itself that *Payam-e-Azadi* started publication in Hindi and Urdu, calling upon the people to fight against the British. The paper was soon confiscated and anyone found with a copy of the paper was presecuted for sedition. Again, the first hindi daily, *Samachar Sudhavarashan,* and two newspapers in Urdu and Persian respectively, *Doorbeen* and *Sultan-ul-Akbar*, faced trial in 1857 for having published a 'Firman' by Bahadur Shah Zafar, urging the people to drive the British out of India. This was followed by the notroius *Gagging Act* of Lord Canning, under which restrictions were imposed on the newspapers and periodicals.

Notable Role

In the struggle against the British, some newspapers played a very notable role. This included the *Hindi Patriot!* Established in 1853, by the author and playwright, Grish Chandra Ghosh, it became popular under the editorship of Harish Chandra Mukherjee. In 1861, the paper published a play, "Neel Darpan" and launched a movement against the British, urging the people to stop cultivating the crop for the white traders. This resulted in the formation of a Neel Commission. Later, the paper was taken over by Ishwar Chandra Vidyasagar. The paper strongly opposed the Government's excesses and demanded that Indians be appointed to top government posts. The *Indian Mirror* was the other contemporary of this paper which was very popular among the reading public.

Yet another weekly, *Amrita Bazar Patrika* which was being published from Jessore, was critical of the government, with the result that its proprietors faced trial and conviction. In 1871, the *Patrika* moved to Calcutta and another Act was passed to supress it and other native journals.

Marathi Press

Mahadev Govind Rande, a leading leader of Maharashtra, used to write in *Gyan Prakash* as well as in *Indu Prakash*. Both these journals helped awaken the conscience of the downtrodden masses. Another Marathi weekly, *Kesari* was started by Tilak from January 1, 1881. He alongwith Agarkar and Chiplunkar started another weekly journal, *Mratha* in English. The Editor of the *'Daccan Star'* Nam Joshi also joined them and his paper was incorporated with *Maratha*. Tilak and Agarkar were convicted for writings against the British and the Diwan of *Kolhapur*. Tilak's *Kesari* became one of the leading media to propagate the message of freedom movement. It also made the anti-partition movement of Bengal a national issue. In 1908, Tilak opposed the Sedition ordinace. He was later exiled from the country for six years. Hindi edition of *Kesari* was started from Nagpur and Banaras.

Press and the First Session of Congress

The Editors commanded a very high reputation at the time of the birth of the Indian National Congress. One could measure the extent of this respect from the fact that those who occupied the frontline seats in the first ever Congress session held in Bombay in December 1885 included some of the editors of Indian newspapers. The firstever resolution at this Session was proposed by the editor of *The Hindu*, G. Subramanya Iyer. In this resolution, it was demanded that the government should appoint a committee to enquire into the functioning of Indian administration. The second resolution was also moved by a journalist from Poona, *Chiplunkar* in which the Congress was urged to demand for the abolition of India Council which ruled the country from Britain. The third resolution was supported by Dadabhai Naoroji who was a noted journalist of his time. The fourth resolution was proposed by Dadabhai Naoroji.

There were many Congress Presidents who had either been the editors or had started the publication of one or the other newspapers. In this context, particular mention may be made of Ferozeshah Mehta who had started the Bombay Chronide and Pandit Madan Mohan Malaviya who edited daily, Hindustan. He also helped the publication of *Leader* from Allahabad. Moti Lal Nehru was the first Chairman of the Board of Directors of the leader. Lala Lajpat Rai inspired the publication of three journals, the *Punjabi*, *Bandematram* and the *People* from Lahore. During his stay in South Africa, Gandhiji had brought out *Indian Opinion* and after settling in India, he started the publication of *Young India; Navjeevan, Harijan, Harijan Sevak* and *Harijan Bandhu*. Subash Chandra Bose and C.R. Das were not journalists but they acquired the papers like *Forward* and *Advance* which later attained national status. Jawaharlal Nehru founded the *National Herald*.

Revolutionary Movement and the Press

So far as the revolutionary movement is concerned, it did not begin with guns and bombs but it started with the publication of newspapers. The first to be mentioned in this context is *Yugantar* publication of which was started by Barindra Kumar Ghosh who edited it also.

When the Ghadar party was organised in Amenca, Lala Hardayal started publication of the journal '*Ghadar*'. Within one year, millions of copies of this journal were published in Hindi, Urdu, Punjabi, Gujarati, Marathi and English and sent to India and to all parts of the world· where Indians were residing. In the beginning the copies of the journal were concealed in parcels of foreign cloth sent to Delhi. It was also planned to smuggle the printing press into India for this purpose. But then the war broke out and it became almost impossible to import printing machinery from abroad. Lala Hardayal was arrested in America and deported to India. One of his followers Pandit Ramchandra started publishing *Hindustan Ghadar* in English. With the U.S. joining the war, the Ghadar party workers were arrested by the American Government. When the trail was on, one of the rivals of Pandit Ramchandra managed to obtain a gun and shoot him dead in the jail itself. The death of Ram chandra led to the closure of this paper.

In 1905 Shyamji Krishna Verma started publication of a journal *Indian Sociologist* from London. It used to publish reports of political activities taking place at the India House in London. In 1909 two printers of this journal were convicted. Shyamji Krishna Verma left England for Paris from where he started the publication of the journal. Later on, he had to leave for Geneva. He continued to bring out the journal from there for two or three years more. In Paris, Lala Hardayal, in collaboration with Madam Cama and Sardar Singhraoji Rana brought out *Vandematram* and Talwar.

After *Yugantar*, it was *Vandematram* that played a significant role in the freedom struggle. This journal was established by Subodha Chandra Malik, C.R. Das and Bipin Chandra Pal on August 6, 1906. Its editor, Aurobindo Ghosh, the editor of *Sandhya*, B. Upadhyay and editor of *Yugantar* B. N. Dutt had to a face a trial for espousing the cause of freedom.

So far as the Hindi papers were concerned, they looked to government for support for some time. Bhartendu Harish Chandra was the first to start a journal *Kavi Vachan Sudha* in 1868. Its policy was to give vent to the misperies of the people of India. When the Prince of Wales visited India, a poem was published in his honour. The British authorities were given to understand that the poem had two meanings and that one word used in the peom could also mean that the Prince of Wales should get a shoe-beating. The government aid to journals like *Kavi Vachan Sudha* was stopped for publishing what was objectionable from the government point of view. Bhartendu

Harish Chandra resigned from his post of an honorary Magistrate. His two friends, Pratap Narain Mishra and Bal Krishna Bhatt started publication of two important political journals *Pradeep* from Allahabad, and *Brahman* from Kanpur. The *Pradeep* was ordered to be closed down in 1910 for espousing the cause of freedom. The *Bharat-Mitra* was a famous Hindi journal of Calcutta which started its publication on May 17, 1878 as a fortnighly. It contributed a lot in propagating the cause of freedom movement. The journal exposed the British conspiracy to usurp Kashmir. Several other papers published from Calcutta which played an important role in freedom struggle included Ambika Prasad Vajpayee's *Swantrtmtra*, Ramanand Chatterjee's *Modern Review'* in English, *Pravasi Patra'* in Bengali and *Vishal Bharat* in Hindi.

One of the foremost Hindi journalist who has earned a name for his patriotism was Ganesh Shanker Vidyarthi. In 1913, he brought out weekly *Pratap* from Kanpur. He made the supreme sacrifice in 1931 in the cause of Hindu-Muslim unity. Krishna Dutt Paliwal brought out *Sainik* from Agra which became a staunch propagator of nationalism in Western U. P. The noted Congress leader, Swami Shradhanand, started the publication of Hindi journal *Vir Arjun'* and Urdu journal *Tej*. After the assassination of Swami Shradhanand, Vidyavachaspathi and Lala Deshbandhu Gupta continued the publication of these journals. They were themselves prominent Congress leaders.

In Lahore, Mahashaya Khushal Chand brought out *Milap* and Mahashaya Krishna started publishing urdu journals which helped a lot in promoting the national cause. In 1881, Sardar Dayal Singh Majitha on the advice of Surendra Nath Bannerjee brought out *Tribune* under the editorship of Sheetala Kant Chatterjee. Bipin Chandra Pal also edited this paper for sometime. Later in 1917, Kalinath Rai joined the paper as its editor.

There is not a single privince in India which did not produce a journal or newspaper to uphold the cause of freedom struggle. A. G. Horniman made the *Bombay Chronicle'* a powerful instrument to promote militant nationalism. He himself took part in the meetings where Satyagraha used to be planned. He published vivid accounts of Jallianwala Bagh carnage for which one correspondent of his paper, Goverdhan Das, was sentenced to three years' imprisonment by a military court. Horniman too was arrested and deported to London even though he was ill at that time. Amritlal Shet brought out the Gujarati journal *Janmabhumi* which was an organ of the people of the princely states of Kathiawad, but it became a mouthpiece of national struggle. Similarly another Gujarati journal *Saanjvartman* played a prominent role under the editorship of Sanwal Das Gandhi, who played a very significant role in the Quit India Movement in 1942. It was soon after independent formed a parallel Government in Junagarh and forced the Nawab of Junagarh to leave the country. The three editors of the Sindhi journal *Hindi* Jairam Das Daulatram, Dr. choithram Gidwani and Hiranand karamchand, were arrested, their press closed and the property of the paper confiscated. In Bihar the tradition of national newspapers was carried forward by Sachidanand Sinha, who had started the publication of *Searchlight* under the editorship of Murtimanohar Sinha. Dev Brat Shastri started publication of '*Nav Shakti* and *Rashtra Vani*'. The weekly *yogi* and the *Hunkar*' also contributed very much to the general awakening.

FREEDOM OF THE PRESS

Freedom of expression has always been emphasised as an essential basis for the democratic functioning of a society. The reasons for this are: the right of an individual to self-fulfilment, which right requires the communication of thought; the importance of constantly attempting to attaint he truth, an attempt which is frustrated if information is suppressed or comment blocked; the inherent democratic right to participate in decision-making, which obviously implies the freedom to obtain, communicate and discuss information,; and the practical importance of maintaining the precarious balance between healthy cleavage and the necessary consensus; "coercion of expression is likely to be ineffective (and).... Conceals the real problems confronting a society... It is likely to result in neglect of the grievances which are the actual basis of the unrest and thus prevent their correction".* Especially because we are compelled to operate our democracy indirectly, it is of great importance that the citizens should be enabled to know what is happening in different regions and different sectors of the functioning of the society, and to listen to different and alternative approaches and comments, so that they can effectively participate in the process of self-government. If facts cannot be freely presented and comments cannot be freely exchanged, there is no way in which the citizens can even attempt to hold the rulers to account. A further dimensions to the freedom of expression is added by the existence of mass society in which communication among citizens can take place only through the use of media like the Press and broadcasting and not directly, except in a limited way. With State monopoly over broadcasting which prevails both technical and, in the Indian context, financial, the importance of the Press is even more crucial.

Our actual experience since Independence, and especially in the last decade or so, also suggests that a free and vigilant Press is vital to restrain corruption and injustice at least to the extent that public opinion can be roused as a result of press investigations and comments. Recently a number of injustices and wrong-doings have been uncovered as a result of the initiative taken by newspapers. Whether it is the question of various types of bonded labour in different parts of the country, the misuse of powers by A. R. Antulay or the existence of smuggling rackets on the West Coast, newspapers have served a very useful purpose by exposing them. The fear that the Press will expose such wrong-doing is a major restraint on potential wrong-doers.

Who Threatens Freedom? Owners Structure

Having accepted that the freedom of the Press is of vital importance especially in our contest, the question arises: is this freedom threatened and, if so, by whom? It has been frequently alleged, especially in India, that the freedom of the Press is in danger because of the ownership of the newspaper industry and the predominance of some newspaper groups and chains. It is also suggested that the editors and journalists cannot have adequate freedom of collecting and disseminating facts and offering comments as they are under the pressure of the capitalist owners. It is further pointed out that free collection and dissemination of facts is not possible in the case of newspapers which depend to a large extent on revenue from advertisements as the advertising interests cannot but influence the presentation of news and comments. Unless this whole structure of ownership and control in the newspaper industry, and also the manner of the economic management of the Press, is changed, it is therefore suggested, the Press cannot be really free.

How far are these Arguments Valid?

It should be conceded at the outset that, like any large private sector industry, the newspaper industry cannot be influenced by the understanding and approach of those who control it. With modern technology, large newspaper organisations enjoy various economies of scale. Groups and chains of newspapers are therefore in a better position to provide richer fare in their newspapers are bound to be businessmen/capitalists, and their overall approach to the society and its problems cannot but be conditioned by this. That is why we inevitably find that the Press which is commercially organised-not run by political pro-business, pro-capitalist as well as usually a pro-Establishment viewpoint. Few newspapers will endorse a philosophy which goes against the established they would hardly raise their voice, or even offer investigative material, about the working of private trade and industry. When those who own or control newspapers are also involved in other lines of business, their stake in the stability of the system is so large that they would not encourage anything which is likely to create problems in the smooth functioning of the society. With maximum emphasis on stability, they would rather connive with oppression and injustice. Unorthodox and anti-establishment vies may not find much place in the columns of such newspapers, while national chauvinism-even jingoism-may come easily. The recent controversy in a country like the United Kingdom with a long democratic tradition about the somewhat subjective stances taken by the B.B.C. in the Falklands crisis shows how difficult it is for the Press or the media to maintain objectivity. The days that we can forget that appalling experience, when the freedom of the press as well as many other freedoms were seriously endangered in the U.S.A.

No Workable Alternative

But what is the possible remedy? Public ownership of newspapers in effect meaning State ownership? Is that what will ensure the freedom of the Press? The idea has merely to be put forward to see how suicidal such a solution can be. Cooperative ownership could be a possible alternative; but there are few examples anywhere in the world of successful cooperative management of large newspaper organisations, or of any large business establishments. A newspaper industry is an increasingly large, technically complex and managerially challenging industry. Unless we want the newspapers to be poorly produced as a result of continuos inefficiency in their management, we can not but permit good and vigorous managers to control major units in this industry. The choice is between having good newspapers even with the shortfalls inevitably arising out of the inadequacies mentioned earlier, or having poor quality newspapers. What our choice will be is obvious.

Competition the Best Policy

One should also point out that our experience in India is not that all those who own and manage the newspaper industry are taking a uniform approach on important issues relating to vital policy-making in the country. There are differences among them and some do take a significantly anti-establishment line. Though they may not necessarily support socialist or communist policies, they may permit a great deal of criticism of the existing system and encourage information as well as comment along critical lines. The degree of such criticism will vary. But our experience does not indicate that all capitalist owners of newspapers will collaborate and operate in some kind of a collusion. In fact, to the extent that there is competition for increasing circulation, a newspaper is bound to attempt to ensure that it is not found wanting in investigating events and giving information which competing newspapers may provide. The owners cannot therefore take an approach which will reduce the circulation by insisting that it reflect his personal viewpoint rather than attempting to present facts and other materials which the readers would be interested in. A capitalist owner may not necessarily be actuated by any lofty motives; but the possibility cannot be ignored that competing newspapers would forge ahead if the paper is allowed to be too sectional or partial. Experience both in India and abroad also suggests that only large newspaper organisations can resist powerful institutions and persons. A small newspaper would institutions and persons. A small newspaper would have found it difficult to face the wrath of a Nixon.

What is therefore of real importance is to ensure that a certain minimum degree of competition exists in the newspaper world. It is true, as mentioned earlier, that, as in many other industries, technology and other aspects give a significant advantage to large scale organisations in the press industry. It is no longer possible for the number of successful newspaper ventures to be very large. We can only have a limited degree of competition and not anything approaching perfect competition. But this is the difficulty in all modern industries. All that can and should be emphasised is that a reasonable degree of competition should be attempted to be maintained.

This can be done in two ways: Firstly, in any effective circulation area which forms a single market for newspapers, careful watch should be kept on dominant newspapers who control a large proportion of the circulation. In the case of such newspapers the normal provisions of the MRTP Act such as special permission being required for their major expansion or setting up of new papers by them etc. should apply. Careful watch should also be kept on the possibility of their indulging in monopolistic and unfair trade practices. It has been already held that the MRTP Act applies to the newspaper industry. What is necessary is to make sure that the provisions of the Act are streamlined and its instruments given adequate teeth so that the anti-monopoly provisions can effectively operate. This is necessary not only in the newspaper industry but in all industries. The difficulty is that throughout the last ten years since the MRTP Act was put on the statute book, the Government has not rally bothered to see that anti-monopoly provisions become effective. In fact, the tendency of Government has been in opposite direction, Viz, to favour the monopoly organisations.

As for large business houses controlling a number of industries and also newspapers, to the extent that such houses represent a significant degree of concentration of economic power, they would come within the purview of the break-up provisions under Section 27 of the MRTP Act. The government would therefore be in a position to have the possibility of such breakup examined by the MRTP Commission and, if such a break-up is advised in public interest, it can take steps in that direction. The difficulty is that the Government has made no use of this section. The Government appears to be merely wanting to have many powers with it so that it can threaten and intimidate those enterprises, including newspaper ones, which are not ready to toe its line. It is significant that the only instance where the Government thought worth looking at; it was only the Indian Express, because it was proving to be a paper not easily amenable to the wishes of those in power at that time. This inference is supported by the fact that, at the Government's instance, R. N. Goenka was replaced as chairman of the Indian Express group by K. K. Birla, and the Government preferred this arrangement in spite of latter's connections with both a large business empire, and with the Hindustan Times. In thinking of any special powers relating to the Press being given to Government, the very real possibility of the powers being mainly used for arm-twisting for partisan interests should not be overlooked.

Positive Assistance to Independent Papers

At the same time, it is important that steps are taken positively to make it possible for independent papers to survive develop. Assistance to them should be provided through general institutions meant to help the growth of independent entrepreneurs, including small ones. The financial institutions as well as promoting organisations-such as the National Small Industries Corporation-can be used for this purpose. Facilities such as subsidised teleprinter services, and facilitating the setting up of small electronic presses, could be other steps in this direction. The assistance should be granted in a manner where no discrimination among individual papers can be easily made, and where the subsidised facility cannot be misused and encashed. For this reason making available a marketable commodity like newsprint at a specially cheaper price should not be supported.

The dependence of newspapers on advertisement revenue may go against the perspective of some puritan minds about an ideal society. But in a world where mass persuasion is becoming respectable even in communist countries like Hungary and Yugoslavia, we cannot think of advertisement as a tainted source of revenue. At a time when the costs of producing newspapers are rapidly raising, advertisement revenue is the only mechanism which can keep the newspaper prices within reasonable limits. Any attempt by Government to put a restriction to advertisement revenue has to be looked upon as an indirect method of upsetting the economy of newspapers and thus an act which would affect Press freedom adversely. To the extent that a newspaper has a large number of sources from which advertisement revenue flows in, it is less likely to be influenced in its coverage by the wishes of any one of them. A smaller newspaper is more likely to be subject to the wishes of an important advertiser, including the Government. It is therefore necessary to realise that larger appears are less likely to be influenced by advertisers. Further, to the extent that the MRTP Act is effectively used, the power of any one advertiser would be limited. Of course, if the Government chooses to continue to keep the MRTP Act should be available to Government to curb undue concentration and misuse of monopoly powers in the Press industry. It should also be obligatory for Government to consult the MRTP Commission before any action under that Act is taken.

The State-The Main Threat

This insistence is necessary because experience all over the world, as well as our own experience since Independence, suggest that the State remains the source of the most potential threat to Press freedom. It cannot be overlooked that, within a short time after passing the Constitution, those in power-who used to swear by Press freedom before Independence-put in provisos to Article 19 (1) of the Constitution so as to clothe Government with powers to curb Press freedom. This was defended on the ground that these powers were likely to be necessary on occasions when the security of the State was threatened; it was emphasised that the powers will not be normally used.

But a special legislation called the Press (Prevention of Objectionable Matters) Act was put on the statute book soon thereafter in 1951. No steps were taken to remove the lacunae which gave Government powers to intercept material going to the Press through the Posts and Telegraphs. Some Chief Ministers thought it proper to take steps against newspapers whose policy they did not like, whether it was a Morarji Desai in Bombay or a Charan Singh in U. P. A persistent attempt to curb Press freedom how ever really began only after 1969. Indira Gandhi felt that the Press was too critical of her ways and she sought to change its approach.

Various threats were held out by Government and steps proposed to curb that section of the Press which was thought to be the most independent. With the aid of some native leftist organisations, a propaganda barrage was mounted against the Press as well as the judiciary both of which appeared to be not easily amenable to the wishes of Government apparently the only reason why the idea of spreading the equity ownership of newspaper companies especially among the workers and the journalists employed therein was not pursued was the feeling that such a measure would give more power in the hands of trade unions who were opposed to the ruling party. On the other hand, arm-twisting of capitalist owners, especially of those who had many other industrial interests and were not very much concerned with the freedom of the Press, was thought to be not so difficult. The antipathy to the Press however continued and got further intensified, especially as most of the important papers expressed their dislike of the acts of the ruling establishment, and many of them advised the Prime Minister to resign after the Allahabad High Court

Judgement in 1975. The antipathy culminated in the pre-censorship imposed in the country for the first time during the internal Emergency. That the pre censorship was used for partisan ends is sufficiently exemplified by the data published as a result of the various enquiries made in 1977-78.* The misuse of powers like pre-censorship was a adequately envisaged by the fact that these powers were even used to black out some unpleasant news about the criminal convictions of an actress, and of some businessmen.

The experience of the Emergency also provided enough evidence to show how weak-kneed a very large part of the Indian Press was when it felt really threatened. One would not have believed that, during the independence movement, a much larger proportion of newspapers had faced difficulties and shown courage. The poor morale of many editors and others concerned was aptly characterised by the Janata Government's Minister for Information and Broadcasting who told the Press that, when they were only asked to bend, they crawled! Nevertheless, there were brave exceptions; and it is important to note who they were. Two of the so-called monopoly papers resisted encroachment on their freedom and faced considerable risks. These were the Statesman and the Indian Express. Of course even a more valiant attitude was shown by independent, small journals like Sadhana (Marathi), Bhoomiputra (Gujrati), Seminar (a monthly journal) and Opinion (a weekly sheet); but these were run by individuals or groups who had a commitment to certain values and where the overall financial stake, the number of employees etc., was not very large. A very large proportion of the regular Press offered little resistance and gradually accepted a kind of self-censorship. That the ruling group was thinking of controls over the Press as a permanent measure was indicated by the putting on the statute book of the Prevention of Publication of Objectionable Matters Act in 1976. It was also known that the spokesmen of Government were threatening newspapers about "consequences", after the censorship was lifted and general elections announced. These threats indicated what might have been in store for the Press in the Congress party had won the elections in March 1977.

The Press began to act with great vigour almost as a rebound after the Emergency was lifted in 1977, and especially after the change brought in as a result of the elections in March 1977. The Janata Government and the short-lived Lok Dal Government, felt the thrust of this vigorous assertion of independence by the Press. This was also the time when the Press specially developed new traditions of investigative journalism, which has now become a major feature of an increasing number of important newspapers.

Since January 1980, with the change of Government, the attitude of the Government of India toward the Press has reverted back to one of antipathy. Many of the new State Governments which came to power in the middle of 1980 have shown active hostility. Instances of threats to the free functioning of the Press are not uncommon. There was the instance in Bangalore when, as a result of the publication of a press report which was disliked by the Chief Minister, there was a kind of gherao of important papers so as to prevent their publication on one day and the police practically pleaded helplessness to do anything about the matter. There was another instance of a former Chief Minister who compared the Press to snakes and scorpions. The Tamil Nadu Government, belonging to a different political party, has put special curbs on contacts between Government officials and the Press, and has stiffened the Cr. P. C. in a manner which would make "scurrilous" writing a nonbailable offence and also one where imprisonment on conviction is made obligatory as a punishment. The Prime Minister herself has indicated more than once her dislike of the manner in which what is called the National Press operates.

Hostile Attitude of Those in Power

The basic attitude of those who are in power has been one of wanting the Press to conform. This is specially clear from the official attitude to the manner in which the broadcasting media under direct Government control are to operate. The demand that broadcasting media be separated from the direct tutelage of Government, and the work be entrusted to an autonomous corporation, has been put forward for a long time.

But this has been resisted by all those who have been in political power at the Centre. The Government of India had appointed in the 60's a committee (the Chanda Committee) to go into this question and it recommended an autonomous set up for the All India Radio. But the Government continued to ignore this recommendation. In fact, during the Emergency, spokesmen of the Government continued to ignore this recommendation. In fact, during the Emergency, spokesmen of the Government made it quite clear that they thought it quite right that the broadcasting media should propagate only the official viewpoint. The Prime Minister herself had clearly state in 1975 that All India Radio is "a Government organ, it is going to remain a Government organ... It is there to project Government policies and Government views. It does not mean we do not give the views of other people, but primarily its function is there to give the views of the Government of India". The Prime Minister justified this by stating that "in no country in the world, in no developing country, do they even allow anybody else to appear or any other viewpoint to be projected'.

Though the Janata Government appointed a committee (B. G. Verghese Committee) to examine this question, and the Committee recommended the setting up of an autonomous body for taking charge of broadcasting, the Janata Government, and also the short-lived Lok Dal Government, took no steps to pursue this recommendation and to make All India Radio autonomous and largely free of Government control. This is an adequate indication of the battles that may always have to be fought, whichever party is in power, to ensure that media of mass communication are permitted to operate freely.

A more recent indication of the Government's indifference to the economic functioning of the Press is provided by the Government's imposing an import duty on newsprint at a time when various costs of the newspaper industry, including the newsprint prices in the major supplying countries, have been rapidly escalating. To impose a duty on newsprint which would further enhance the costs of producing newspapers, in a country where the incomes of the common people are very low and where the circulation of newspapers is still very small, is hardly calculated to ensure wider circulation of newspapers. The proceeds of the wider circulation of newspapers. The proceeds of the import duty form such a minor part of the Central Government's revenue that if the duty was not imposed it would have meant no real difficulty for the Government. In spite of widespread demand in the Press, the Government continues the import duty for a second year, only making it specific instead of advalorem.

State Powerful in India

A further point of importance in this context is that, because of the necessity to ensure planned development of our economy, considerable powers regarding various aspects of the economy have been conferred on Government. With the attitude of the Government of intolerance of criticism as indicated earlier, the possibility of the Government misusing these powers against the newspapers whom it considers hostile is very real. Not only that Government misusing these powers against the newspapers whom it considers hostile is very real. Not only that Government has considerable powers which can be used at its discretion under statutes like the IDRA and MRTP Act, but here are also other powers such as under import control, the grant of credit through banks the bulk of whom are in the public sector, and even services provided by public utilities like Posts and Telegraphs (including telephones), and power supply.

Normal credit facilities may be denied, power supply may be cut off or made irregular (ostensibly on technical grounds), or postal and Telegraphic facilities may be discriminatingly used, to harass newspapers whose policies are disliked by those in positions of political power. Government advertisements and advertisements by the large and expanding public sector business organisations may be denied or they may be used in such a discriminating manner as to favour or disfavour particular newspapers. The overall powers of the State may be used to create difficulties for independent newspapers and news people. Even police protection may mysteriously disappear when well organised mobs gherao newspaper offices and threaten it with violence. Enough data are available to show that these are not merely theoretical possibilities but realities which face the Indian Press. It is therefore clear that the main threat to press freedom in India arises from the executive power of the State, both at the Centre and in the States. What is likely is not so much a direct and overt act of nationalisation as what may be culled salami tactics of putting curbs in an increasing and steady manner through various obstructions and threats.

Legislators' Attitudes

It is also necessary not to ignore the fact that the traditions of democratic polity and essential freedoms have not had a very long innings in India. Intolerance of inconvenient speech or writing therefore comes easily to many people in the country. Enough data are available even about happenings in recent years to illustrate this, Chhabirani episode in Orissa being one of the most notorious ones. Investigative journalism, when it touches some vested interest or the other-whether it is in politics, castes, property rights, trade unions, or any other-is in special danger as a result of persistent threats of violence. It would not be wrong to say that the greater the distance of the journal or the journalists from metropolis the greater the risk, though it is not as if such danger is quite absent even in metropolitan areas.

The intolerance of critical references is further exemplified in the attitude shown by many legislators to the question of legislative privileges. Even though it is now more than 30 years since the Constitution was passed and the idea then was that the privileges of legislatures would be codified within a few years, no legislature in India has yet taken any steps in that direction and there appears to be almost a consensus among legislators to avoid such codification. The result is that the possibility that a legislature may treat a particular reference as an infringement of legislative privilege is a kind of Damocles' sword on the heads of newspapers. It does not infrequently happen that legislators utter obscenities, trade in abuses and generally behave in an undignified manner. If the presiding officer expunges such words, or decides that nothing will go on record, the idea is that publication of such part of the proceedings, even if it has taken place, is not to be reported; and if it is, is may be treated as a contempt of the legislature. This is strange logic indeed. What actually happens, is actually said, is treated as if it is wiped out by the decision of the presiding officer and is not to be reported. Unlike in some foreign legislatures such a sin the U.K., it is not an odd word here or there which is expunged but, frequently, whole passages. A citizen who is present in the visitors' gallery is obviously a witness to what happens; but those who are not present are not expected to be informed through the Press of what actually happened. One does not understand by what logic such an approach is taken. On the other hand, it is only proper that the citizen should have the maximum access to information about what his representatives do, the manner in which they behave, or misbehave.

THE MUSLIM PRESS AND THE INDEPENDENCE MOVEMENT

The history of the modern press is closely linked with the invention of the printing press. However, the subcontinent as the cradle of one of the very old civilisations of the world had long had a news gathering mechanism in place through the ages. But even in recorded history, there existed a well-organised system for the collection of news. At various periods the subcontinent came up with a variety of well-knitted news-gathering systems.

The institution of newsletters came much later. Dr. Abdus Salam Khurshid's pioneering work on "Newsletters in the Orient" throw light on the origin of newsletters in the subcontinent. It was the Ghaznavid Muslim rulers who are said to have introduced the system in India towards the end of 10th century. The system soon gained ground with the Sultanate at Delhi and the institution of news gathering was streamlined and made highly efficient. During the Mughal rule, the system became highly mature. It was, however, during Aurangzeb's reign that newsletters were at their peak and the news-writers or "waqai-nawees" as they were called, earned the epithet of the "eyes and ears of the emperor" Newsletters existed in the Mughal courts in India till as late as 1857, when the great war of independence was waged.

Bengal, a part of which is now Bangladesh, was the forerunner in modern journalism in the whole of the subcontinent. It was in Bengal that the first newspapers in India made their appearance and then the seeds of awakening were spread over the length and breadth of the rest of the country, beginning of course, with some pockets of British colonies such as Madras and Bombay. Almost from its birth, the all absorbing interest of the Indian press had been politics. James Augustus Hickey started The Bengal Gazette in 1780, some eighty years after the first daily newspaper in England had commenced publication. Perhaps it would be stretching the analogy too far to term Hickey's "loads of abuse" as purely political but he did write this; "Mr Hickey considers the liberty of the press to be the very existence of an Englishman and free government" and he did set a precedent, followed devotedly by many editors after him. He went to prison rather than abandon that belief.

Sir Syed Ahmed Khan, by sponsoring and running the Tahzibul Akhlaq and the bilingual Scientific Society Magazine laid the foundations of the press as an institution of Muslim Indian society as he had a message to deliver and had no motive to make profit. Politics was significantly tabooed as Sir Syed had persistently asked Muslims not to participate in politics till they were properly educated. The salient feature of the Muslim press during this period included education of Muslims on western lines, reform of Muslim society, modern interpretation of religion, promotion of a purposeful literature, demand for the due share of Muslims in public service and an informed interest in the affairs of the Muslim world.

Muslim interest in politics began from the partition of Bengal (1905) when a new province of dominant Muslim majority (Eastern Bengal and Assam) emerged. Next year, a deputation of Muslim leaders met the governor-general and obtained the promise of introducing separate electorate. In December 1906, the All India Muslim League was established and in 1909, the Morley-Minto Reforms included the principle of separate electorate. It seemed that Muslims were having a smooth sailing in politics, and that there was a close understanding between them and the rulers.

The British government announced the undoing of the partition ofBengal, in 1911, that caused deep resentment among Muslims. Then followed the kanpur mosque agitation. A Muslim procession was fired upon ruthlessly and as a result hundreds of people died and received injuries. That added a lot to Muslim resentment,. As Muslims were deeply interested in the Muslim world, the loss of Libya as a consequence of the Italo-Turkish war and the secession of large slices of European territories from the Turkish empire as result of the two Balkan wars, caused humiliation. Muslims felt that they were beaten both at home and abroad. That gave birth to a new and vociferous Muslim Press.

During this phase of disillusionment and convulsion, four political personalities entered the domain of journalism. They were Hasrat Mohani, Muhammad Ali Jauhar, Abul Kalam Azad and Zafar Ali Khan. While Azad was a master of oriental learning, the others were graduates of the Aligarh College, while Muhammad Ali was, in addition, a graduate of Oxford University as well. All were poets and writers of repute but none was a professional journalist. They adopted the profession of journalism in order to promote political objectives. All were pan-Islamists and anti-Imperialists.

With the promulgation of the Government of India Act of 1935, elections to provincial assemblies were held in 1937. Congress won in six Hindu majority provinces and in the NWFP while Muslim League held sway over Bengal and Sindh; in Punjab the Unionist Party won the election. The power-drunk Congress did not include representative Muslims in its majority provinces, and depended on puppets with no respect in the community and trampled upon Muslim rights in such a ruthless manner that there was no course left for Muslims except to demand and a separate state of their own. The result was the Lahore Resolution of the All India Muslim League aiming at the establishment of independent sovereign states in the North-West and North-East of the subcontinent comprising Muslim majority areas. Later a single state was envisaged.

The closing years of the movement gave birth to a number of newspapers. The independent ventures included Nawa-i-Waqt of Lahore and Jang and Anjam at Delhi and The Pakistan Times of Lahore that appeared six months before partition. In addition the Quaid-i-Azam collected a "Create a Muslim Press Fund" and established Dawn at Delhi under the auspices of a trust, with himself as the managing trustee and also sponsored an Urdu daily named Manshoor from the same city as an official organ of the All India Muslim League. Of these Nawa-i-Waqt of Hameed Nizami and Dawn, later edited by Altaf Hussain were the most important and influential. Together with the old newspapers, they struggled hard in mobilising Muslim public opinion in support of the Pakistan Movement until Pakistan appeared on the map of the world as a sovereign state.

During this phase, starting from 1937 to 1947, the Muslim press grew rather rapidly. A number of English language newspapers sprang up while the Urdu press, too, had new additions. Together with the old newspapers, they voiced Muslim political aspirations with still greater force and played a major role in the mobilising public opinion in support of the Pakistan Movement. From Lahore also appeared Eastern Times, originally sponsored by Feroze Sons under the temporary editorship of Allama Abdullah Yusuf Ali. He was followed by Mr. FK Khan Durrani who had written a number of books on Muslim politics. Though shabby in appearance and deficient in equipment, it did play a role in the projection of Muslim view point. For a couple of years there existed in Lahore and New Times a weekly started by Malik Barkat Ali. This paper, too, acted as the spokesman of the Muslim League. Muslims were greatly handicapped by the fact that API and the UPI, two Indian news agencies, were both controlled by Hindus. Muslims' news was blacked out and distorted; therefore, a news agency named the orient Press of India was sponsored. Though financially weak and under-equipped, it did help in circulating news about Muslim politics.

After the Lahore Resolution was passed the Quaid-i-Azam sponsored the "Create a Muslim Press" campaign and collected funds for the purpose. Dawn came about in October 1942. The paper's broad policy was to support the league but it was allowed to make independent criticism within the framework of its policy. Its first editor was Pothan Joseph but after a couple of years Altaf Hussain replaced him. Altaf Hussain wielded a trenchant pen and his editorials were widely appreciated. The paper's entry was banned by the Khizr Ministry into Punjab during the League's civil disobedience movement in Punjab, but thousands of its copies were smuggled and sold at a high price in several cities of the province.

The Quaid-i-Azam also stared Manshoor as an Urdu daily from Delhi which was the official organ of All India Muslim League. This bright and fancy daily was edited by Syed Hasan Riaz. However, this could not succeed and had to close down after a couple of years. Lahore had been an important newspaper centre from the late 19th century. From 1939 to 1947 Muslim press here, too, grew rapidly. A number of English newspapers appeared while the Urdu press also had new additions. Together with the old newspapers they voiced Muslim political aspirations with greater force and played a major role in mobilising public opinion. Lahore witnessed new trends for a couple of years. A weekly was started by Malik Barkat Ali which also acted as an organ of the All India Muslim League.

Some underground papers were also taken out from Lahore when the Khizar government banned publication of the news of civil disobedience movement in Punjab. These papers were cyclostyled and distributed on a large scale. Thus Muslim press became a power to be reckoned with side by side the old Lahore newspapers like Zamindar of Maulana Zafar Ali Khan and Inqilab of Maulana Abdul Majid Salik. It is an interesting historical fact that after the adoption of the Lahore Resolution the name Pakistan was used for the first time by two Hindu newspapers of Lahore namely daily Milap and Partab.

Till 1942 the All India Muslim League leadership had not used the term Pakistan. But when these two Hindu communal newspapers sarcastically mentioned that the Lahore Resolution was a resolution for the creation of Pakistan and the movement by the All India Muslim League was a movement for Pakistan; the Quaid-i-Azam accepted. He declared that if they called it a Pakistan movement, then let it be so. Zamindar, Inqilab and Nawa-i-Waqt from Lahore and Dawn from Delhi played a yeomen's role in advancing the Pakistan movement. The Pakistan Times came in the months of the struggle for independence but still it played its innings in whatever little time it had. In the 1947 riots Hindu mobs burnt the offices and the printing press of Dawn in Delhi. As a result it close down temporarily, only to reappear from Karachi at the inception of Pakistan. The trust later ceased to exist and it was owned by the Pakistan Herald Publications with a majority of shares possessed by the late Muslim League stalwart Haji Sir Abdullah Haroon. It can easily be summed up about the performance of the press during the independence movement that the press owned by Muslims contributed to furthering Muslim politics even as what political institutions and leaders were later to fail to achieve. Although the press owned by Muslims lacked financial and technical facilities on the days of its inception, the enthusiasm of the owners and workers of these newspapers compensated for the lack of resources.

IMPORTANCE OF JOURNALISM AND JOURNALISTS IN A DEMOCRATIC INDIA

Important journalists like MJ Akbar and Anita Pratap established themselves as fearless leaders in the field. MJ Akbar is single handedly responsible for redesigned and edited The Telegraph in Calcutta. Anita Pratap became the first journalist to interview LTTE leader Prabhakaran in the 1980's and she also covered the 1983 Sri Lankan internal riots. But it was Chitra Subramanian and her coverage of the Bofors scandal that firmly established the fact that the Indian media should also act as a whistle blower of the society in order to keep the government in check. Her investigative articles first started appearing in The Hindu, down south and then when then it was later published in The Indian Express. The repercussions of that story were still felt in the 2009 General Elections in India. Magazines such as Tehelka have since established themselves as leaders in investigative journalism since.

The Current Scenario and the Future

With the emergence of the television and the new media (internet), it can be argued that newspapers are becoming irrelevant in terms of providing the latest news. However, many newspapers in India and the world to some extent have started providing analysis of the news as well. The coverage of the 2009 General Elections is the proof of that. Most newspapers had their own supplements dedicated to the elections and they scrutinised every detail of the elections in a way the television channels cannot provide. As of 2000, there are at least 41,705 newspapers in India and growing every day. The media whilst flawed is one of the most precious commodities in any democracy and as India celebrates another year of its emancipation, the media has a lot to celebrate as well – everyday for millions all over the country it makes this independence count substantial instead of some word uttered as a cliché at some cocktail party.

HINDI NEWSPAPERS: ON THE CUSP OF A MEDIA REVOLUTION

Hindi newspapers catering to local needs are creating new audiences and 'a different kind of public sphere' in towns and districts in the Hindi belt, media critic Sevanti Ninan says. 'These changes have both positive and negative aspects,' the New Delhi-based Ninan told IANS in an interview. Her latest book, 'Headlines from the Heartland: Reinventing the Hindi Public Sphere', has been described by author and critic Robin Jeffery as a 'remarkable... draws readers deep into the media revolution that is changing India'.

Ninan said that in the 1990s, a 'newspaper revolution began blowing across northern and central Ninan, a columnist on media, is founder-editor of the journalism centric site TheHoot.org. She began her career at the Hindustan Times and worked for several years at the Indian Express. 'I don't think the quality of journalism in this age of booming media gets anywhere near the kind of attention it deserves. But television localization has been getting some attention,' said Ninan. Ninan feels her book completely supports the view that localising helps readership. In her book, she said that Hindi journalism flowered in 'unexpected and unorthodox' ways. 'I encountered village store-keepers both on the road to Jagdalpur (in Chhattisgarh) as well as in Udaipur and Banswara districts in Rajasthan who called themselves news agencies,' she explained. They would solicit handouts from the local populace about functions, felicitations and events, solemnly stamp these handouts with the name of their news agency and send the items onward to the newspaper which had asked them to supply such news, she explained. The common mode of sending the news was to give the items to the local state transport driver who would drop them into mailboxes, which the newspapers had installed at major transport depots. 'This is an example of how localisation democratised access. Anyone could give news about themselves, from even a far flung corner of the state, and it would find its way into the paper, more or less unchanged,' Ninan told IANS. She noted that in Chitrakoot and Banda districts of Uttar Pradesh there are a group of women, some of them Dalits, who bring out a newspaper called 'Khabar Lahariya' -- which focuses on village level news of all kinds.

This includes articles about 'ration shops without rations, about wells drying up, about a man who thought he was buying a pregnant cow but found that it had a tumour and he had been duped'. In her view, these women manage to corner local government functionaries and quiz them if there are public complaints against them. 'It is sterling grassroots journalism of the unexpected kind,' she Copyright 2009 IndiaeNews.com. All Rights Reserved. Another unexpected example of handout journalism came from Chhattisgarh where, in 2002, Maoists embarked upon a public relations exercise and would have handouts delivered to newspaper offices.

'These would be used in a matter of fact manner. Occasionally, they would take a journalist whom they trusted on a field visit to areas which they controlled,' said Ninan. She believes her work 'looks at a particular language, in a particular part of the country, and I focus quite a lot on the socio economic basis for the spread of newspapers as well as the linkages between political awareness and newspaper growth'. Ninan sees her work as being a 'content analysis based on chunks of monitoring done in Madhya Pradesh and Jharkhand, to write about the content of local news'.

Others have written on this issue too, though with a differing emphasis. Francesca Orsini wrote 'The Hindi Public Sphere, 1920-1940', from a scholarly take, focused on language and literature. In his 1999 book 'Apne Gireban Mein', Yashwant Vyas of Dainik Bhaskar looked at some of the changes coming in with localisation in the Hindi press.

Robin Jeffrey looked at the newspaper revolution in the regional press throughout the country in his book 'India's Newspaper Revolution: Capitalism, Politics and the Indian-Language Press'. 'The south Indian newspapers led the way. Robin Jeffrey begins his book with an anecdote about the impact of Eenadu on local crime. Both Eeenadu in Andhra Pradesh and Malayalam Manorama in Kerala used local editions to expand starting from the 1980s,' said Ninan. 'The Times of India, I think, led the way in English-language localisatio by having different editions for the suburbs of Mumbai. But in the English-language press localisation remains confined to metropolitan cities and their suburbs. Both Hindustan Times and the Times of India have separate pullouts for Gurgaon,' she noted.

Ninan's earlier books include 'Through the Magic Window', 'Television and Change in India' (Penguin India, 1995), 'Plain Speaking with Chandrababu Naidu' (Viking, 2000) and 'Rajasthan' (Roli Books 1980).

IMPORTANCE OF HINDI NEWSPAPER IN INDIA

has became the important tool of distributing news on various fields through the most descriptive of manners. Since the time that the worlds first newspaper was born, there has been much progress in the way they presented their news to the readers. Newspapers are the most popular choice when it comes to grasping news simply because newspapers cater to readers of all ages and communities. The newspaper industry in India have achieved greater prestige days by days because of the existence of newspapers of various regional languages. The Indian newspaper industry witnesses the flourishing of newspapers in English, Hindi, and other regional languages, which cater to people speaking different languages. This multilingualism in newspapers increases the hits of newspaper reading in the country. Indian Hindi newspaper, for instance, has the largest number of circulation since Hindi is the national language of India and is spoken in most parts of the country.

We found since newspapers in the country have innovated their approach in targeting more readers by using colored pages, better paper materials, etc., the scope of growth in newspaper advertising and marketing has also become more possible. Newspapers serve as perfect platform for advertisers and advertising agencies to promote their products in print in the most creative manner possible. Keeping in mind the popularity of newspapers and their readability, advertisers are targeting popular newspapers more and more.

We have seen that Hindi newspaper, being avery popular choice because of reaching out to the masses at all levels has become an option that has caught the attention of advertisers and marketing companies. Moreover, advertisers and marketing agencies have the opportunity to showcase their concepts and ideas in the most constructive and creative manner in print. The scope for a commendable progress in newspaper advertising and marketing makes major popular Indian newspapers, including an Indian Hindi newspaper, a strong contender as an impressive platform for advertisements and marketing concepts.

Now we can say that many competitor has came in the market for their newspaper.But we see that The Indian advertising and marketing scenario has witnessed a steep increase because of the application of such platforms as newspapers, magazines, television, Internet advertising, and so on. However, the conventionalism and undying popularity of newspapers makes them the favoured choice for advertisers to promote their products. Pitch on Net is an online advertising agency that provides various forms of advertisements, marketing and public relations services on its website. Its website www.pitchonnet.com highlights necessary details on various modes of advertising and marketing, including newspaper as one of them.

6

Mass Media and Culture in a Democratic Society

The starting point is that the conditions for democracy imply a new conception of citizenship: economic, political, social and cultural. Thus, political citizenship involves new political structures and the return to the classical conception of politics (direct democracy). Economic citizenship involves new economic structures of community ownership and control of economic resources (economic democracy). Social citizenship involves self-management structures at the workplace, democracy in the household and new welfare structures where all basic needs (to be democratically determined) are covered by community resources, whether they are to be satisfied in the household or at the community level. Finally, cultural citizenship involves new democratic structures of dissemination and control of information and culture (mass media, art, etc.), which allow every member of the community to take part in the process and at the same time develop his/her intellectual and cultural potential.

It is obvious that the above new conception of citizenship has very little in common with the liberal and socialist definitions of citizenship, which are linked to the liberal and socialist conceptions of human rights respectively. Thus, for the liberals, the citizen is simply the individual bearer of certain freedoms and political rights recognised by law which, supposedly, secure equal distribution of political power. Similarly, for the socialists, the citizen is the bearer not only of political rights and freedoms but, also, of some social and economic rights, whereas for Marxists the citizenship is realised with the collective ownership of the means of production. Furthermore, the conception of citizenship adopted here is not related to the current social-democratic discourse on the subject, which, in effect, focuses on the institutional conditions for the creation of an internationalised market economy 'with a human face'. The proposal for instance for a redefinition of citizenship within the framework of a "stakeholder capitalism" belongs to this category. This proposal involves an 'active' citizenship, where citizens have 'stakes' in companies, the market economy and society in general and managers have to take into account these stakes in the running of the businesses and social institutions they are in charge of.

The conception of citizenship adopted here, which could be called a democratic conception, is based on our definition of inclusive democracy and presupposes a 'participatory' conception of active citizenship, like the one implied by the work of Hannah Arendt. In this conception, "political activity is not a means to an end, but an end in itself; one does not engage in political action simply to promote one's welfare but to realise the principles intrinsic to political life, such as freedom, equality, justice, solidarity, courage and excellence". It is therefore obvious that this conception of citizenship is qualitatively different from the liberal and social-democratic conceptions, which adopt an 'instrumentalist' view of citizenship, i.e. a view which implies that citizenship entitles citizens with certain rights that they can exercise as means to the end of individual welfare.

Although the above conception of citizenship implies a geographical sense of community which is the fundamental unit of political, economic and social life, still, it is assumed that it interlocks with various other communities (cultural, professional, ideological, etc.). Therefore, the community and citizenship arrangements do not rule out cultural differences based on language, customs etc, or other differences based on gender, age, ethnicity and so on; they simply provide the public space where such differences can be expressed. Furthermore, these arrangements institutionalise various safety valves that aim to rule out the marginalisation of such differences by the majority. What therefore unites people in a political community, or a confederation of communities, is not a set of common cultural values, imposed by a nationalist ideology, a religious dogma, a mystical belief, or an 'objective' interpretation of natural or social 'evolution', but the democratic institutions and practices, which have been set up by citizens themselves.

However, as I attempted to show elsewhere this cultural pluralism does not mean a kind of cultural relativism where 'everything goes'. In other words, it is possible to derive an ethical system and correspondingly a set of cultural values which is neither 'objective', (in the sense that it is derived from a supposedly objective interpretation of social evolution-Marx, or natural evolution---Bookchin), nor just a matter of individual choice. There can be a set of common or general moral criteria by which individual actions could be judged, i.e. a code of democratic ethics, which would be based on the fundamental principle of organising a democratic society around a confederal inclusive Democracy, (i.e. a democracy based on a confederation of demoi, or democratic communities).

DEMOCRATIC ETHIC CODE

This code of democratic ethics may be derived out of the two fundamental principles of organisation of a confederal inclusive Democracy, i.e. the principle of autonomy and the principle of community. Thus, out of the fundamental principle of autonomy one may derive a set of cultural values about equality and respect for the personality of every citizen, irrespective of gender, race, ethnic identity etc. Out of the same fundamental principle one could derive the principle of protecting the quality of life of each individual citizen--something that would imply a relationship of harmony with nature. Similarly, out of the fundamental principle of community life one may derive a set of values involving solidarity and mutual aid, caring and sharing. These values should constitute an integral part of the dominant social paradigm so that democracy can reproduce itself. This of course does not exclude the possibility, or rather the probability, of the existence of alternative cultural values, or perhaps even of a conflict between personal and collective values---particularly with respect to those citizens who cannot reconcile themselves with the tragic truth that it is we who determine our own truth and might still adhere to moral codes derived from irrational belief systems (religions, mystical beliefs etc). However, as long as these people are in a minority, (hopefully, a dwindling one, through the Paedeia of a democratic society), the conflict in their personal values with the collectively defined values should not be a problem for the community as a whole.

THE REFORMIST APPROACH

The reformist approach claims that it can bring about systemic change through either the conquest of state power (reforms 'from above') or through the creation of autonomous from the state power bases which would press the state for reforms (reforms 'from below'). The main example of the former strategy is the social democratic approach, whereas the main example of the latter is the civil societarian approach. The social democratic approach reached its peak during the period of statism and particularly in the first thirty years after WWII, when the social democratic consensus was dominant all over the Western world. However, the internationalisation of the market economy since the mid '70s brought about the end of this consensus and the rise of the neoliberal consensus-which, in my view, is irreversible as long as the market economy is internationalised, in other words, as long as the market economy reproduces itself. The recent deletion from the program of the British Labour Party (which was the last socialdemocratic party still committed to full socialisation of the means of production) of 'clause four', which committed it to full socialisation, marked the formal end of socialdemocratic claims towards real systemic change.

In fact, the neoliberal agenda for 'flexible' labour markets, minimisation of social controls on markets, replacement of the welfare state by a safety net etc has now become the agenda of every major socialdemocratic party in power or in opposition.

The parallel degradation of social democracy and the reversal of most of its conquests (comprehensive welfare state, state commitment to full employment, significant improvement in the distribution of income) has clearly shown that supporters of the revolutionary approach were always right on the impossibility of bringing about a systemic change through reforms.

As regards the civil societarian approach, the strategy here is to enhance 'civil society', that is, to strengthen the various networks which are autonomous from state control (unions, churches, civic movements, co-operatives, neighbourhoods, schools of thought etc.) in order to impose such limits (i.e. social controls) on markets and the state, so that a kind of systemic change is brought about. However, this approach is based on a number of unrealistic assumptions.

Thus, first, it implicitly assumes a high degree of statism where the state can still play the economic role it used to play during the socialdemocratic consensus. Second, it assumes, in effect, an almost closed market economy where the state can ignore the instant movement of capital in case a government attempts to meet demands of civil societarians which threaten capital's interets. No wonder that civil societarians usually deny (or try to minimise) the importance of the present internationalisation of the market economy. It is also indicative that when civil societarians attempt to internationalise their approach the only limits on the internationalised market economy that they view as feasible are various 'regulatory controls'. But, such controls have very little in common with the sweeping social controls that they have in mind when they discuss, abstracting from the present internationalised market economy, the limits that civil society networks should impose on markets (drastic reduction of inequalities, massive creation of jobs etc).

So, the civil societarian approach is both a-historical and utopian. It is a-historical, since it ignores the structural changes, which have led to the present neoliberal consensus and the internationalised market economy. And it is utopian because it is in tension both with the present internationalised market economy and the state. So, given that civil societarians do not see the outcome of this inevitable tension in terms of the replacement of the market economy and the state by the civil society, it is not difficult to predict that any enhancement of the civil society will have to be compatible with the process of further internationalisation of the market economy and the implied role of the state. In other words, the 'enhancement' of civil society, under today's conditions, would simply mean that the ruling political and economic elites will be left undisturbed to continue dominating society, while, from time to time, they will have to try to address the demands of the civil societarians--provided, of course that these demands are not in direct conflict to their own interests and the demands of oligopolistic production.

In conclusion, enhancing the civil society institutions has no chance whatsoever of either putting an end to the concentration of power, or of transcending the present multidimensional crisis. This conclusion may be derived from the fact that the implicit, although not always explicit, aim of civil societarians is to improve the functioning of existing institutions (state, parties, market), in order to make them more responsive to pressures from below when, in fact, the crisis is founded on the institutions themselves and not on their malfunctioning! But, in the present internationalised market, the need to minimise the socio-economic role of the state is no longer a matter of choice for those controlling production.

It is a necessary condition for survival. This is particularly so for European capital that has to compete with capital blocks, which operate from bases where the social-democratic tradition of statism was never strong (the United States, the Far East). But, even at the planetary level, one could seriously doubt whether it is still possible to enhance the institutions of civil society within the context of the market economy. Granted that the fundamental aims of production in a market economy are individual gain, economic efficiency and growth, any attempt to reconcile these aims with an effective 'social control' by the civil society is bound to fail since, as historic experience with the statist phase has shown, social control and market efficiency are irreconcilable objectives. By the same token, one could reasonably argue that the central contradiction of the market economy today is the one arising from the fact that any effective control of the ecological implications of growth is incompatible with the requirements of competitiveness, which the present phase of the marketization process imposes.

THE LIFE-STYLE APPROACH

The second type of approach which claims capable to bring about systemic social change is the presently fashionable, particularly among Anglo-Saxon anarchists, life-style strategy. There are several versions of this strategy. Sometimes this approach involves no intervention at all in the political arena and usually not even in the general social arena--other than in struggles on specific 'Green' issues, like animal rights campaigns etcetera. Alternatively, this approach may involve a process which, starting from the individual, and working through affinity groups, aims at setting an example of sound and preferable life-styles at the individual and social level: alternative media, Community Economic Development projects, 'free zones' and alternative institutions (free schools, self-managed factories, housing associations, Local Employment and Trading Systems (LETS), communes, self-managed farms and so on).

However, this approach, in any of the above versions, is, by itself, utterly ineffective in bringing about a systemic social change. Although helpful in creating an alternative culture among small sections of the population and, at the same time, morale-boosting for activists who wish to see an immediate change in their lives, this approach does not have any chance of success--in the context of today's huge concentration of power--in building the democratic majority needed for systemic social change. The projects suggested by this strategy may too easily be marginalised, or absorbed into the existing power structure (as has happened many times in the past) whereas their effect on the socialisation process is minimal--if not nil.

Furthermore, life-style strategies, by usually concentrating on single issues which are not part of a comprehensive political program for social transformation, provide a golden opportunity to the ruling elites to use their traditional divide and rule tactics (the British elites, for instance, frequently use security guards recruited from the underclass to fight Green activists rather than 'exposing' the police on this role!) Furthermore, systemic social change can never be achieved outside the main political and social arena. The elimination of the present power structures and relations can neither be achieved "by setting an example", nor through education and persuasion. A power base is needed to destroy power. But, the only way that an approach aiming at a power base would be consistent with the aims of the democratic project is, to my mind, through the development of a comprehensive program for the radical transformation of local political and economic structures.

A variation of the life-style strategy which however has, also, elements of the civil societarian approach is, to my mind, the strategy proposed by Noam Chomsky, Michael Albert and the group around Z magazine. Thus, Albert sees the setting up of alternative media institutions just 'as part of a project to establish new ways of organising media and social activity', without even mentioning the need to incorporate them into a comprehensive political program for systemic change. In fact, what differentiates the alternative from the mainstream media in his argument is, basically, their internal structure:

Being alternative can't just mean that the institution's editorial focus is on this or that topical area. And being alternative as an institution certainly isn't just being left or right or different in editorial content. Being alternative as an institution must have to do with how the institution is organised and works... An alternative media institution sees itself as part of a project to establish new ways of organising media and social activity and it is committed to furthering these as a whole, and not just its own preservation.

Similarly, Chomsky does not raise either the issue of incorporating alternative institutions into a comprehensive political program for systemic change. Thus, to the question whether we should just continue supporting efforts to set up alternative media institutions etc, or whether, instead, we should direct our striving towards integrating such attempts in a struggle to build a new political and social movement that will fight for alternative systems of social organisation, his reply is that these two possibilities 'should not be regarded as alternatives... these are not conflicting goals; rather, mutually supportive efforts, all of which should proceed'. It is therefore obvious that for Chomsky and Albert the establishment of alternative media is seen as a kind of life-style strategy, rather than as part of a political strategy and a comprehensive program for systemic change. Similarly, Chomsky's argument above that, even within the existing institutional framework, we could reverse the present concentration of power involves elements of the civil societarian approach. It is illustrative how Chomsky justifies his argument on the matter:

These are not the operations of any mysterious economic laws; they are human decisions that are subject to challenge, revision and reversal. They are also decisions made within institutions, state and private. These have to face the test of legitimacy, as always; and if they do not meet that test they can be replaced by others that are more free and more just, exactly as has happened throughout history.

However, although it is true that there are no historical or natural laws determining social evolution this does not mean that 'anything goes' within the existing institutional framework, as Chomsky seems to assume. The institutional framework does set the parameters within which social action takes place. This means that both the nature and the scope of radical social action cannot transcend these parameters-unless social action explicitly aims at the institutional framework itself. The neoliberal consensus was not just a policy change, as social democrats assume, but a structural change imposed by the needs of internationalisation of the market economy.

This implies that the basic elements of the neoliberal consensus and particularly flexible markets and minimisation of social controls on markets will not go away, as long as the present internationalised market economy exists. But, today, the market economy can only be internationalised, since the growth (and therefore profitability) of the multinationals, which control the world market economy, depends on enlarging their markets worldwide. And as long as the market economy has to be internationalised, markets have to be as open and as flexible as possible. All this means that, as long as the system of the market economy and representative democracy reproduces itself, all that reforms ('from above', or 'from below') can bring about today is temporary victories and reversible social conquests like, for instance, those made during the period of the social democratic consensus which are now being systematically dismantled by the neoliberal consensus.

THE REVOLUTIONARY APPROACH

Coming now to the revolutionary strategy, by 'revolution from above' I mean the strategy, which aims at systemic change through the conquest of state power. The Marxist-Leninist tradition is a classical example of this type of strategy. This approach, implied that the change in the social paradigm even among a minority of the population, the vanguard of the proletariat, (organised in the communist party and equipped with the 'science' of socialism, i.e. Marxism), could function as a catalyst to bring about a socialist revolution.

The socialist revolution would then lead to the conquest of state power by the proletariat (effectively by its vanguard, i.e. the communist party) which would bring about a change in the institutional framework as well as a change in the dominant social paradigm. The socialist society would give way to a communist society only when the rapid development of productive forces, through the socialisation of production relations, would lead to the abolition of scarcity and division of labour and the withering away of the state.

History however has shown that this strategy could only lead to new hierarchical structures, as the vanguard of the working class becomes at the end the new ruling elite. This was the main lesson of the collapse of 'actually existing socialism' which has clearly shown that, if the revolution is organised, and then its program carried out, through a minority, it is bound to end up with new hierarchical structures rather than with a society where concentration of power has been abolished. By 'revolution from below', I mean the strategy which aims at systemic change through the abolition of state power and the creation of federations of communes, or of workers' associations. The various trends within the anarchist movement (community-oriented versus worker-oriented) aim at revolution, in order to abolish state power and transform society 'from below', rather than in order to conquest state power and transform society 'from above'. But, attempts for revolutions from below in History have usually ended up either as insurrections, which failed to lead to a systemic change (the major recent example being the May '68 insurrection in France) or to civil wars, where the superior means, organisation and efficiency of their enemies (either the state army and/or statist socialists) led to the suppression of revolutionaries (the major recent example being the Spanish civil war in 1936).

To my mind, the major problem of any revolutionary strategy, either from above or from below, is the uneven development of consciousness among the population, in other words, the fact that a revolution, which assumes a rupture with the past both at the subjective level of consciousness and at the institutional level, takes place in an environment where only a minority of the population has broken with the dominant social paradigm.

Then, if it is a revolution from above, it has a good chance to achieve its first aim, to abolish state power and establish its own power. But, exactly because it is a revolution from above with its own hierarchical structures etc, it has no chance to change the dominant social paradigm but only formally, i.e. at the level of the official ideology. On the other hand, although the revolution from below is the correct approach to convert people democratically to the new social paradigm, it suffers from the fact that the uneven development of consciousness among the population may not allow revolutionaries to achieve even their very first aim of abolishing state power. Therefore, the still unresolved problem with systemic change is how it could be brought about, from below, but by a majority of the population, so that a democratic abolition of power structures could become feasible.

THE INCLUSIVE DEMOCRACY APPROACH

The Inclusive Democracy (ID) project does offer a strategy, which aims at resolving this problem. It starts first with the assumption that radical systemic change would never come about through reforms, or life-style strategies. This is because systemic change requires a rupture with the past, which extends to both the institutional and the subjective level. Such a rupture is only possible through the development of a new political organisation and a new comprehensive political program for systemic change. This means that the various activities to set up communes, co-ops, alternative media institutions etc are just irrelevant to a process of systemic change---unless they are an explicitly integral part of such a comprehensive political program. It is in this sense that one may argue that the two strategies are not complementary as Chomsky argues, but mutually exclusive.

The ID political strategy comprises the gradual involvement of increasing numbers of people in a new kind of politics and the parallel shifting of economic resources (labour, capital, land) away from the market economy. The aim of such a transitional strategy should be to create changes in the institutional framework, as well as to value systems, which, after a period of tension between the new institutions and the state, would, at some stage, replace the market economy, statist democracy, and the social paradigm "justifying" them, with an inclusive democracy and a new democratic paradigm respectively.

The immediate objective should be the creation, from below, of 'popular bases of political and economic power', that is, the establishment of local public realms of direct and economic democracy which will confederate in order to create the conditions for the establishment of a new society. Contesting local elections (the only form of elections which is not incompatible with the aims of the ID project) could provide the chance to put into effect such a program on a massive social scale, although other forms of establishing new types of social organisation should not be neglected, as long as they are part of a program which explicitly aims at systemic change.

Once the institutions of inclusive democracy begin to be installed, and people, for the first time in their lives, start obtaining real power to determine their own fate, then the gradual erosion of the dominant social paradigm and of the present institutional framework will be set in motion. A new popular power base will be created.

Town by town, city by city, region by region will be taken away from the effective control of the market economy and the nation-state, their political and economic structures being replaced by the confederations of democratically run communities. A dual power in tension with the state will be created, an alternative social paradigm will become hegemonic and the break in the socialisation process--the precondition for a change in the institution of society--will have occurred. The legitimacy of today's 'democracy' will have been lost. The implementation of a strategy like the one outlined above requires a new type of political organisation, which will mirror the desired structure of society. This would not be the usual political party, but a form of 'democracy in action', which would undertake various collective forms of intervention at:

- the political level (creation of 'shadow' political institutions based on direct democracy, neighbourhood assemblies, etc.),
- the economic level (establishment of community units at the level of production and distribution which are collectively owned and controlled),
- the social level (democracy in the workplace, the university etc.), and
- the cultural level (creation of community-controlled art and media activities).

However, all these forms of intervention should be part of a comprehensive program for social transformation aiming at the eventual change of each municipality won in the local elections into an inclusive democracy. The alternative media established as part of this program would play a crucial role in developing an alternative consciousness to the present one, as regards the methods of solving the economic and ecological problems in a democratic way. They should connect today's economic and ecological crisis to the present socio-economic system and make proposals on how to start building the new society. For example: by setting up a democratic economic sector, (i.e. a sector owned by the demos); by creating a democratic mechanism to make economic decisions affecting the demotic sector of the community; by 'localising' decisions affecting the life of the community as a whole (local production, local spending, local taxes, etc.).

Without underestimating the difficulties involved in the context of today's all-powerful methods of brain control and economic violence, which, in fact, might prove more effective methods than pure state violence in suppressing a movement for the inclusive democracy, I think that the proposed strategy is a realistic strategy on the way to a new society.

DEMOCRATIC MEDIA

The sufficient condition which has to be met so that democracy will not degenerate into some kind of "demagocracy", where the demos is manipulated by a new breed of 'professional' politicians, is crucially conditioned by the citizens' level of democratic consciousness. This, in turn, is conditioned by Paedeia. It is therefore obvious that the cultural institutions, particularly the media, play a crucial role in a democracy, given their role in the formation of Paedeia.

So, let us now consider the nature and role of the mass media, as cultural institutions, in a democratic society. First, there is no reason why the mass media in a democratic society will distort rather than reflect reality. As political and economic power would be equally distributed among citizens and therefore the existence of institutionalised elites would be excluded, the media would face none of the present dilemmas whether to reflect the reality of the elite, or particular sections of it, versus the reality of the rest of the population. Still, even in an inclusive democracy there is still the problem of the possible emergence of informal elites, which may attempt to exercise some sort of control over the information flows. It is also clear that no democracy is possible unless its citizens are fully informed on anything affecting their life. Therefore, a way has to be found to organise the decision-taking process in the media so that, on the one hand, citizens are always fully informed and, on the other, the media are under the real control of the community.

It is obvious that it is citizens as citizens, through their assemblies, who should determine the overall operation of mass media and supervise them. This function could not just be assigned to the councils of media workers because in that case the democratic society will run the double risk of media not expressing the general interest, as well as of the possible emergence of new media elites within, at least, some of them. This does not, obviously, mean that the assemblies will determine every day what the content of TV news bulletins will be, or what the papers would say next day. What it does mean is that the community assemblies would set strict rules on how full diversity and accountability could be achieved and then supervise the application of these principles in media practice.

Diversity implies that all sorts of views should be given full access to the media, provided that that they have been approved by the community and media workers' assemblies. Assuming that these assemblies have internalised the dominant democratic social paradigm, one could expect that they would not give easy access to views which contradict the democratic values (e.g. views promoting racial, sexist, religious values etc). However, the decision will always rest with the assemblies and if they see no contradiction involved in giving full access to such views this will simply herald the degradation and eventual collapse of the democratic society itself.

Accountability implies that the media workers would be accountable for their decisions to the media workers' assemblies in the first instance and, next, to the community assemblies. Such a structure of accountability would be compatible with the lack of hierarchical structures in the media and the fact that it will be the communities themselves that would 'own' the media institutions.

So, this dual system of decision-taking, whereby overall decision-taking and supervision rests with the community assemblies, whereas the determination of detailed operational functioning of the media is left to the media workers' assemblies, to my mind, guarantees that not only the general interest is adequately taken into account but also that the day-to-day decisions are taken democratically by the media workers themselves.

DEMOCRATIC MEDIA ORGANIZATION

Democratic media is a form of media organization that strives to have the principles of democracy underlying not only the production of content, but also the organization of the entire project.

Definition of the Term

Democratic Media is the concept of organising media along democratic lines rather that strictly commercial and/or ideological lines. Like the idea of democracy itself, democratic media looks to concepts such as transparency, inclusiveness, one-person-one-vote and other key concepts of democracy as principals of operation. This is in contrast to the idea that media should be run by commercial operations and with a agenda to make profit from providing media and where the media reflects the opinions and values of the owner and/or advertisers It is also in contrast to state-run operations where the media reflects the value system of the state itself.

Edward S Herman laysout what he thought the form that democratic media would take, "A democratic media can be indentified by its structure and functions. In terms of structure, it would be organized and controlled by ordinary citizens or their grass roots organisations....As regards function, a democratic media will aim first and foremost at serving the informational, cultural and other communications needs of members of the public which the media institutions comprise or represent.

Background of the Term

The idea of democratic media stems from the belief that media is a vital part of a democratic society;

"First, media perform essential political, social, economic, and cultural functions in modern democracies. In such societies, media are the principal source of political information and access to public debate, and the key to an informed, participating, self-governing citizenry. Democracy requires a media system that provides people with a wide range of opinion and analysis and debate on important issues, reflects the diversity of citizens, and promotes public accountability of the powers-that-be and the powers-that-want-to-be. To therefore, if media is vital for democracy, democratic media argues that media itself needs to be organized along different lines to the existing forms;

" The evidence is clear: if we want a media system that produces fundamentally different results, we need solutions that address the causes of the problems; have to address issues of media ownership, management, regulation, and subsidy. Our goal should be to craft a media system that reduces the power of a handful of enormous corporations and advertisers to dominate the media culture.

The idea of democratic media is still in its infancy as noted by Carroll & Hackett (2006 where they term it 'democratic media activism' however the idea does have older roots; In 'Triumph of the Market: Essays on Economics, Politcs, and the Media' Edward S Herman wrote that democratic media was a condition of democracy;

A democratic media is a primary condition of popular rule, hence of a genuine political democracy. Where the media are controlled by a powerful and privileged elite, whether of government leaders and bureaucrats or those of the private sector, democratic political forms and some kind of limited political democracy may exist, but not genuine democracy.

The term has been used to describe a number of new media projects from Wikipedia to the Indymedia movement to describe how it saw itself;

Indymedia is a democratic media outlet for the creation of radical, accurate, and passionate tellings of truth.

Democratic media differs from similar (and related) concepts such as citizen media, media democracy and independent media (aka alternative media) in that it puts as much emphasis on the organization of the media project as it does on the content. (Note; this definition means that an independent media or citizen media project can also be a democratic media project, but being an independent media or citizen media project does not mean it is automatically a form of democratic media. It also means there could be a project that promotes the concepts of media democracy without it itself explicitly claiming to be a form of democratic media.) For a media project to be considered democratic media it must have (or strive towards) the following characteristics:

- Open publishing
- Transparency (humanities)
- Accountability
- Open access (publishing)
- Non-commercial.

SOCIAL DEMOCRATIC JOURNALISM IN DEVELOPING SOCIETIES

In developed media systems, one response to globalization and to the excesses of the liberal journalism model has been to give renewed emphasis to the social democratic model typified by public broadcasting. Speaking at the spring conference, the Aspen Institute's Charles Firestone asked whether governments could not play a valuable role in facilitating and safeguarding diversity of expression, and particularly in the modern era, whether government might not be a necessary countervailing force against the large concentrations of private economic power in the media marketplace. Through direct or indirect intervention, government may-among other things-promote public access to the means of communication, encourage and regulate competition, and subsidize high-quality news, public affairs, and cultural fare that the market may not support.

Participants had mixed feelings about the government's ability to play a positive role in news and public affairs. Even where governments are ostensibly acting in the "public interest," said Maciej Wierzynski, the legacy of state control makes for an uneasy partnership. "Anytime we try to discuss the role of government in media it leads to political questions," he said. "Who controls? Who sets the priorities? In the case of Poland, state-owned media have played the decisive role in electronic media on the rationale that they are protecting 'national culture' against foreign television. As a result, we have a situation where national culture is not so much protected, but the government makes political appointments to state radio and television."

It is not uncommon for journalists in democratizing nations to reject the social democratic journalism model, which in their experience has been used primarily as a tool of domination. But more recent experience with privatization has led some to modify this view: Albeit imperfect, government involvement in the news media at least allows for public scrutiny and accountability. Discussing the possibility of privatization of state broadcasting in Ghana, Kwame Karikari worried that privatization would result in a system peopled by "cronies" of the ruling party.

"If broadcasting is still a civil service, we can demand that it really serve the public interest. If it is just a front, we can do nothing."

PARTICIPATORY JOURNALISM IN DEVELOPING SOCIETIES

Participatory journalism-much scorned in developing nations-has obvious appeal in developing societies. It emphasizes the kinds of civic associations that promote civil society, and in societies emerging from authoritarian pasts no single institution can advance the cause of democratization. Participatory journalism also reaches out to the large numbers of people, particularly in rural areas, who have traditionally been both socially marginalized and beyond the reach of virtually every public affairs medium except state radio.

Critics of participatory journalism charge that it is susceptible to abuse. This may be especially true in societies without a tradition of independent media. Further, the impediments to independent journalism in developing societies-poverty, high illiteracy rates, scattered populations, and poor infrastructure-are particularly injurious to the goals of participatory journalism. The Internet, for example, has been widely praised as the first mass medium that allows for interactivity and community building-and thus ideally suited to participatory journalism-but poverty and limited information infrastructure make the Internet unavailable to a majority of people in many developing societies.

The Role for International Organizations in Promoting Free Press and Civil Society

Because so many of the conference participants were from the international development community, a great deal of discussion focused on what international organizations could do to support the enabling conditions of press freedom and civil society. Generally, the participants agreed that IGOs and NGOs need to place greater emphasis on local and regional programs that will sustain themselves after crises and start-up funding are passed. Indigenous media, in turn, must better identify and articulate their own needs to the international community. Specifically, the conferees identified two categories of need that require focused attention: infrastructure development and professional development (training and institutional support) for journalists. The two are in some obvious ways mutually supporting and, as discussed below, the participants thought of professional development as less an exercise in instruction than one in social engineering, in building the civil society.

Infrastructure Support

Some infrastructure needs are clearly material ones. Particularly in societies in conflict, said Kwame Karikari, "Media houses have become targets, as in Sierra Leone and Liberia." International organizations, he urged, should make capital investments if they want to make a lasting difference. "Invest in a printing press and get a journalistic organization to run it as an independent company," he said. "Support it with management training." Such investments do not have to be large. Still another material need identified by several participants-and one clearly linked to journalism professionalism-are journalism schools. In some developing regions, Central

Europe and Russia especially, journalism schools tend to be highly theoretical places staffed by professors with little newsroom experience and almost no practical knowledge of free-enterprise journalism. Upgrading these institutions, or inventing new ones, is a key to building a level of professionalism that well-meaning but short-lived programs cannot.

As Sheila Coronel of the Philippines Centre for Investigative Journalism said, "We need support that's not a seminar here or there, but where you identify intellectuals in a region and you equip them with books and other materials, and some pay, and you let them teach." David Makali appeared to second this view: "I hold a dim view of short-term training programs. After you train people they disappear and results disappear. It would be better to invest in self-teaching aids, in education as part of infrastructure. I would like to see resource centers that journalists can access and that are stocked with materials for self-teaching."

Several participants did mention training programs they thought valuable, such as a World Bank project on health issues in developing nations that was coupled with an extensive reporting project. Lin Neumann described successful efforts in Thailand to first pass a national open-records law, then to train journalists how to use it.

Andreas Harsono argued for specialized reporting programs that would provide journalists substantive expertise in several areas-health care, the military, religion, and finance. Another need that might be considered under infrastructure is simple protection. Journalists who are subject to harassment, physical harm, or expulsion need both somewhere to go and a way to publicize their plight. A number of participants urged the creation of organizations or facilities that would provide physical relief and professional support to journalists in such situations.

7

The Concept of Press Freedom and Democracy

A free press is a cornerstone of (liberal) democracy. It is essential for holding government accountable, and for citizens to get informed, to communicate their wishes, to participate in the political decisionmaking. In principle, and on the analogy of democracy, press freedom has been accepted worldwide as the norm. The Soviet mass media enjoyed, in contrast with 'bourgeois' mass media and on the analogy of 'real democracy', 'real freedom'. Hence, media were freed from the obligation to be profitable: 'Freedom of the press was equated with freedom from private ownership: being freed from the profit motive, the media were free to do their duties as instruments of the state and the Party' (Siebert et al., 1956).

The communist model embraced the notion of the so called 'positive freedom', namely the freedom *to*, whereas in the liberal view, common in the West, the concept of 'negative freedom' or freedom *from*, prevailed: freedom from external goals (eg. building of a communist society, class homogenization) and external control and pressures (eg. government, parties, industry). A free press, in other words, is an autonomous press: free to determine its own tasks and policies. In line with this view of freedom, 'traditional free press theory (..) lacks a prescriptive character. It does not in its simple and most basic form say anything of what the press ought to do' (McQuail, 1976). Media autonomy, or independence, implies that the media are clearly separated from state and political institutions and free from/of inhibiting forms of economic, political or other dependency. Karol Jakubowicz (2000) distinguishes three levels of media independence:

1. External independence of media organizations, that is freedom to establish and operate media outlets without legal, political, or administrative interference or restraint.
2. Internal independence of editorial staff, that is editorial autonomy, respected by owners, publishers and managers.
3. Personal/professional independence of media practitioners, both management and journalists, which implies their impartiality and detachment from social, political and economic interests in their performance of journalistic duties and a sense of high professionalism and dedication to journalistic ethics.

Whereas laws, codes and institutions can contribute a lot to the first two levels of independence (media institutions and editorial staff) – one could speak of a 'formal press freedom' in accordance with the notion of 'formal democracy' – the third level, that is the individual level, is situated more on the field of (political) culture (t.i. attitudes, norms, values). And whereas the first two levels can be possibly realized without the third, absence of the third level on the other hand makes external and internal independence to a large degree meaningless. In other words: as democracy, press freedom is not considered a dichotomic but a continuous variable.

The choice is not between press freedom or no press freedom but between more or less press freedom. In every country and every system one can distinguish factors that spur press freedom on the one hand and factors that curtail press freedom on the other hand. The American organization Freedom House (2002) concentrates on the external factors that endanger press autonomy as the most measurable criteria: laws, regulations and administrative decisions that influence media content, political pressures and controls on media content, economic influences over media content and repressive actions (censorship, physical violence, arrests, killing of journalists). On the basis of these criteria Russia enjoys a 'partial press freedom'.

Very often the issue of 'press freedom' is linked to the issue of 'press responsibility' or 'social responsibility'. Together with Freedom House (2002) we want to stress the demand for 'freedom' above the demand for responsibility. Hence, the issue of 'press responsibility' often is voiced to defend governmental control of the press. It is linked more with the concept of 'positive freedom' than with the concept of freedom as such ('negative freedom'). Another frequently made association is that of press freedom with 'freedom of information' and the 'right to know'. This aspect is crucial indeed and complementary to press freedom as it relates to the perspective of the citizen. We'll come back to it later.

The Paradox of Democracy and Press Freedom

The process of democratization in Russia paradoxically became a justification to curtail press freedom and to keep the media instrumentalized. The instrumental use of the mass media in postcommunist Russia is a continuation of the communist past. Although the external (societal) goal has changed from the building of the communist society into support for the democratic society, the mobilization of the mass media as a means to a goal remained unchanged. Gorbachev considered the mass media main instruments in promoting his politics of glasnost and gaining support for his reforms. As before, mass media mobilized people for the ideology of socialism but now in a more dynamic way. Yassen Zassoursky, dean of the Faculty of Journalism of the Moscow State University, has labelled the mediamodel in the glasnost era (1985-1991) successively the 'glasnost-model' (Zassoursky, 1997) and the 'instrumental model'. The first label (glasnostmodel) points out an element of change, namely the break with the previous 'administrative-bureaucratic model'. Also in this model, however, Zassoursky points at the instrumental use of the mass media. In the name he later used (instrumental model), this aspect of continuity is brought to the forefront. The first Yeltsin-years received from Zassoursky the label of 'fourth power model'. The expectations, however, were pitched too high, and from 1995-'96 onward this label was changed in for that of 'authoritarian-corporate model.

It seems that the press could not meet the requirements for being called an independent 'Fourth Power'. 'Whatever good or bad happened to the Russian media in the 90s was directly tied to Yeltsin's views and acts in the information sphere', states media law specialist Andrei Richter (2000). Yeltsin presented himself as the self-constituted personal guarantor of democracy and press freedom. While it is obvious that Yeltsin 'allowed' more freedom than any of his predecessors, he never questioned his presumed right to allow such freedom. And in exchange he expected loyal support from the mass media for his policy. Yeltsin embodied the belief that in order to improve the democratic procedures one has to step 'beyond' these procedures.

In the name of democracy he fired upon Parliament in October 1993 and banned opposition newspapers. In the name of democracy he ruled largely by decree thus ignoring a whole series of 'horizontal checks'. In times of elections-'the lifeblood' of democracy – the mobilization of mass media reaches a peak. In the name of democracy Yeltsin blatantly expected the mass media to support and arrange his re-election as President in 1996.7 The mass media were comitted to an anti-communist crusade. The whole election campaign was reduced to a duel between President Yeltsin and oppositional candidate Zhuganov, between the future and the past, between democracy and communism, between press freedom and press control.

The tone of the campaign was set by the sacking on 15 February 1996 of Oleg Poptsov, head of the state-owned television station RTR (Belin, 1997). The right to appoint and dismiss media functionaries is one of the most powerful means of *direct* influence in the media for the executive. The President appoints the chairman of the 'public' television channel ORT and the government channels RTR and *Kul'tura*. The government appoints the chairmen of the central radio channels. Another way of direct control are the state organizations directly subordinated to the executive, especially the Media Ministry but also an *ad hoc* institution such as Boris Yeltsin's 'Federal

Information Center of Russia' (December 1992 – December 1993) or an institution with no direct authority over the media such as the Security Council. The possibilities for *indirect* control are even greater.

There is the reliance of many media outlets on economic sponsorship, either through state subsidies or by businesses, either open or secret. There is the use of courts as weapons deployed against journalists (esp. libel and slander). There is the dependency on the Kremlin – instead of an independent agency – for the issuance and revoking of broadcast and publishing licenses. There is the dependency on state facilities such as printing houses, transmission facilities, and distribution systems. There is the accreditation of journalists and the inequal access to information. There is the use of violence against journalists. To this we can add the legal insecurity caused by the rapid succession of decrees, government orders and procedures, and the upredictable changes in policy and practice of, for example, tax collection (eg. massively tolerated tax-evasion, followed by repressive controls on a large scale).

The paradox of democracy and press freedom : the media's side It does not appear fair to exclusively blame the authorities for the described system. The label 'authoritarian-corporate model' implies next to the 'authoritarian' aspect (that is, the media subordinated to the authorities) also the 'corporate' aspect (that is, the cooperation and alliances). The distinction comes down to the question whether the media are 'forced' rather than 'free' partners of the authorities. The question of quilt is inappropriate. We can only observe and conclude. In the early years of the Russian Federation (1992-'93), marked by the conflict between President and Parliament, 'most of the Russian media appeared to adopt a strongly progovernment stance'. A content analysis of central television programs in the run-up to the referendum of 25 April 1993, showed 'the obtrusive partisanship of state television'.

The majority of media *voluntarily* opted for the new, hence democratic partiality. Their leaders approached Yeltsin on their own initiative for protection and promised loyalty. In the presidential elections of 1996, the majority of journalists and media professionals rallied behind Yeltsin again and *voluntarily* agreed with the mobilization function of the media. As Shevelov, vice president of television channel ORT, stated: 'you can only refer to pressure if there is resistance. There is none.'. The journalists adhered to partisanship not only for material reasons but also out of normative considerations. Igor Malashenko, president of the private television station NTV, who joined the Yeltsin re-election campaign in April 1996 as chief media advisor, explained this logic as following: if the private media provided "unbiased, professional, and objective" campaign coverage, Zyuganov would win the election, and journalists would lose their freedom permanently. Better to become a temporary "instrument of propaganda" in the hands of the Kremlin, Malashenko argued. *Partijnost'* was justified for the protection of democracy and consequently for press freedom. In the name of democracy the journalists voluntarily gave up their autonomy and their freedom.

Elections in general, and the 1996 elections in particular, can be considered critical but not atypical periods. Hence, it is not possible to treat the electoral period as being distinct from the context in which media normally operate. Quite the reverse, if we may believe Brzezinski (1970): 'A perceptive formula is easier to articulate in a moment of special stress. (..) The situation of crisis permits sharper value judgments'. In general, and apart from election context, research has shown that many Russian journalists do not reject the paternalistic character of power and therefore accept its tutelage in mass communication. The journalist considers himself, in line with the tradition, a missionary of ideas, not a neutral observer or autonomous information disseminator. The concept adhered to is that of the active or participant journalist as decribed by the Hungarian writer Janos Horvat : someone who wants to influence politics and audiences according to his political beliefs. The restriction to the presentation of mere facts is even commonly regarded as a devaluation of the profession of journalist.

The attitude of the individual journalists suits the media-owners who like to use the argument of press freedom to protect their own freedom and their particular interests. As the majority of media-holdings form part of larger financial-industrial groups and as money is still made through political connections, political, economic and media-interests go closely together. Political and economic elites try to secure via the media their own positions. Oligarchs and media magnates like Boris Berezovsky and Vladimir Gusinsky are the classic examples. When the media outlets of Vladimir Gusinsky became the target of prosecution, Gusinsky immediately alarmed that press freedom and in extension even democracy was endangered. His alarm was taken over by other journalists in Russia as well as in foreign countries (the USA in the first place). There were, however, also sceptical voices. Robert Coalson (2000) wrote in a column in *The Moscow Times*: 'Gusinsky has shown very little genuine concern for press freedom. Like the other oligarchs, he only appears when his own interests are directly at risk'.

In the same way Sergej Markov (2001) noticed with reference to a rally on freedom of speech, organized in connection with the NTV-case: '.. all speeches by NTV stars were about NTV's freedom. Such egoism could not inspire champions of freedom of expression'. Also in line is the following reflection: 'Where were the voices of protest from this 'independent' press when Yeltsin attacked the legitimate Russian parliament with military force, when the Soviet Union became dissolved by the signatures of a few officials, when the country's resources passed into the hands of a few oligarchs, and when corruption allowed Yeltsin's chosen family and friends to suddenly acquire wealth and transfer this wealth out of the country? That 'independent' press manipulated a government that served its interests'. 'The concept of freedom of speech has become hackneyed after Gusinsky and somewhat awkward to use' concludes the however not neutral General Director of Gazprom-Media, Alfred Kokh (2001).

As Price and Krug (2000) state : 'for free and independent media to 'work', the community in question must value the role that the media play'. The public however seems to accept the 'Russian interpretation' of press freedom. Or, in any case, is adapted to it. The people react to mass media information by asking themselves not 'is this true' but '*komu eto vygodno* ?' (to who's advantage ?). News is interpreted in function of the news source, whether 'Berezovsky's channel', 'Gusinsky's channel' or 'the government's channel', or whether Potanin's newspaper, LUKoil's newspaper or the Communist Party's newspaper. It is telling that 'independent' media in Russia are identified with 'opposition' media. Media independence is considered illusory, and partisanship the norm. Many Russians endorse the proposition that the mass media have the obligation to support 'the system'. A poll at the end of 2000, for example, shows that 34% of the Russians agrees that the mass media have to give 'full support' to the President and that opposition is not desirable. 'In today's Russia, media freedom is (..) not the most fashionable and popularly supported notion' declared television presentator and journalist Evgeny Kiselev in an interview with Jeremy Drukker (*Transitions Online*, 10 juli 2000). And Elena Androunas (1993) points to the absence of 'freedom as a state of mind'.

MEDIA DEMOCRACY

Media democracy is a production and distribution model which promotes a mass media system that informs and empowers all members of society, and enhances democratic values. The term also refers to a modern social movement evident in countries all over the world which attempts to make mainstream media more accountable to the publics they serve and to create more democratic alternatives.

It is a concept and a social movement that has grown as a response to the increased corporate domination of mass media and the perceived shrinking of the marketplace of ideas. Its proponents advocate monitoring and reforming the mass media, strengthening public service broadcasting, and developing and participating in alternative media and citizen journalism.

Definition of the Term

Media democracy is a difficult term to define, since in addition to being a concept, it is also an advocacy movement being advanced by a number of academics and grassroots organizations, each with its own methods and goals. It is also difficult to define because the term [democracy] itself is contested.

Market liberals would claim that democracy is best served by the media if there is a minimalist state that allows for private media ownership, does not censor content, or require public-interest broadcasting. In this way, the market would facilitate technological innovation and provide whatever fare the consumer demands. By contrast, media democracy advocates argue that corporate ownership and commercial pressures influence media content, sharply limiting the range of news, opinions, and entertainment citizens receive. Consequently, they call for a more equal distribution of economic, social, cultural, and information capital, which would lead to a more informed citizenry, as well as a more enlightened, representative political discourse.

More radical thinkers argue that media democracy remains an under-defined concept because of deliberate structural pressures that prevent individuals from questioning the connection between media and democracy. A leading proponent of this view is Noam Chomsky, who argues that

> The concept of "democratizing the media" has no real meaning within the terms of political discourse in the United States. In fact, the phrase has a paradoxical or even vaguely subversive ring to it. Citizen participation would be considered an infringement on freedom of the press, a blow struck against the independence of the media that would distort the mission they have undertaken to inform the public without fear or favour... this is because the general public must be reduced to its traditional apathy and obedience, and driven from the arena of political debate and action, if democracy is to survive.

Despite the difficulties in defining the term, the concept broadly encompasses the following notions: that the health of the democratic political system depends on the efficient, accurate, and complete transmission of social, political, and cultural information in society; that the media are the conduits of this information and should act in the public interest; that the mass media have increasingly been unable and uninterested in fulfilling this role due to increased concentration of ownership and commercial pressures; and that this undermines democracy as voters and citizens are unable to participate knowledgeably in public policy debates. Without an informed and engaged citizenry, policy issues become defined by political and corporate elites. A related element of this concept examines the lack of representation of a diversity of voices and viewpoints, particularly of those who have traditionally been marginalized by mass media.

British and European Cultural Studies has spawned a range of alternative definitions of 'media democracy', including the idea that media audiences are the source of a new form of creative cultural politics. These are not simply audiences of public, Internet or alternative media, but include mass media audiences as well. This radical idea suggests that a cultural democracy emerges through the everyday experiences and meaning-making of audiences. Clearly, such a notion of media democracy extends the familiar conception of institutionally-derived representative democracy. A key theorist in this area is Jeff Lewis (2005), who coined the notion of a globalizing mediasphere..

Key Principles: Media Ownership Concentration

A key idea of media democracy is that the concentration of media ownership in recent decades in the hands of a few corporations and conglomerates has led to a narrowing of the range of voices and opinions being expressed in the mass media; to an increase in the commercialization of news and information; to a hollowing out of the news media's ability to conduct investigative reporting and act as the public watchdog; and to an increase of emphasis on the bottom line, which prioritizes infotainment and celebrity news over informative discourse. This concentration has been encouraged by government deregulation and neo-liberal trade policies. For example, the U.S. Telecommunications Act of 1996 discarded most media ownership rules that were previously in place, leading to massive consolidation in the telecommunications industry. Over 4,000 radio stations were bought out, and minority ownership of TV stations dropped to its lowest point since the federal government began tracking such data in 1990. In its review of the Telecommunication Act in 2003, the Federal Communications

Commission (FCC) further reduced restrictions and allowed media corporations to grow and expand intc other areas of media.

The past decade has also seen a number of media corporate mergers and takeovers in Canada. For example, in 1990, 17.3% of daily newspapers were independently owned; in 2005, 1% were. These changes, among others, caused the Senate Standing Committee on Transport and Communications to launch a study of Canadian news media in March 2003. (This topic had been examined twice in the past, by the Davey Commission (1970) and the Kent Commission (1981), both of which produced recommendations that were never implemented in any meaningful way.)

The Senate Committee's final report, released in June 2006, expressed concern about the effects of the current levels of news media ownership in Canada. Specifically, the Committee discussed their concerns regarding the following trends: the potential of media ownership concentration to limit news diversity and reduce news quality; the Canadian Radio-television and Telecommunications Commission]] (CRTC) and Competition Bureau's ineffectiveness at stopping media ownership concentration; the lack of federal funding for the CBC and the broadcaster's uncertain mandate and role; diminishing employment standards for journalists (including less job security, less journalistic freedom, and new contractual threats to intellectual property); a lack of Canadian training and research institutes; and difficulties with the federal government's support for print media and the absence of funding for the internet-based news media. The report provided 40 recommendations and 10 suggestions (for areas outside of federal government jurisdiction), including legislation amendments that would trigger automatic reviews of a proposed media merger if certain thresholds are reached, and CRTC regulation revisions to ensure that access to the broadcasting system is encouraged and that a diversity of news and information programming is available through these services.

Media democracy advocates argue in favour of such legislative policies that encourage a stronger commitment to serving the public interest and a commercial framework that facilitates independent media ownership.

The 2004 documentary film *Outfoxed: Rupert Murdoch's War on Journalism* treats criticism about corporate media concentration.

Alternative and Citizen Media in the World

As a response to the shortcomings of the mainstream media, proponents of media democracy often advocate supporting and engaging in independent and alternative media, in both print and electronic forms as well as video documentary. Through citizen journalism and citizen media, individuals can produce and disseminate information and opinions that are marginalized by the mainstream media. In the book *We the Media: Grassroots Journalism by the People, for the People*, Dan Gillmor urges individuals who are concerned about media ownership concentration and the decreasing amount of public-interest broadcasting to use technology like the internet to create and distribute information they believe is not properly reported in the mainstream news media. This book details strategies that individuals and groups can use to democratize the media.

THE CONCEPT OF DEMOCRACY

Press freedom and democracy are words with a highly positive emotional value. Amartya Sen (1999) has pointed out that while democracy is not yet universally practiced, nor indeed uniformly accepted, in the general climate of world opinion, democratic governance has now achieved the status of being taken to be generally right. Because of its positive emotional value the word is highly vulnerable for abuse and 'cooptation' which leads to a shift, and in the end an emptiness, of meaning. In the Soviet Union a distinction was made between the real 'socialist democracy' (*sotsialisticheskaya demokratiya*) and the fake 'bourgeois democracy' (*burzhyuaznaya demokratiya*). The meaning of the word democracy became even more obscured by the use of the prefixes pseudo-, new-, or 'not consolidated' in combination with democracy. Postcommunist Russia has been labelled all of this, due to the gap between its democratic quality and its democratization rhetoric. Other labels have been used that question the genuineness of Russian democracy even more:

Russia as 'delegative democracy', 'totalitarian democracy' (Goble, 2000) or 'authoritarian democracy' (Sakwa, 1998). With the same half-heartedness, Olcott and Ottaway (1999) speak of 'semi-authoritarianism', Zhelev (1999) of 'a multiparty authoritarian system', Sergej Kovalev of an 'authoritarian-police regime that will preserve the formal characteristics of democracy and market economy' (in *RussiaReform Monitor* nr. 742, 31 January 2000) and the Russian commentator Mikhail Delyagin of a 'liberal dictatorship' and 'manipulative democracy' (in *RussiaReform Monitor* nr. 742, 31 January 2000). Koshkareva and Narzhikulov (1998) speak of a 'nomenklatura democracy'. Diamond (1996) calls this a characteristic of the 'third wave' of democratization (Huntington, 1993): the gap between the so called electoral (formal, political) and liberal (substantial, social) democracies.

At a minimum, democracy is a political system based on free, competitive and regular elections. This 'electoral' democracy presumes space for political opposition movements and political parties that represent a significant range of voter choice and whose leaders can openly compete for and be elected to positions of power in government. The concept of 'liberal' (eg. Diamond, 1996) or 'substantial' democracy extends the key element of free competition with a bunch of political and civil rights (freedom of speech, freedom of association, freedom of religion, etc.) and the notions of the rule of law, inclusive citizenship and civil society.

The concept of substantial democracy cannot easily be reduced to a set of procedures and institutions but is described as 'a way of regulating power relations in such a way as to maximize the opportunities for individuals to influence the conditions in which they live, to participate in and influence debates about the key decisions that affect society'. Democracy in this sense is not a dichotomic but continuous variable. The choice is not between democracy or no democracy but between more or less democracy, which comes down very often to 'old' and 'new' democracies

(Mayer, 1989). Linz and Stepan (1996) distinguish 'consolidated' and 'transitional' democracies. Consolidation is attained to when democracy became 'the only game in town', constitutionally as well as behaviourally and attitudinally (Linz & Stepan, 1996). At this stage, institutions and laws alone are not sufficient anymore, and the element of political culture joins in. The concept of political culture builds largely on the book of Almond and Verba, *The Civic Culture,* and experiences some renaissance in the last decennia.

The idea however, that one 'culture'-one constellation of values, norms, belief systems, and attitudes-fits democracy closer than the other, is not new. Plato already pointed out that forms of government (oligarchy, democracy, tyranny, aristocracy) differ according to dispositions of men (Störig, 1985, vol. I). More recently, Miller, White and Heywood (1998) have expressed this as 'democracies require democrats'. The concept of political culture provides a link between the macro level of the society and the micro level of the individual. The concept of culture also suggests some continuity over time: 'neither an individual's values nor those of a society as a whole are likely to change overnight. Instead, fundamental value change takes place gradually' (Inglehart, 1997). The value has singled out as most contributive to a 'civic' or 'democratic' culture is trust, and more specifically impersonal trust, in contrast with personal trust.

In the 'democratic' culture, the individual is considered an end in itself and a rational being, capable of making independent judgments and choices (eg. voting) and able to construct his own 'truth' out of widely divergent messages. 'Authoritarian culture', in contrast, places truth in the hands of a few 'wise men' whereas the common man is distrusted and considered a dependent, irrational being, a 'cog in the wheel', not capable of making independent judgments and choices. Merrill and Lowenstein (1990) speak of a 'democratic orientation' (with examples such as John Locke and John Milton) versus an 'elitarian orientation' (with examples such as Plato, Machiavelli, Hegel, or Nietzsche). The former can be linked to individualism, pluralism and trust; the latter to collectivism, dominance (unitary truth) and distrust. Russia has traditionally been an elitist country. Tsarist Russia was characterized by a wide gap between the ruling elite and the common men (Krug, 1990). Communist Russia was, despite its claims to be egalitarian, very elitist oriented. Lenin stressed the role of the Communist Party as a vanguard party.

Hence, the mass lacked class consciousness and organization and had need of the guidance of the Party (Lenin, 1972). According to Kropotkin, Lenin's attitude was dictated by a fundamental distrust in mankind. The American journalist Robert Kaiser (1976) has stated it very crude when he wrote: 'The Soviet system is built on the assumption that the citizenry cannot be trusted'.

The sharp dichotomy between the Party and the people outlived Lenin. Pavao Novosel (1995) speaks of a division of the Soviet society in 'first and second class citizens', formalized through the *nomenklatura* system. Postcommunist Russia is characterized by a more diversified social stratification but the contrast between the 'elite' (oligarchs and rulers) and 'the people' remains. The distinction is expressed more frequently than before in terms of money and standard of living, but remains present in the mentality of the Russians as well. Also Zhelev (1996) sees this as a constant between the past and the present: 'the sense that 'we, the people' are of no consequence' and the tension between 'us' and 'them'.

Truth has traditonally been unitary in Russia and so was the community, as words like *sobornost'* (a kind of mystic unity) testify to. In the Marxist interpretation too there was only one right position. Opposition and diversity were considered falsehood and therefore deserved no hearing (McDaniël, 1996). William Zimmerman (1995) has called this 'synoptic thinking': 'the view that there is only one correct philosophy'. This view is diametrically opposed to the pluralistic view of truth and the parliamentarian model that 'by contrast is based on the assumption that the existence of groups or factions that express and defend particular interests in a representative institution is not only natural but its sole justification' (Sergeyev & Biryukov, 1993).

PRESS FREEDOM AND CIVIL SOCIETY

For many of the conferees the discussion about expression theory reduced to a practical question: Which is more urgent, establishing freedom of expression or establishing the conditions of civil society that make expression meaningful? Effectively circumventing the chicken and egg nature of the question, Sheila Coronel, executive director of the Philippine Centre for Investigative Journalism, put the matter this way:

It is a general thinking that freedom of expression is good for its own sake, regardless of the consequences. But, it doesn't guarantee anything. It doesn't guarantee fulfillment; it doesn't guarantee stability. We take the risk and we can have the exact opposite results of what we hope for. The social good that comes from free expression depends on social contexts-basic survival is necessary first or else free expression becomes a right of the elite. Many of us come from countries that lack a number of important enabling conditions-a diversity of media outlets, peace, and stability, a culture of tolerance, an economic system that meets people's basic needs. This raises some questions about what our role is as journalists.

How do we use our freedoms to make free expression available to a majority of citizens? Coronel's formulation of the issues fits well within the tradition of civil society thought, which is concerned with the institutions that comprise the non-governmental sector of society-churches, neighbourhoods, families, clubs, and civic groups, and so on. These institutions are characterized by voluntary association and perform a number of important social functions: they provide a buffer between the individual and the power of the state and the market; they create social capital; and they develop democratic values and habits.

Civil society, in short, provides to democracy what the law, with its rules and sanctions, cannot-social trust, social authority, civic virtue, and vision-the stuff of citizenship. It is an oversimplification, but not too much of one, to say that fundamentally civil society is about social responsibility. This idea as it has developed in modern times stands in opposition to the Western tradition of liberal individualism and its tendency to see people either as bundles of legal rights and entitlements, cut off from any higher moral claims, or as consumers motivated only by economic self-interest.

Journalism, depending on how one defines the term, fits awkwardly into the mix of institutions that comprise civil society. One view of journalism sees its role as building civic consciousness and social solidarity (for example, the "public journalism" movement in the United States). A more traditional view-the so-called "fourth estate" view-follows closely on free expression theory and sees journalism as institutionalizing the expressive freedoms that provide a moderating influence on sources of power.

A third model of journalism, one often promoted with respect to developing nations, is less democratic than it is developmental; it sees journalism as promoting socio-economic change through education, economic expansion, and growth. This model is not necessarily anti-democratic, but places politics second to development, which is its priority.

In each of these models, journalism is a business, sometimes of a kind that links it financially or editorially to government. By being linked to government, journalism usually lacks the characteristic of voluntary association that defines civil society institutions. Ideally, however, journalism shares with those institutions devotión to a larger public purpose. Still, in a society where free association is possible, journalists have organized themselves into numerous voluntary associations whose broad purposes are to improve press performance and enhance public service.

Typically most of these organizations acknowledge that the corollary of press freedom is press responsibility, and some-press councils, for instance-also provide mechanisms for the public to hold journalists accountable for shoddy work. With respect to responsibility, journalism again fits uneasily in traditional norms of civil society. To many journalists, and non-governmental organizations (NGOs) concerned with media, "responsibility" is a code word that signals government restrictions on media activity whenever the government deems such activity "irresponsible."

Several NGOs, for instance, have objected to the provision on free expression in the European Convention on Human Rights, which begins "Everyone has the right to freedom of expression," and continues "the exercise of these freedoms, since it carries with it duties and responsibilities, may be subject to such formalities, conditions, restrictions, or penalties as are prescribed by law and are necessary in a democratic society, in the interests of national security, territorial integrity or public safety, for the prevention of disorder or crime, for the protection of health or morals, for the protection of the reputation of the rights of others, for preventing the disclosure of information received in confidence, or for maintaining the authority and impartiality of the judiciary."

Despite the obvious potential for government abuse in such language, forty member countries of the Organization for Security and Cooperation in Europe (OSCE) subscribe to it. Many new democracies in Europe have used the same or similar language in drafting their media laws, and throughout the Aspen Institute conference several participants spoke-as Kwame Karikari, executive director of the Media Foundation for West Africa, did-of the need "to balance the rights of individual and community."

Most developed democratic governments officially view "freedom" as the result of non-restrictive government policies towards the media and "responsibility" as the product of self-regulation-a view that most of the journalists at the conference shared. However, in both established and emerging democracies, this principle probably works better in theory than it does in practice. One of the common features of an emerging democracy is an increasing number of people who call themselves journalists, but who are untrained and unprofessional. In both established and emerging democracies, the Internet exacerbates this trend.

Finally, in many developed media systems the ever widening acceptance of the marketplace as the best arbiter of press performance has led to greater reliance on sensational over serious journalism and many well publicized compromises in journalism ethics; not surprisingly, it has also led to renewed focus on press accountability. Presumably governments and journalists will in time mature and come to grips with their new freedoms, meanwhile, both must deal with the very real grievances and dangers that define the present.

Many journalists categorically reject the view that journalistic performance is in any way compromised by complete freedom in favour of a more absolutist approach to free expression. Americans in particular take this view, and indeed raised it in the 1997 negotiations with the Council of Europe that gave rise to the OSCE's creation of an office to promote freedom of the media. The United States' experience with free expression is unique in that to a degree unmatched anywhere the First Amendment protects speech that, in Supreme Court Justice Oliver Wendell Holmes' words, "we loathe and believe to be fraught with death."

Beyond the example of the First Amendment, the absolutist approach to free expression suffers from defects both as theory and as history. Despite Holmes' words (indeed, perhaps because of them) the American system of free expression is not absolutist, nor could it be. All speech is conduct but not all conduct is speech, and taken literally, absolutism is unable to distinguish between the two. Thus absolutism not only makes a civil society impossible, but it plays into the hands of authoritarian governments that promise freedom of speech but arbitrarily punish dissenting or controversial speech as prohibited conduct.

Historically, the liberal American position on speech is relatively new. In the nineteenth century-the United States' own emerging democracy period-free speech law was state law, and state constitutions typically linked the right to speak freely with the obligation to speak responsibly. Beginning in 1931 and particularly since 1964, the United States Supreme Court has moved far from that view with respect to the press, but its legacy is still evident in some core doctrinal areas (prior restraint, for instance), and in the Court's respect for the police powers of the state (for example, the use of time, place, and manner restrictions).

Another feature of the American media system-and increasingly media systems everywhere-that runs counter to civil society thinking is its heavy reliance on the purchasing and viewing habits of consumers as the most credible measure of press performance. American journalism has historically eschewed critical evaluation both from within its ranks (ombudsmen and media critics) and from outside (commissions and academic studies); self-regulation is informal and, to the public, pretty much invisible.

This leaves the law as the only meaningful tool of redress for alleged press wrongs. The result, several legal commentators have noted, is ironic: It is primarily judges-officers of the state-who establish the de facto rules of press accountability in the United States, not the news media themselves. This enlarges the role of government in public life and strains it beyond its competency, both roles being anathema to civil society adherents. Whether for those reasons or others, participants at the conference saw self-regulation as a means of maintaining press independence from the state.

FREEDOM OF OPINION, NOT OF INFORMATION

The result is a pluralist but not an independent (autonomous) press. Pluralist, in the sense of representation in the media system of a broad range of political expression, opinions and interests. In this sense, postcommunist Russia is hardly less pluralistic than older democracies and probably even more, as it is not hindered to the same degree by 'political correctness' or 'la pensée unique'. Peter Humphreys (1996) points in his book on media policy in Western Europe at a systematic decline of pluralism in the 20st century, caused by a de-ideologization of the traditional politics and commercialization, standardization and concentration of the media. While the Russian media system is characterized by a high degree of concentration as well, this concentration is not at all linked with depolitization: 'money in the CIS is still made through connections in the government, and in this game it helps to own newspapers and stations as instruments of political influence' (Pankin, 1998). Ivan Sigal (1997) has named Russian news coverage 'a part of politics'. 'In such circumstances', says Izvestiya-journalist Sergej Agafonov, 'a free independent press is doomed, but an unfree and dependent press can flourish'. Alexei Pankin speaks of a unique result: 'a genuinely pluralistic unfree media'. However, a pluralism that derives the right to exist from the presence of different power groups in society is an uncertain pluralism. Hence, when the different power groups join forces because they feel threatened in their positions, as was the case in the 1996 presidential elections, this pluralism dies.

The greatest victim of this kind of pluralism is the (factual) information. Every newspaper and every television channel brings its own *versiya* of the facts. In order to get an accurate picture of what happened, one has to read daily about six newspapers and watch several television stations, claims Andrei Fadin (1997). But who does? 'What we have is not freedom of information, and this 'freedom' is not exhaustive stimulating readers to buy half a dozen newspapers, but rather discouraging them from reading anything other than gossip columns and cheap sensations, and even more importantly, from organising their own actions on the basis of information received' reacts Alexei Pankin (1997). The scepticism of the public is illustrated by its small confidence in the media: down from 70% in 1990 to only 13% in 2000 (Fossato, 2000).

To fulfil their information function, the media need not only to break with the view of journalism as 'politics conducted with other means'. They also are in need, more concretely, for guaranteed access to information and transparency of governance. Press freedom presumes that, though independent, the press is not shielded away from government and industry. Worldwide, a correlation is determined between press freedom and transparency, and consequently between transparency and democracy: 'Information gathering is a vital component of freedom of information. Without access to information, journalists are engaged primarily in the presentation of opinions. And while openness in the statement of opinions is an important element of democratic society, it is not sufficient for its development and maintenance. The possibility for an informed citizenry depends on the ability of journalists to have access to sources. Without this kind of journalistic effectiveness, a society can have free and independent media, but their utility toward advancement of democratic institution-building might be severely limited.' (Krug & Price, 2000)

A climate of open access clings to the principle of information as a universal *right*, adjudged to everyone on an equal basis according to laws and procedures (universalism) whereas a culture of secrecy considers information a *privilege*, dependent on position or connections (particularism). Laws concerning transparency include those that recognize and guarantee public access to government-controlled information and institutions, with limited exceptions for national security, protection of personal privacy, crime prevention, and other goals. Laws concerning the licensing and accredititation of journalists also relate to his question.

Russia has always been characterized by a culture of secrecy rather than transparency. Always in Russian history, information was considered a privilege not a universal right-a property of the 'elite' who could dispose of it arbitrarily. In the Soviet Union, access to news sources depended on one's hierarchical (Party) position. The privileges of the nomenklatura 'first class' citizens (Novosel, 1995) not only included material goods, such as high salaries, access to 'diplomatic' shops, country houses, and the like, but also enhanced access to information: from the right to see foreign movies, or to read books, declared unsuited for general distribution to the receipt of special foreign news bulletins, on a daily basis compiled by TASS and distributed on paper of different colours according to the degree of detail and the intended public. Though the high-placed functionaries received significantly more information, they too received their information on a 'need-to-know' basis. The result of this information policy was an information deficit: information became one of the most sought after commodities in the Soviet Union. Informal networks and rumours filled the vacuüm. Parallel to the official information circuit, and on the analogy of the 'black market', an unofficial information circuit (eg. *samizdat*) was functioning. The use of personal networks and informal contacts for obtaining scarce information, services or goods is indicated in Russian by the word *blat* or the term *ZIS (znakomstva i svyazi)*.

In the Soviet Union, the use of informal information networks primarily had an economic function, namely the survival in an economy of scarcity (Ledeneva, 1998). In the transition to a free market economy, privileged access to information played a key role in the process of privatizations, which became indicated as 'insider privatizations'. Personal (particularistic) relations (eg. corruption, loyalties, privileges) continue to dominate the post-communist Russian economy and politics alike. Postcommunist leaders continue to see secrecy as a method to control the information flow. The panellists that IREX brought together to discuss the media situation in Russia agreed unanimously that 'access to some publicly relevant information is not free: authorities continue to view information as their property, and want to control access.' Defence-related security topics that are not state secrets have the status of classified information. As a result 'obtaining publicly relevant information has become an increasingly challenging and dangerous job for Russian journalists, especially in cases of investigating authorities' abuses, corruption, fraud during election campaigns, and the war in Chechnya'. Banai sums up the three most efficient processes of information gathering in Russia as 'trust, relationship and integration'. Authorities still offer privileges to some periodicals and journalists. Mikhail Gulyaev names as 'privileged media' under President Yeltsin the news agencies ITAR-TASS and Interfaks, the newspapers *Kommersant'* and *Izvestiya*, and the weekly *Argumenty i Fakty*.

More recent examples support the enduring culture of secrecy. The way in which the Kremlin handled the disaster with the sunken submarine Kursk in the summer of 2000 fuelled speculations that the government was trying to withhold information from the public. Media coverage of the disaster was restricted, only state-controlled television channel RTR was granted full access to the disaster scene. The dissemination of false and misleading information led to confusion and government officials provided obscure answers to justified questions. The adoption by the Security Council of the 'Doctrine of the

Information Security of the Russian Federation' (*doktrina informatsionnoj bezopasnosti Rossijskoj Federatsii*) on September 9th, 2000 roused fear that the government intended to limit the free flow of information and conceal information from the public. Among others, the doctrine promotes a feeling of distrust towards the foreign press whereas the unrestricted access to foreign media nowadays is guaranteed by the Russian mass media law of 27 December 1991.

The Russian mass media law (*zakon Rossijskoj Federatsii o sredstvakh massovoj informatsii*) gives the citizens only an indirect right to information, that is they have the right to efficient reception *through* the mass media of correct information on the activities of state organs, societal organizations and their functionaries. Mass media however have guaranteed access to government and administration information. Unlawful refusals from government or administration functionaries to communicate information requested upon are punishable by law. In reality however, refusal of information remain a problem. Since 1993, the Glasnost Defence Foundation (*Fond Zashchity Glasnosti*, 1997) draws up an inventory of all infringements of the rights of journalists and mass media. The majority of violations is tied up with precisely the refusal and restriction of access to information. What's more, the number of infringements increases throughout the 90s. Very few journalists however, claim their rights before court. Again, we have to conclude that the existence of laws alone is not a sufficient condition for their implementation. Kathryn Hendley (1999) points out that the 'demand for law' lags behind the 'supply of law'. The demand for law implies respect for the law and trust in law, or, in other words a 'juridical culture'.

CONSTITUTIONAL HISTORY OF INDIAN PRESS FREEDOM

Democracy can flourish only where its citizens enjoy full freedom of speech and expression subject only to reasonable restrictions. Hence due to this anxiety only the press council of India was born in 1954. But if, we look to the historical background of the Media law, we will find that, it was as early as in 1799 that first time, Lord Wellesley promulgated the "Press Regulations", which had the effect of imposing pre-censorship on an infant newspaper publishing industry. Thereafter, in 1835 the "Press Act" was passed. Then in 1857 the government passed the 'Gagging Act', which among various other things, introduced compulsory licensing for the owning or running of printing presses; empowered the government to prohibit the publication or circulation of any newspaper, book or other printed material and banned the publication or dissemination of statements or news stories which had a tendency to cause a furor against the government, thereby weakening its authority. The process continued, but the constitution makers brought the most significant change, by inserting Article 19 (1) (a) in the part III, as fundamental right of the constitution. This speaks about the freedom to express & expression. This only led to the formation of Press Council of India. Although, the Indian Constitution does not expressly mention the liberty of the press, it is evident that the liberty of the press is included in the freedom of speech and expression under Article 19(1) (a). As it was also observed by the apex court of India in the case of Indian Express Newspapers (Bombay) Private Limited vs UOI.

CONSTITUTIONAL PROVISIONS IN U.S., U.K. AND SWEDEN

Freedom of press also found a place in the American Constitution which has been greatly influenced by the English Common Law. An expressed provision was made for freedom of press in the Bill of Rights which was incorporated into the American Constitution by the First Amendment. This Amendment was largely influenced by section 12 of the Virginian Declaration of Rights in which press was described as "one of the great bulwarks of liberty which were not to be restrained by despotic governments".

Freedom of Press in U.K.

In U.K., since Parliament is sovereign, the subjects cannot possess guaranteed rights such as are guaranteed to the citizens of USA, India and many other countries. The right of freedom of speech or discussion, which means that the person may write or say as he pleases, has been well reorganized in England. A subject may say or do what he pleases, provided he does not transgress the substantive law. Or infringe the legal rights of others. A citizen has completed liberty to do anything unless the public authority by some rule of common law or statute law prevented his action.

Freedom of Press in Sweden

Swedish Constitution is one of the few other Constitutions which have made expressed provisions for freedom of press in its Constitution. The law of freedom of press in Sweden which was first promulgated in 1810 was replaced in 1949 by a new Act which enjoyed the sanctity of being a part of the Constitution. Most of the Articles of Freedom of Press Act are to be found in the Constitutional documents of Sweden along with the amendments made. It is also a well known fact that the Scandinavian countries have always been in the press freedom.

PRESS FREEDOM-CURRENT SCENARIO

Freedom of press or rather the lack of it as an issue has gained importance in the last 2-3 years. Some of the recent incidents which have brought the issue to the forefront are as follows:

Spearheading the list is the Tehelka episode where the news portal was forced to shut down completely following the continued harassment of its [Tehelka.com's] journalists for having exposed the 'scam' in the defence department involving ex defence Personnel's and central government ministers. Another issue which created a lot of hue and cry over press freedom was the threat to expel Alex Perry of the TIME magazine which questioned Prime Minister Vajpayee's physical fitness to lead the country. Journalists working in Gujarat and Kashmir have also been susceptible to frequent attacks for reporting on the political scene there.

But the latest controversy which has brought the perennial problem of protection of freedom of speech and press from arbitrary exercise of the power of punishing for contempt possessed by the legislature, back in to limelight, is the action of the Tamil Nadu Legislative Assembly, of punishing the editors and journalists of The Hindu for publishing reports of speeches in the Assembly and for editorial comments on its action of referring those reports to its privilege committee.

The root and justification for the existence of the power of the Parliamentary Privilege given by our Constitution lies in the ancient privilege given to English House of Commons in 1689. But these powers of the house which have been referred to as "insult laws", have been condemned and scrapped in most of the nations. The powers of commitment to prison which were described in England as the keystone of Parliamentary Privilege are not longer in use. The Joint Director of International Press Institute Parliamentary Committee recommended in 1999 that Parliament's power to imprison persons, whether members or not who are in contempt of Parliament should be abolished.

But as far as the situation in India is concerned there exists constitutional contradictions as to whether the Parliamentary Privileges are limited by Fundamental Rights. It has been held that the transitional provisions in the first part of Article 105(3) and 194(3) are provisions independent of Part III of Constitution and are therefore not controlled by Part III. But as we see, in the 'Reference Case', it has not been possible for Supreme Court to maintain this proposition in toto, as it questioned the theory that the exercise of the Legislature's right to punish for contempt was absolute and uncontrolled as it held that any action of the Legislature was examinable by the Court if it was violative of the fundamental right to freedom embodied in Article 21 [right to life and personal liberty] of the Constitution.

The result is that this uncertain situation will continue, until the Supreme Court launches into the area and clarifies its previous decisions which are conflicting and legislators come forward to codify the privileges. Mean while the power of Parliamentary privilege can be subjected to judicial scrutiny [judicial review] as every authority or power should be exercised within the constitutional limits.

As Chief Justice (retd.) P.N. Bhagwati had put it "Every organ of the government, be it executive, legislature or the judiciary, derives its authority from the Constitution and it has to act within the limits of its authority. No one, howsoever highly placed, and no authority, howsoever lofty can claim that it shall be the sole judge of the extent of its power under the Constitution." A permanent solution is necessary as despite the Courts' earlier decisions matter has been raised again and again. The seriousness of the matter also calls for an urgent need for codification of Parliamentary Privilege as there is no other alternative. The legislators' reluctance to codify has been attributed to the reason that it would mean limiting their powers; as the Court has made it quite clear that if the Parliament or a State Legislative enacted a law under Articles 105(3) or 194(3) respectively to define its privileges then such a law would be subject to Article 19(1) (a) and a competent Court could strike down that law under Article 13 of the Constitution if it violated or abridged any of the fundamental rights.

PRESS NEEDS TO IMPROVE

It may be asked: Would this be enough to ensure that the Press is left genuinely free to carry out the functions that it must perform? Would it not be necessary to think of some other, more positive, steps to ensure that the press does not remain a hand-maid of only the powerful in the country? The inadequacies of the Indian Press need not be connived at.

There is no doubt that private business-and those who control it-are treated by most newspapers with kid gloves. This partly because of the ownership of many newspapers and therefore the philosophy of those who are appointed to senior journalistic positions. The trade union side of industrial disputes, the approach of the political parties on the left side of the political spectrum and the difficulties of the unprivileged and the dispossessed have received far less attention than other smaller but influential sections and vested interests in the vast bulk of our newspapers. It should, however, be said that the situation is changing for the better. Competitions, and also the increasing influence of professional journalists, are making it difficult for newspapers to ignore these various aspects. It is well known that the bindings at Bhagalpur, the treatment of workers as bonded servants by many landed interests, the exploitation of child labour in slate factories, or of female labour in bidi factories ore even of adult workers in asbestos factories have been brought to light not by small newspapers but by large ones which are many times dubbed by critics as belonging to the Monopoly or the Jute Press category. This tendency shows that to the extent that at least some degree of competition can be ensured in every circulation area chances are that there would be a fair degree of investigation of different types of events.

A part of the answer to the difficulties lies in making it possible for independent newspapers and especially periodicals to operate without too much handicap. But, even then, such newspapers may not be as successful as the large ones operated as capitalist undertakings. Their workers, including journalists, may have to work at a sacrifice. But unless there are elements in the country which are ready to work with self sacrifice and zeal for causes in which they believe, new and unorthodox ideas cannot develop and new political groups cannot emerge. There have been examples of such efforts such as the daily Shramik Vichar run by some trade union groups in Pune. There was even an attempt at running a paper devoted to the requirements of the district of Pune which however did not continue for long. Real entrepreneurship in this field would consist of such efforts and, except for direct and discretionary subvention, various other steps can be taken to help the whole category of such newspapers and periodicals. This would make it possible for the larger newspapers to be kept on their toes. Even though investigative journalism is fast developing in India, the quality of the Indian Press in many respects leaves much to be desired. Even though, as a result of various awards, the emoluments of journalists have considerably improved in the last few years, adequate talent is not still attracted to this field.

There is also a great deal of lethargy which leads to large scale reproduction of speeches as well as gossip from the corridors of power instead of well organized news. The tendency even of some of our top newspapers to rely on articles from the foreign Press when dealing with world affairs shows a lack of initiative in developing Indian talent for analysing world problems from the Indian point of view.

With some exceptions, there has also not been enough effort to develop interest in news, other information and comments on aspects of life other than politics, crime and sports. Investigative news collection can be of great use in matters like the operation of Plan programmes and projects. In some newspapers, useful reports of investigations in sectors like power and irrigation have recently appeared. But this is still experimental and confined only to a few papers. Such inadequacies can be overcome only with better training, more competition and greater professionalisation. There are no short-cut remedies for this.

The most serious inadequacy relating to the Indian Press is to be found in newspapers published in Indian languages. Most of them are poorer in quality as compared to newspapers in English. This is so even in respect of Indian language papers belonging to same groups. This obviously happens because the managements of such groups contihue to think that the prestige of the group depends more on the English language newspapers than on the Indian language ones.

It is quite obvious that the number of those proficient in English will not expand as rapidly as that of the literate in various Indian languages. The demand for Indian language newspapers is already expanding faster and this trend will be further accelerated in future. As the number of legislators who understand English declines, it is essential in public interest and for the proper functioning of our democracy that the quality of the more important Indian language newspapers improves rapidly. Special steps such as the development of teleprinter services in Indian languages and support to the adaptation of the best techniques for printing Indian language newspapers should be taken by the Government so as to help.

8

Power of Audience and Media

Power in communication normally means power of the communicator. The one who sends the message seems to be the one who has the power to select topics, to decide what is relevant for the addressee and what is not, to determine who is addressed and to determine time, duration and location of the speech or communicative event. The outcome of this communicator-centred paradigm are the different communication models, like the "propaganda model", the "ideology model" of the Frankfurt School in the 1940s and 1950s, the mathematical "sender-receiver-model" (Weaver 1949) or the "stimulus-response-model" (Hovland 1949). Despite some striking differences all these models have in common that they picture the mass audience as a more or less passive and helpless victim of media influence from the side of the communicator.

Of course there are communicative events, which legitimise this kind of perspective, for example manipulating forms of media communication in totalitarian societies, or different strategies of information politics in the communication of war and crisis. Taken for example the propaganda via newspaper and radio by the Nazis, the press control by the NATO in the Kosovo-conflict, or the press politics of the USA in the Golf war, it seems to be naïve, to talk about the power of the audience. The power of the communicator seems to be overwhelming in these cases. However, despite these counter-examples it still makes sense from different reasons to focus on the role of the audience. One group of reasons can be traced back to the nature of media communication as a special form of intercultural communication, the other group of reasons grounds in the specific character of internet-communication.

To refer to the audience as an instance of power is not meant metaphorical. The audience, for example the internet user, decides what websites he visits, how he interacts with this website, how deep he understands it or whom he trusts as a partner/interactor. These "what", "how", "how deep" and "whom" are deeply rooted in the cultural knowledge and competence of the user. But it is not determined by culture in a causal sense or in a sense of culture as a kind of super power. Nor has the communicator the power to command the addressee to believe him, to understand or to trust him. Understanding, believing, attentiveness and trust are strictly individual and therefore under the power of the audience. Of course we could see culture as an instance of power by itself, for example as structural power (Castells 1997) or symbolic power (Bourdieu), which limit the wiggle room of the respective audience. But from an action theoretical point of view, we have to focus on the user and his acquisition activities, to find out, how the interplay of culture and interaction in internet communication works.

The relevant instance for what happens is the user himself or, as we can learn from Manuel Castells, the people's mind: "The new power (of the information age, H-J. B.) lies in the codes of information and in the images of representation around which societies organize their institutions, and people build their lives, and decide their behaviour. The sites of this power are people's mind".

This shift of focus from the communicator and the message to the audience has wide ranging consequences for the theoretical approach of communication analysis and for the design of empirical research. One of the most famous model in this user-centred approach is the so called use-and-gratification approach: The main factors of media use are the gratifications, for example information or entertainment values, that websites, radio or television programs offer in the eyes of the audience. That means: the power to decide, what and how media are used, is clearly seen on the side of the audience, not on the side of the communicator.

Another model within a audience-centred paradigm is the so call interactional or transactional model: "My proposal that we look at communications as a transactional relationship (..) encourages us to look at the initiative of the audience as it goes about its own business of getting the information it wants and avoiding what it does not want, at how the audience affects what will be said, and at the changes which take place in the communicator in the process of communication". From this point of view the audience has not only the power to select information but the power of influencing the communicator and the message as well. It is quite clear that a model which focus on the perceptions of the audience as constructions of meanings and sense, and of a mutual influencing relationship between audience and communicator is more open to questions of cultural and intercultural understánding than causal theories of media influence. So it is logical that Dennis McQuail labelled this family of theories as "cultural tradition" and he states: "The clearest line of development in audience theory has been a move away from the perspective of the media communicator and toward that of the receiver" (McQuail 1997, 16).

Trust is a powerful means of the audience in every form of communication: No communicator can force the addressee to trust him. Trust is a voluntary gift of the addressee to the communicator. If we summarize the different approaches on the problem of trust in communication we can find three functional explanations: Trust is a constitutive feature of successful communication because of complexity, risk and time-space-distance. Niklas Luhmann defines trust as a "mechanism to reduce complexity"; Ulrich Beck sees trust as a means to communicate under the conditions of social risk and for Anthony Giddens "trust is related to the absence in time and in space". All these types of definitions and explanations fit exactly on human-computerinteraction and on internet communication. Therefore we can use these concepts to get a better understanding of these specific forms of communication and of the role of the audience. Risk and trust are not objective categories but subjective categories. And they are subjective in a deep sense: neither you can command a person, to trust in you or someone or something nor you can command a person not to feel uncertain or risky. Risk and trust are built up in communication. They are, to say it in words of constructivism "constructs of the observer". Media communication has a double connection with risk and trust: First media communication should transfer the knowledge which helps us to minimize uncertainty and build up trust. Second: media communication has itself become a risk, a risk of information and therefore minimizes trust. As Anthony Giddens said in an interview:

"An alarming phenomena is that the old Enlightenment assumption that uncertainties were dissolved by the acquisition of knowledge is increasingly giving way to the realization that the present production of knowledge produces uncertainty. A lot of the uncertainties of the world come not from ignorance, but from knowledge. If you consider the new risk environments, they come from scientific breakthroughs as much as from a lack of them." And one can add: they come from media coverage and information outlets as much as from the lack of them. One of the main reasons for that is the times pace-difference especially in global forms of communication. Giddens describes this feature of communication under the aspect of "disembedding": "By disembedding I mean the lifting out of social relations from local contexts of interaction and their restructuring across indefinite spans of time-space" (Giddens 1990). From this point of view all media communication is disembedded, as it leaves behind the direct face-to-face-communication. Media communication is a clear example for what Giddens called "faceless commitments" in "abstract systems". But internet is the most disembedded media and the most abstract system as it has moved most far away from face-to-face-communication:

In internet communication we first do not have limitations of space: there are no borders for circulation and there is unlimited memory space for content. This dimension of disembedding constitutes the globalisation of the medium. Second: we have no limitations of time, which means messages can be posted at every time, communicators do not have to wait for datelines of publishing. Coverage can happen in real-time, without any delay of production and distribution, and as one should add: without any quality control. (real-time character of the media) And third: we have no limitations of communicators and participant roles: whoever has the technical capacities to receive messages with a computer, is able to send them. And he can do that without restrictions on his or her role, be it as a commentator, a reporter, a businessman, citizen, or a politician. (Interactivity)

And forth, in the internet there are no limitations of content. "All the news, that fit to print" is no longer the limitation of internet content. Whether are we limited on content, which fit to print – we can also present content, which fit to be videotaped, audiotaped or visualized in other ways, nor are we restricted to "news". E-business offers, games, stock brokerage are also parts of internet communication. (Multimediality an Multimodality).

This high degree of disembeddedness makes internet communication a highly risky one, because disembedding always means loss of control: control over sources and their reliability, control over selection, or control over verification.

The audience has to cope with the problem of informational risk and of communication collapse. Trust is normally a means to compensate for our lack of knowledge in handling complex systems. Trust reduces uncertainty. It does not make up for lack of knowledge, but it allows us to believe and act as if we were in a state of full and certain knowledge. But trust is at the disposal of the audience, not at the disposal of the communicator. To understand the role of trust in internet communication we need a user-centred approach Interactivity in internet-communication: research design and empirical results

THE INTERNET AND INTERCULTURAL COMMUNICATION

In traditional media, like newspaper, radio or television we normally have a defined audience, be it a local, a regional or a national one. Things for the first time chanced with global television programs like for example CNN or Sky News. In the case of the Internet global reach of communication has become the standard feature of the media. The question arises, if this strengthens or weakens the power of the audience. One can find reasons for both answers. On the one side one could suggest, the more programs or websites we have for selection, the more cultural differences we get presented the more alternatives the audience has. We are not limited for example to read only our daily regional or national newspaper, but we can compare different newspapers world wide to get a better understanding of international affairs.

On the other side one could argue: the more alternatives a single user has to deal with, the more he depends on help from the communicators to make a rational choice. Without deciding which of the two alternatives is the right one, one can state that the communicative and intercultural competence of the audience is a decisive feature for its power or its weakness. If we follow a communicative interpretation of globalisation, as for example Anthony Giddens defines this concept, one can say that global communication is always intercultural: "Globalisation can thus be defined as the intensification of worldwide social relations which link distant localities in such a way that local happenings are shaped by events occurring many miles away and vice versa".

To emphasize this function of global communication some authors are using the concept of "glocalization" (Beck, Robertson) which should indicate that the main effect of global communication is not (yet) the evolution of a global public sphere but the connections between distant local cultures. With reference to intercultural communication the power of the audience has become visible in the actions of the anti-globalisation movement on the different economy summits in Seattle, Genoa or New York. Without the internet as a communication tool the mobilisation of the movement in different parts of the world would not have been possible.

Another example for the power of the audience is the emancipation from traditional media in cases of international news coverage. For the first time during the Kosovo war in 1999 there was a constant coverage of the conflict besides classical media of newspaper, radio and television and without references to the official sources of the NATO or the different national governments. This new power of the audience could be observed on two levels: on the level of information seeking and on the level of information distributing: „For the first time (during the Kosovo war, H-J. B.) anyone on the Internet can receive a flow of combatant news, comments and pictures (...) But the real point is that anyone with such an equipment could also transmit their news, comments and pictures to a global audience, by passing the traditional mass media".

Although this is not "the end of journalism" as Elihu Katz stated in respect to the Golf war coverage, the multiplicity of sources of information leads in deed to a change in the role of journalism. Journalism is in the act of losing its power of information and interpretation to the internet audience. Media is about to change from push communication to pull communication.

The crisis of the 11th September attack on the WTC and the Pentagon is another striking example of an active audience in internet communication. The New York Times commented on the 12th of September 2001: "More than news, what people all over the world craved in the wake of yesterday's terrorist attacks was connection to each other, and many of them found that most easily achieved by going online."

Data from log file analysis and polls show, that internet traffic had increased heavily after the terror attacks. Traffic to US-sites from other countries doubled during the weeks of the attacks, from 6 Million visitors to about 12 Million on a weekly average. 64 percent of Americans used the internet to find information on the attacks. They went online to find more detailed information, to find information they could not get elsewhere, to find more up to date information, and to find out what was happening while they were at work. 64 percent used the internet as a secondary source of information, whereas television remains the most used primary information source. More than 17 Million user visited the CNN website. The number of German online surfers who used us-American Websites, doubled between the 10th and 16th of September. Traffic to the Web site for the Centre for Disease Control surged by more than 118 percent during the week of Oct. 7, according to Nielsen/Net Ratings, a Web audience measurement company. The Web site drew about a half million visitors, and more than 250,000 looked up pages containing information on the symptoms, diagnosis and treatment of anthrax. The data not only show the increase of internet traffic but also that internet traffic had become more international, more intercultural. And that is maybe the most interesting aspect of the whole issue.

Normally, as is stated in empirical research on linking patterns of the internet from the year 2000, "national cultures continue to exert a substantial influence on how transnational connections are made. So normally 90 percent of links on US websites are directed to other US-sites, in European countries about between 60 and 70 percent of the links refer to website at home. If they refer to websites across the national borders, 70 percent of links from Europe are directed to US websites. In case of the information habits after the September 11th event this seems to have changed:

Data from Hitwise, which tracks traffic to the most popular news sites, show that traffic to sites such as Islamic Gateway, Dawn.com (Pakistans national newspaper), ExpressIndia.com, HindustanTimes.com, and Haaretz.co.il (isreali newspaper) grew noticeably in the aftermath of the September 11 attacks. The biggest increase in traffic was that of Afghanistan Online (Afghan-web.com), which jumped more than 11 000 places in the Hitwise rankings. Traffic to Al Jazeera.net, the site of the independent Middle East television station, has also soared. The Online edition of Germany's most influential news magazine "*Dear Spiegel*" covered a story, in which they portrayed some of the online news sites from Islamic countries, to support German online user in searching foreign news. The regional newspaper in Minneapolis, the "*Pioneer Press*" presented its readers the same service of portraying some of the Arabic and Islamic websites.

Of course it is assumed that the activities of the audience in internet communication are interrelated with the respective cultural background. This becomes rather evident if we compare, for example, internet user profiles and patterns of use in Germany an in the People's Republic of China (PRC). According to the data of CNNIC the typical Internet user in China is currently a 20-30-year old male, living in a urban area at the cost, well educated with a bachelor degree and uses the internet more then 10 hours a week. In Germany the picture is much more complex: nearly half of the Internet user are female, internet use differs little between country and city, the rate of the highly educated with BA or MA is not higher than the rate of the users with the lowest education, the rate of the persons between 20 and 30, between 30 and 40, between 40 and 50 years old is nearly the same and only one third of the internet user are still in school or at university or college.

And also the patterns of internet use are different between the two cultures: Entertainment is a much more import motive for Chinese Internet users than it is for German users; in both countries seeking for information is the main intention, although the two groups are interested in different kinds of information: in China for example user are, beside news, very interested in hard-and software information, in Germany user are, besides news, more interested in economical information and service information. About 70 percent of the visited sites in China are domestic sites and the most serious problem for Chinese user is slow access speed, whereas in Germany the most bothering aspect is advertising. The relevant question in regard to the problem of audience power is, how patterns of use and profile of users correlate with content and design of websites and how they influence the intercultural communication via Internet.

What became rather clear from the presented data: a full understanding of the power of the net is only available if audience research does not take a back seat but becomes an independent part of an overall research design.

How Interactive is Human-computer-interaction?

The concept of interactivity has become a buzzword in human-computercommunication. Its use is so inflationary that sometimes even a cigarette machine seems to be interactive.

The different approaches to disambiguate the concept of interactivity roughly speaking can be divided into two groups: members of the first group try to define interactivity technically, what leads to a rather wide concept. Members of the second group define interactivity on the basis of sociological or psychological theories. Crucial for these definitions is the idea of reciprocity: If it is the case that A interacts with B then that implies that B interacts with A. As this definition does not fit to human-computerinteraction representatives of the latter group normally argue against using the term "interactivity" for this kind of communication an try to restrict it to human-human-interaction.

To escape this dilemma I will try to define interactivity and usability based on action theory and a theory of problem solving in a hypertext environment. Within this perspective interactivity in human computer communication is defined as a kind of "as-if-activity": a user who is communicating for example on an internet platform – be it a learning system, an e-business-platform or an online-newspaper – implies that he acts with the online program as if it was a real partner in a face-to-face-interaction. Especially the thinking aloud procedure provides a lot of evidence for this kind of as-if-interaction. The utterances and the behaviour of the user show that interaction in human-computer-communication is not virtual but that it is a natural implication, with real consequences for the acquirement of websites. We can get a better understanding of interactivity in human-computercommunication if we look at that process as a kind of problem solving in a hypertext environment.

- the problem of navigation: Where can I go to and how to manage?
- the problem of orientation: Where did I come from and where am I?
- the problem of coherence: What has this page to do with the preceding ones?
- The problem of framing: Which parts of a page form a functional unity and which parts serve different functions on different levels of structure?

These types of problems of online communication form a good basis for systematic research on the one hand and for defining aspects of usability on the other hand: The more a website enables a user to solve the named types of problems the higher the usability of that website. From that we can deduce the most central dimensions of quality for evaluating a nonlinear hypertextual program: coherence – on the macro and the micro level, clarity, orientation quality, navigation quality and open-up quality.

The typology of problems is not only of theoretical interest but is used as a starting point for empirical usability research. It provides an orientation of what features of a website are relevant for usability research and it provides standards as to what degree a website fulfil criteria of usability. So the data of the empirical research can be analysed in two ways: they can be analysed for building up a theory of media reception including a better understanding of usability and interactivity. And the data can be analyzed in respect to an evaluation of a website: to what degree does it fulfil the criteria of usability.

METHODS AND TESTING DESIGN

An adequate strategy for empirical research, which tries to generate user Centred data is to follow qualitative methods. Data from quantitative methods like counting click rate or page views, log file analysis, standardized questionnaires for users or experts only generate secondary data, from which one has to deduce hypothesis about the how and why of using an online program.

The following approach combines different qualitative methods and could therefore generate primary data on how, why and to which result website is used. The empirical results which are presented are based on tests with about 150 users, each one tested between 60 and 90 minutes.

The websites for audience research were different kinds of online newspapers, e-business sites, information sites of television and radio stations. The procedure for the test persons was a mixture of free surfing an solving some retrieval tasks so that a quite natural situation of online communication was modelled.

The methodological design of the test combines the following methods:

- a pre-analysis of the site to specify the most relevant or most problematic Parts
- a moderated testing session of 60 to 90 minutes during which the test person can explore the site in a free surfing style and has to solve some specific tasks.
- the thinking aloud procedure
- Video and audio documentation of the test person
- the digital documentation of the visited sites and the navigation actions of the test person
- questionnaire or interview at the beginning and at the end of the session Starting point for the analysis is a videotape which combines the digital documentation of the web navigation, the video documentation and the audio documentation of the thinking aloud utterances.

This kind of research design guaranties primary data and direct access to the human-computer-interaction. Findings in the process of interactivity can be deduced from a wide range of different indicators: *action indicators* (curser moves, *navigation actions* like scrolling or clicking), *utterance indicators* (comments from the thinking aloud method), *behavioural indicators* (mimic and gesture, signals of surprise and of being asked too much of), *problem solving indicator* (scrolling, back navigation, repeated reading).

The interplay of these different indicators allows highly reliable assumptions on the reception of online programs and of course guarantee highly user-centred results for questions of usability and interactivity.

Empirical Results

First the empirical data show that using online programs is indeed a case of "asif-interaction". Utterances of the test person, their actions, their difficulties and the corresponding strategies to solve them show clearly that acting on an internet platform is indeed inter-acting with an implied partner on the assumption that he re-acts on what the test person is doing.

Second, results of the empirical research prove a tight interrelation between knowledge or competence on the side of the user and their navigation strategy. Especially knowledge of the structure of a website-on a micro and a macro level – knowledge of rules and patterns of online communication and knowledge of the communicator prove as central factors of the chosen problem solving strategies.

Third, On the level of exploring a single website – for example the entering page – as well as on the level of navigating from page to page one can observe patterns and rules, which guide the actions of the test person.

Although internet is a new media, we already can find standardization and prototyping in a high degree. Users try to build up special "scripts" to have standard solutions for the above mentioned typical problems of browsing in non-linear, hypertextual and multimodal communications. A script – in the words of Schank and Aberlson "is a predetermined, stereotyped sequence of actions, that defines a well-known situation".

Fourth, the consequences of the results may not be the most joyous for creative web designers: Under the aspect of usability and user orientation and in the light of the empirical results the basic principle of web design should not be innovation but standardization.

For most of the users the new media is full of surprise so that it is more economical to meet their "scripts" than to present them another surprise. The more similar a website is to this prototype the higher the usability rating by the audience in the reported tests. That must no be the end of creativity in web design. But each deviation from the standard form must be reasonable and understandable from the point of view of the audience.

Fifth: There is a strong correlation between usability and trust. The higher the usability of a website and the acquaintance with it, the more trustworthy a website is. We can see online communication as highly disembedded in the sense of Anthony Giddens which means "the lifting out of social relations from local contexts of interaction and their restructuring across indefinite span of time-space" (Giddens 1990) Especially for these forms of communication trust is a crucial feature to compensate the risk of communicative failure.

AUDIENCES BEFORE WORLD WAR II

Prior to the 1930s, knowledge of media audiences consisted of little more than anecdotal impressions coupled with basic demographics. The advertising sales departments at firms like the Chicago Tribune and the Curtis Publishing Company were among the earliest pioneers in the field of marketing research, conducting door-to-door interviews and "pantry surveys" to collect data about household product purchases. But because the goal of this research was to encourage national manufacturers to spend more on print advertising or to allocate more of their budget in a particular geographic market, these surveys compiled data about neighbourhoods, cities, or regions. There was little effort to describe or measure media audiences as distinct social groups.

In their own market evaluations, advertising firms adopted the custom of dividing cities and towns into neighbourhoods, assigning each a grade ("A," "B," "C" or "D") based on home values or the average family income of residents. Predictably, publishers tried to emphasize the number of their subscribers hailing from the more desirable "A" and "B" neighbourhoods, suggesting that greater resources would translate into more active consumers who comprised a better audience for advertising. But publishers had little information about how their periodicals were actually used and no real insights about what persuaded readers to spend money. Advertising experts suspected that the answers to these questions might determine if their commercial messages were effective.

In the absence of any credible information, advertisers fell back upon anecdotes, trade wisdom, and "professional instincts." Indeed, despite an avowed respect for new "scientific" methods, advertisers tended to rely on subjective impressions of media audiences in deciding where to place their messages and how to frame their pitch. Over time, those impressions were assembled into a more general vision of American society.

Advertising historian Roland Marchand argues that in practice, advertisers conceived of the public in terms of two broad groups, the "mass" and the "class." These working divisions, writes Marchand, were largely based on the audiences imagined for popular media.

The sensationalism and excess of tabloid newspapers, confession magazines, and Hollywood romances did not hold up well against the cosmopolitan standards of Madison Avenue executives, and many harbored an image of the masses as uncultivated and impressionable. Yet, crucially, gender tended to trump all other characteristics when it came to imagining readers, since the trade wisdom during this era held that up to 80 percent of household purchases were made by women. The advice offered by advertising authorities and the trade press in the 1920s and 30s reveal that descriptions of the "masses" were highly feminized, sharing the qualities of irrationality, emotionalism, and susceptibility that were so often attributed to women.

The complacency that media firms and advertisers displayed in distinguishing audience information from more general market data was upset by the rapid growth of radio as a medium. Hidden behind the walls of the home, radio audiences represented a mystery both in terms of their numbers and in terms of how listeners interacted with the new medium. From the beginning, Marchand suggests, advertisers believed that there was something special about the radio, an unique intimacy that newspapers or magazines could not begin to match. For a time, in fact, many advertisers were wary of commercializing radio, fearing that if product appeals entered the home by this means, a backlash might develop against their industry. As radio promoters struggled to resolve these questions—of how many were tuning in and what they were experiencing—media audience research witnessed its first major divide along qualitative and quantitative lines.

The first radio rating service, the Cooperative Analysis of Broadcasting, was formally launched in 1929. Inspired by George Gallup and other public opinion experts, CAB researchers telephoned a selection of homes at set intervals during the day, asking the respondent what he or she had listened to in the preceding two hours. Some advertisers immediately raised doubts about the accuracy of these ratings, extending their low opinion of the masses to a distrust of audience recall. The first refinement in radio audience measurement was therefore the invention of "coincidental ratings" which polled household members about what they were listening to at the time of the call. The pursuit of a foolproof measure of radio audiences would continue throughout the 1930s and beyond, culminating in the A.C. Nielsen company's introduction of its "audimeter" in 1942. By mechanically recording when a radio set was on and which channel it was tuned to, the audimeter eliminated the need for self-reporting from the unreliable masses.

Questions remained about how radio effected its listeners and whether the medium enjoyed a special relationship with its audience. Advertisers, network executives, and researchers shared a belief that radio might be a instrument of social uplift, a means of elevating popular tastes by bringing high culture to the masses.

As Susan Douglas suggests, the research conducted by Paul Lazarsfeld and his colleagues at the Bureau of Applied Social Research was strongly influenced by this vision. From their offices on the fringes of Columbia University, these research entrepreneurs conducted studies for the government, private corporations, and media industry groups throughout the 1930s and 40s.

In their studies of radio audiences, Bureau researchers pioneered the use of qualitative methods including focus groups, participant observation, and structured and unstructured interviews. Invariably, these studies frustrated hopes that radio would cultivate a taste for high culture, revealing, for example, that many listeners didn't mind commercials and actually regarded them as educational. Fans of advice programs believed they were improving themselves by learning about manners or how to conduct themselves in public. Other researchers found that soap opera listeners regarded their favorite programs as teaching lessons in how to live a better and more moral life.

AUDIENCES IN THE NEW MILLENNIUM

When today's working audience models are held up against those of the past, the lines of continuity that run throughout the history of audience research are marked by crucial differences. Multiplying media options and the ambient clutter of advertising have intensified the anxiety that media executives and advertisers feel at the prospect that people today lead increasingly diffuse lives. As a result, media and advertising professionals have increasingly focused attention on controlling the spaces of media interaction, in part to offset persistent fears about having lost control over the audience's time schedule. As early as the 1950s, Alfred Politz recognized that if radio was to survive alongside television and its national audiences, radio executives needed to establish in convincing terms what their medium could do better. He emphasized the ways in which radio "seeped into the crevices of peoples' lives," finding them at moments when the attention required of TV viewing was simply not feasible.

The widespread acceptance of this reasoning may well have allowed radio to survive as a commercial medium. Today, the most highly prized (and priced) time slot for radio advertising is during the 4 p.m.-7 p.m. "drive time." Reports by companies like Arbitron, which specializes in the measurement of radio audiences, now read like pop sociology investigating how listeners in markets like Los Angeles use the automobile to manage their challenging schedules. Arbitron has good reason to expand its research program beyond program choices and the number of listeners; as commuters spend increasing amounts of time in their automobiles, hours spent with the radio have increased while overall time of exposure to most other forms of media have decreased.

Changes within the "Nielsen Family" system for calculating television ratings offer another example of how media executives, following prompts and an occasional threat from advertisers, have responded to the perception that people lead increasingly frenetic lives. The last major advance in ratings technology was the launch of the Nielsen "People Meter" in 1987. As cable television, VCRs, and channel-changing remotes came into wide use, advertisers and television executives began to fear that existing methods of measuring the audience were inadequate. Despite the installation of "audimeters" that recorded television use and channel selection, the Nielsen system still relied heavily on self-reported diaries to ascertain which family members were present in the audience.

Advertisers had long been suspicious of this information source, doubting respondents' commitment to recording their viewing behaviour. Technology that allowed channel surfing, muting, and the "zapping" of commercials in recorded programs only intensified the feeling that diaries were a hopeless cause. In response to these grumblings, Nielsen introduced the People Meter, a remote control unit featuring a separate button for each member of the family. In theory, when a family member sits down to watch TV, he or she presses a button to log in and presses a second time when through viewing. In minimizing the active participation of respondents, the People Meter joins a long line of measurement innovations that have attempted to correct for the unreliable nature of the mass audience.

But by the late-1990s, advertisers and media executives had begun to worry that even the People Meter required too much of TV viewers. Moreover, researchers were increasingly aware that home was only one of the places where people came into contact with television, and was increasingly a place that represented a diminishing share of many people's time. Efforts to improve and streamline the means of tracking viewing habits began. This spring, with financial support from A.C. Nielsen, Arbitron has embarked on a trial of the newest audience measurement technology, the Portable People Meter. Costing upwards of $20 million to develop and field-test, the system consists of small pager-sized personal recorders which each participating family member carries with them as they go about their day.

The unit records inaudible coded signals from every radio, TV, or cable TV program that the wearer comes into contact with. At night, each portable unit is "docked" in a home console from which the collected data is transmitted to a central processing station. In an obvious concession to the distrust that has long characterized the interactions of researchers and media audiences, each Portable People Meters contains a built-in motion detector to insure that the unit is worn.

But the nature of the distrust researchers have of the audience has assumed new forms as well. Where in the past, researchers had questioned the memory of audience members or suspected that irrational drives often motivated behaviour, the latest fears center, ironically enough, on the audience's self-conscious participation in a highly mediated world. This is evident in the growing reservations that researchers have about the use of focus groups, which had been perhaps the single most popular information gathering method of the 1980s and 1980s, Recently, experts in qualitative market research have raised the discouraging possibility that some focus group participants are not responding in a spontaneous manner, but rather, are acting according to media generated ideas about how focus group participants are supposed to act. In what some regarded as the beginning of the end for focus groups, a mail-order book entitled *The Focus Group and Mystery Shopper's Participant Information Manual and Directory* was published in 2000; the book helpfully instructs people on how to be a professional focus group respondent.

Qualitative research still offers a means of investigating trends like the accelerating pace of daily activity and the audience's increased awareness of their media involvements. But when compared to the work that Lloyd Warner and his proteges were conducting in the 1950s, today's qualitative research contains an important difference.

Researchers today emphasize the "fragmented" and "contradictory" nature of identity. While this perception poses a challenge to reductive computer "lifestyle" catalogs, it also undercuts further any remaining belief in media as an instrument of social integration. Since the mid-1980s, a group of consumer theorists based in business schools have promoted an "interpretive turn" in consumer research. Adopting the principle that all truth is socially-constructed, these theorists propose that the goal of consumer research is not to uncover the universal laws of the market, but rather, to understand the multiple, overlapping, and contradictory identities of consumers.

These self-described "postmodern" consumer experts embrace methods like ethnographies, close readings, discourse analysis, and personal introspection. Their articles and papers have come to resemble presentations listed in the MLA convention program, with titles like "Libratory Postmodernism and the Reenchantment of Consumption," "Deconstructive Strategy and Consumer Research," "Post-structuralism and the Dialectics of Advertising: Discourse, Ideology, Resistance.

Although consumer research is not synonymous with audience research, it is important to note that the domains of media and marketing have steadily converged over the past three decades. Beyond the familiar warnings that commerce and culture have become increasingly indistinguishable, it is worth asking what the implications may be when media and marketing share—and mutually act upon—a vision of the fragmented public.

Communications scholar Joseph Turow has suggested that "narrowcasting" and other, more subtle ways of tailoring the audience for radio, TV, cable, and the web have created the equivalent of "electronic gated communities." Though expressly designed for an audience reading outside of the home, a newspaper like *USA Today* shares in this exclusivity; the imagined settings that help to define its audience are privatized spaces like hotel lobbies, skymalls, college campuses, and the business class section of the New York-to-Washington shuttle. In the past, media designed for specific segments of society (ethnic newspapers, women's magazines, Christian radio stations) have co-existed alongside other forms of media that at least paid service to the ideal of being allinclusive.

Turow suggests it has become increasingly difficult to find examples of such "society making" media, as there are fewer media enterprises that do not self-consciously target particular audiences. Insofar as heightened media segmentation has opened up new possibilities for groups like gays and lesbians, African Americans, and Latinos who have been historically underserved by the media, this is a trend with some undeniably positive results. But the segmentation of media audiences into "lifestyle" groups defined by consumer researchers, advertisers, and marketers also threatens to pose a particular, classbound perspective of social life as a universal.

While the accelerating pace of life, a more self-conscious relationship with the media, and the fragmented and fluid nature of identity are understood as socially pervasive trends, the management strategies practiced by many media firms demonstrate that certain audiences—and their corresponding ways of seeing and experiencing the world—receive a disproportionate share of the attention.

Even newspapers, once the medium that claimed to have "something for everyone" (and historically, the form of published material with the highest number of working-class readers) actively court affluent members of the professional middle class through their lifestyle, consumer, and personal finance coverage.

The content of these pages is used, in turn, to present advertisers with "upscale" images of who their messages will be reaching. The danger in accepting the notions about social change that are circulated in much of today's media is that these cultural drifts and "trends" are increasingly reported from the perspective of an audience that is imagined in greatly limited terms—especially in their class positioning. Meanwhile, media management strategies of "controlled circulation" in publishing, or "signalling" and "tailoring" in cable television, take tangible steps to use distribution and content to exclude those populations who are deemed less desirable by advertisers.

9

Power and Responsibility of Media Communication

Power, authority, and responsibility--both assuming responsibility and allowing others to assume responsibility--are delicate issues in communicative media education. Power as exercised by the teacher is sometimes divided into four different categories: authoritative, autonomous, authoritarian, and abdicated power.

As far as MICT are concerned, power is constantly a topical issue which should be studied carefully in various research settings. Another way of thinking of power is the continuum from monologue to dialogue and polylogue. In order to facilitate dialogue, the teacher has to be able and willing to give up his own monologue. Dialogue will change into an authentic polylogue only if constructivist principles are respected and mutual discussion encouraged.

Polylogue is basically a fundamental way of conversation and an exchange of ideas in computer conferencing, but it can be hampered if the technical or pedagogical manager of the conference occupies too much scope of the conference's virtual space. Consequently, the question can be traced back to the role of monopoly or the teacher's (the manager's authority) in comparison to authentic dipoly (two communicators' authority) or tripoly, in which several communicators respect each other's right to express themselves. In many respects, this is closely connected to the question of electronic leadership, which appears to be one of the most important factors as far as the success of an electronic conference is concerned.

At Once Individualised and Networked vs. Mass Communication

Most of the above factors are also linked to the question of whether communication and instruction are being individualised or oriented towards mass communication. Modern information and communication technologies give access to individualised learning tools and make it easy to organise an individualised or learner-focused learning environment which, however, takes advantage of extensive physical and conceptual networking. In the same way, dyadic forms of work are facilitated as well as small group constellations. As stated above, telelogic communication emphasises small specialised group communication or target group communication, while traditional mass media (radio, television or the so-called electronic media in comparison to telematic media, such as e-mail, computer conferencing, WWW, gophers, Archie, FTP, etc.) aim at reaching large audiences.

The benefits of networked computers are accepted as a new starting point. Sawyer (1992) cites America 2000 (1992) in that "[b]y far the most promising benefit of networked computers for education lies in extending the network to include access to computing from the homes of teachers and students. This would address head-on one of the most difficult roadblocks to educational improvement ... Non-classroom access to a significant learning tool would be especially important in the case of disadvantaged students ... access to a personal computer in the home ... could provide a powerful alternative to entertainment television or the street. If students had home access to personal computers integrated into the curriculum and linked to the schools' library resources, they would be able to extend their classroom exposure by repeating lessons missed in class, retrying simulation-based `lab experiments,' and preparing homework using the computer for library access, word processing, drawing, music study, and computation. ... The home time available to students during each week of the school year could easily equal the time spent in the classroom. During the summer vacation, the same computer facility would be available for educational gaming, electronic mail, summer projects, and adult literacy or other training programs."

COMMUNICATION/EDUCATION/TEACHING

In the final analysis, the question is about the subtle differences between media communication education, communicative media education and educational media communication on one hand, and about communication as communication or communication as educational communication on the other hand, and, in the final analysis, between teaching, studying, and learning as well as about the shifts of emphasis in learning paradigms, concepts of learning and knowledge in connection with the changes in teachers', students' and schools' status.

Communication, implicitly, covers everything as everything is communication per se, verbal, non-verbal or at least paralingual or extralingual. Teaching may include studying and learning, but there has been a strong shift of emphasis from teaching-based approaches towards learner-centered or learner-sponsored approaches. When speaking about open multimedia-based and networked learning environments or about virtual schools (e.g., Tella 1995), we have to bear in mind that the word `learning' in the English language also implies studying, while in Finnish it mostly refers to the product of studying. Or perhaps we should start to underline the importance of education as an overall term; speaking of primary, secondary, adult and lifelong education may also lead us to start talking about computer-based education with a special emphasis on computer-mediated communication, which seems to cover most of the features human-to-human communication has always included. Consequently, open learning and distance education are terms whose role and significance are likely to increase in the years to come.

We are to a large extent dependent on regular contact with the mass media for information, entertainment, ideas, opinion and many other things all of which are connected to our attempts to 'make sense' of who and what we are. Our cultural experiences are affected by the development of systems of mass communication. A look at current research shows that we spend from 18 to 35 hours per week watching TV, for example. It is 'normal' to spend 3-4 hours per day in the company of a TV set. Large amounts of our time are spent in a range of media related activities.

To study 'media' is to study also how we define our own sense of who and what we are. What do we mean by 'culture'? How does a media text shape or construct or change cultural identity? What exactly is 'mass media' or 'mass communication'?

We all inhabit particular situations and things like our surroundings, family, friends; school, work, neighbourhood and so on shape our individual identities. In media-speak we refer to this aspect of our cultural identity as our situated culture. In other words, the small-scale communications and interactions we have on a day-to-day basis with the place we live in and the people around us. This kind of culture is primarily an oral one-it is passed on and formed largely by intimate word-of-mouth communication.

Since the mid 19th century, we have come to live not only in a situated culture, but in a culture of mediation. The press, film and cinema, television and radio and more recently, the Internet, have developed to supply larger scale means of public communication. So now our situated culture exists within a much wider mediated world. The introduction of the term 'global village' in the 1960's illustrates how much our world has changed and the change is due almost entirely to the development of mass communications. So what do we mean by 'mass communication' or 'mass media'?

Think of it as the transmission (sending) and reception of 'messages' on a very large scale. Most communication is done on a direct face-to-face basis in a situated cultural context and it is a two-way process. The received message can be responded to instantly. There is 'feedback'.

With mass communication there are four main distinctive features, as follows:

1. There is a gap or an institutional break between the 'sender' of the message and the 'receiver'. The makers of the media texts, the 'senders' of the messages, do not have an obvious feedback relationship with the audience. (Shouting at the TV screen does not count as feedback!) Audience responses are rarely 'heard'. This means that mass-mediated culture tends to be a one-way process. Producers have to target imaginary, generalised or stereotypical audiences. They can (and do) 'shape' products accordingly. They also make assumptions about audiences that are based on conceptual ideas of what people are like, rather than how they really are. Look at any glamour magazine and you can see what the makers of the texts think men and women should look like, for example.
2. Specialised technologies, especially the internet, have begun to affect the one-way system of communication described above. In addition, these technologies have made it possible to 'capture' messages in a very physical form (photographs, film, tape-recordings) which in turn has led to historical permanence or records. Our sense of 'history' is thus affected (and some would say, constructed.)
3. Media messages can be extended 'outwards', so that events taking place regionally or locally now have global coverage (9/11, for example) Audiences are frequently calculated in billions! This has major significance in terms of media institutions. Lots of profit to be made from selling syndicated rights to the whole world's media!
4. Media messages have therefore become a modern commodity-an industry-a product. Market forces thus have a definite impact on the production and distribution of media texts. It is argued that as mass media have become 'facts of life' and we have all become socially and culturally more dependent on them.

It is argued that the media now occupy a central role in defining and interpreting the very nature of the world according to certain values, cultural principles and ideologies. We inhabit an information and consumer society as a result and concerns are expressed about exactly what effects the media have on society.

Ideology-a set of ideas or a view of the world that is selective and gives a particular version of reality. Sometimes seen as deliberately constructed by powerful groups in order to maintain power and control.

There are three major areas of concern, as follows:

1. Mass media has a political and a persuasive power over us. Radio, TV, the press and film can manipulate whole societies. Political propaganda, advertising and the so-called 'mind-bending' power of the media are long-standing causes of debate and concern.
2. Since the 19th century there has been a mistrust of so-called 'popular culture', which is thought to debase or degrade cultural traditions and standards. The ongoing debate about the future of public service broadcasting in Britain in the 1990's is an example of this. What exactly is 'quality' and cultural value in broadcast output?
3. The most contentious issue concerns the effects of the mass media on social behaviour, in particular violence and delinquency. The media have regularly been accused of 'causing' outbreaks of unrest in society.

RELATION OF CULTURE AND MASS COMMUNICATION

Culture can be defined as the beliefs, values, or other frameworks of reference by which we make sense of our experiences. It also concerns how we communicate these values and ideas. Mass media are centrally involved in the production of modern culture. Media production, media texts and media reception are like a series of interlinked circuits. What is produced is influenced by cultural values; how the texts are formed and represented are influenced in the same way and the readings of the texts are also subject to both abstract and particular cultural viewpoints.

Popular Culture

Historically (until the 19th century, at any rate) the term 'popular' was quite a negative thing, with overtones of vulgarity and triviality. Something not 'nice' or 'respectable'. In the modern world, the term means 'widespread', liked or at least encountered by many people. It has also come to mean 'mass-produced', i.e. made for the 'mass' of people. There is a downside to this, of course, in that it can also be interpreted as 'commercial' or 'trashy'. This leads into a further consideration, which is the definition of 'popular culture' as 'low' culture, something not for the elite, but for the 'common' people. Cultural value ('high' culture) has been traditionally associated with dominant or powerful groups-those who have appreciation of classical music, art, ballet, opera and so on. 'Low' or popular culture is everything not approved of as 'high'. It is vulgar, common, or 'easy'.

Another definition of 'popular' is literally 'of the people', a kind of 'folk' culture and this is an interesting area, because it encompasses the idea of an 'alternative' culture which includes minority groups, perhaps with subversive values. The 'indie' music scene is an example of this. So 'popular' culture can and sometimes does, challenge the 'dominant' cultural power groups.

Postmodern Culture

It is argued that modern culture has entered a so-called 'post-modern' phase. Put simply there are four areas of definition here:

1. Because popular culture and media images dominate the age, they dominate our sense of reality. The world is now 'intertextual' (images, copies, simulations and so on are so global that there are no authentic originals any more) The result is that popular culture has replaced art and 'high' culture and the contrived and the simulated has replaced the reality of experience and history. How and what we consume has become more important than what and how we produce.
2. Postmodernism is about style. Pastiche, collage, bricolage (the mixing and re-using of images, signs and symbols) are emphasised at the expense of content or substance.

3. Time, space history and place have become less secure-more confused. The forces of global communications and networks are eroding national cultures. This causes tension and uncertainty.
4. Postmodernism is sceptical about absolute truths, artistic, scientific, historical or political, so a secure sense of time and place is becoming more difficult to sustain. Once secure theories are now open to question and doubt.

COMMUNICATION HISTORY

The history of communication dates back to the earliest signs of life. Communication can range from very subtle processes of exchange, to full conversations and mass communication. Human communication was revolutionized with speech about 200,C00 years ago. Symbols were developed about 30,000 years ago, and writing about 7,000. On a much shorter scale, there have been major developments in the field telecommunication in the past few centuries. Humans are not the only one to master communication. Various animals are engaged in different forms of communication of their own. Animal communication is any behaviour on the part of one animal that has an effect on the current or future behaviour of another animal. The study of animal communication (zoosemiotics) has played an important part in the development of ethology, sociobiology, and the study of animal cognition. Animal communication, and indeed the understanding of the animal world in general, is a rapidly growing field, and even in the 21st century so far, many prior understandings related to diverse fields such as personal symbolic name use, animal emotions, animal culture and learning, and even sexual conduct, long thought to be well understood, have been revolutionized.

COMMUNICATION BETWEEN HUMANS

Evolution of the brain differentiated humans from animals, as among other things it allowed humans to master a very efficient form of communication-speech. The FOXP2 gene, which appeared in homo sapiens about 200,000 years ago, was likely responsible for much of this change. Speech greatly facilitated the transmission of information and knowledge to further generations. Experiences passed on through speech became increasingly rich, and allowed humans to adapt themselves to new environments-or adapt the environments to themselves-much more quickly than was possible before; in effect, biological human evolution was overtaken by technological progress and sociocultural evolution. Speech meant easier coordination and cooperation, technological progress and development of complex, abstract concepts such as religion or science. Speech placed humans at the top of the food chain, and facilitated human colonization of the entire planet.

Speech, however, is not perfect. The human voice carries only so far, and sign language is also rather limited in terms of distance. Further, all such forms of communications relied on human memory, another imperfect tool: memory can become corrupted or lost over time, and there is a limit to how much one can remember. With the accidental death of a 'wise man' or tribal elder, a primitive tribe could lose many generations of knowledge.

The imperfection of speech, which nonetheless allowed easier dissemination of ideas and stimulated inventions, eventually resulted in the creation of new forms of communications, improving both the range at which people could communicate and the longevity of the information. All of those inventions were based on the key concept of the symbol: a conventional representation of a concept.

The oldest known symbols created with the purpose of communication through time are the cave paintings, a form of rock art, dating to the Upper Paleolithic. Just as the small child first learns to draw before it masters more complex forms of communication, so homo sapiens' first attempts at passing information through time took the form of paintings. The oldest known cave painting is that of the Chauvet Cave, dating to around 30,000 BC. Though not well standardized, those paintings contained increasing amounts of information: Cro-Magnon people may have created the first calendar as far back as 15,000 years ago. The connection between drawing and writing is further shown by linguistics: in the Ancient Egypt and Ancient Greece the concepts and words of drawing and writing were one and the same (Egyptian: 's-sh', Greek: 'graphein').

The next step in the history of communications is petroglyphs, carvings into a rock surface. It took about 20,000 years for homo sapiens to move from the first cave paintings to the first petroglyphs, which are dated to around 10,000 BC.

It is possible that the humans of that time used some other forms of communication, often for mnemonic purposes-specially arranged stones, symbols carved in wood or earth, quipu-like ropes, tattoos, but little other than the most durable carved stones has survived to modern times and we can only speculate about their existence based on the observation of primitive cultures such as those of Africa or Oceania.

A pictogram (pictograph) is a symbol representing a concept, object, activity, place or event by illustration. Pictography is a form of proto-writing whereby ideas are transmitted through drawing. Pictorgaphs were the next step in the evolution of communication: the most important difference between petroglyphs and pictograms is that petroglyphs are simply showing an event, but pictograms are telling a story about the event, thus they can for example be ordered in chronological order. Pictograms were used by various ancient cultures all over the world since around 9000 BC, when tokens marked with simple pictures began to be used to label basic farm produce, and become increasingly popular around 6000-5000 BC. They were the basis of cuneiform and hieroglyphs, and began to develop into logographic writing systems around 5000 BC.

Pictograms, in turn, evolved into ideograms, graphical symbols that represent an idea. Their ancestors, the pictograms, could represent only something resembling their form: therefore a pictogram of a circle could represent a sun, but not concepts like 'heat', 'light', 'day' or 'Great God of the Sun'. Ideograms, on the other hand, could convey more abstract concepts, so that for example an ideogram of two sticks can mean not only 'legs' but also a verb 'to walk'. Because some ideas are universal, many different cultures developed similar ideograms. For example an eye with a tear means 'sadness' in Native American ideograms in California, as it does for the Aztecs, the early Chinese and the Egyptians. Ideograms were precursors of logographic writing systems such as Egyptian hieroglyphs and Chinese characters. Examples of ideographical proto-writing systems, thought not to contain language-specific information, include the Vinca script and the early Indus script. In both cases there are claims of decipherment of linguistic content, without wide acceptance.

The oldest-known forms of writing were primarily logographic in nature, based on pictographic and ideographic elements. Most writing systems can be broadly divided into three categories: logographic, syllabic and alphabetic (or segmental); however, all three may be found in any given writing system in varying proportions, often making it difficult to categorise a system uniquely.

The invention of the first writing systems is roughly contemporary with the beginning of the Bronze Age in the late Neolithic of the late 4th millennium BC. The first writing system is generally believed to have been invented in prehistoric Sumer and developed by the late 3rd millennium into cuneiform. Egyptian hieroglyphs, and the undeciphered Proto-Elamite writing system and Indus Valley script also date to this era, though a few scholars have questioned the Indus Valley script's status as a writing system.

The original Sumerian writing system was derived from a system of clay tokens used to represent commodities. By the end of the 4th millennium BC, this had evolved into a method of keeping accounts, using a round-shaped stylus impressed into soft clay at different angles for recording numbers. This was gradually augmented with pictographic writing using a sharp stylus to indicate what was being counted. Round-stylus and sharp-stylus writing was gradually replaced about 2700-2000 BC by writing using a wedge-shaped stylus (hence the term cuneiform), at first only for logograms, but developed to include phonetic elements by the 2800 BC. About 2600 BC cuneiform began to represent syllables of spoken Sumerian language. Finally, cuneiform writing became a general purpose writing system for logograms, syllables, and numbers. By the 26th century BC, this script had been adapted to another Mesopotamian language, Akkadian, and from there to others such as Hurrian, and Hittite. Scripts similar in appearance to this writing system include those for Ugaritic and Old Persian.

The Chinese script may have originated independently of the Middle Eastern scripts, around the 16th century BC (early Shang Dynasty), out of a late neolithic Chinese system of proto-writing dating back to c. 6000 BC. The pre-Columbian writing systems of the Americas (including among others Olmec and Mayan) are also generally believed to have had independent origins, although some experts have noticed similarities between Olmec writing and Shang writing that seem to suggest that Mesoamerican writing was imported from China.

The first pure alphabets (properly, "abjads", mapping single symbols to single phonemes, but not necessarily each phoneme to a symbol) emerged around 2000 BC in Ancient Egypt, but by then alphabetic principles had already been incorporated into Egyptian hieroglyphs for a millennium.

By 2700 BC Egyptian writing had a set of some 22 hieroglyphs to represent syllables that begin with a single consonant of their language, plus a vowel (or no vowel) to be supplied by the native speaker. These glyphs were used as pronunciation guides for logograms, to write grammatical inflections, and, later, to transcribe loan words and foreign names.

However, although seemingly alphabetic in nature, the original Egyptian uniliterals were not a system and were never used by themselves to encode Egyptian speech. In the Middle Bronze Age an apparently "alphabetic" system is thought by some to have been developed in central Egypt around 1700 BC for or by Semitic workers, but we cannot read these early writings and their exact nature remain open to interpretation.

Over the next five centuries this Semitic "alphabet" (really a syllabary like Phoenician writing) seems to have spread north. All subsequent alphabets around the world with the sole exception of Korean Hangul have either descended from it, or been inspired by one of its descendants.

The transmission of signals over a distance for the purpose of communication-began thousands of years ago with the use of smoke signals and drums in Africa, the Americas and parts of Asia. In the 1790s the first fixed semaphore systems emerged in Europe however it was not until the 1830s that electrical telecommunication systems started to appear.

IMPORTANCE OF COMMUNICATION CHANNELS

The problem of which channels are focused upon when discussing the question of communication is essential. In this context, three channels are often taken up, i.e., monologic communication (i.e., traditional mass media), dialogic communication (i.e., face-to-face human communication), and telelogic (or computer-mediated human) communication.

The role of communication can also be approached from other perspectives. We can for example talk about primary, secondary or tertiary communication. Primary communication can be considered as face-to-face communication, mostly in real time, for instance when having a dialogue with somebody or when delivering or listening to a speech.

Secondary communication can be represented by a number of art forms, such as theatre, while tertiary communication consists of mediated communication or, in more general terms, of computer-mediated human communication (CMHC).

Dimensionality of Communication

Another way of looking at communication is the dimensionality or directionality of communication, in which several components can be distinguished. Basically, if communication is intended to go in one direction only, we can refer to it as one-way or monodirectional (unidirectional) communication. Two-way (bidirectional) communication emphasises the fact that both the sender and the recipient of the message can play an active role in the communication act.

Electronic mail is often considered as an example of bidirectional communication as the roles of both communicators (transceivers) are essential. A third dimensionality contains pluridirectional communication, such as computer conferencing or networking in general, in which communication is spread on several levels of communicators, either simultaneously or asynchronously, i.e., independently of time and space.

There is an eminently clear demand for clarifications as far as the classification of various combinations is concerned. In this article only a few anticipatory examples will be given. An example of primary unidirectional communication would include giving an order, while an example of primary bidirectional communication could be a dialogue. In foreign language teaching, primary unidirectional communication often characterises teacher-centered lessons, during which the teacher tends to limit his use of foreign language to so-called "teacher-talk" commands. The primary target should, however, be primary bidirectional communication, in which the teacher, for instance, aims at more communicative use of the target language, relying on learners' language proficiency as much as possible.

Secondary unidirectional communication is mainly represented by traditional mass media communication, i.e., monologic communication media as they were up till the mid- and late-1980s. Secondary bidirectional communication includes telecommunications, CD-ROMs, CD-Is, etc. Network-based communication can be depicted as secondary pluridirectional communication, which, at the moment, is growing fast.

Another way of dividing communication is through the communication channel vs. its representation. This division includes oral production (via the phone, for instance), textual production (e.g., letters, faxes), textually produced but emulating oral production (e.g., e-mail), and iconic production (e.g., graphics, audio-graphics). Two other dimensions are worth mentioning as well: the continuum from stationary to nomadic and from isolating to networking. Educational technology, in the traditional sense, was mainly synchronous and stationary. A language laboratory represents traditional educational technology at its best--or at its worst. However, technological progress has advanced towards more nomadic products and media, which are independent of time and place, asynchronous, transferable, light, inexpensive, and which gradually become invisible.

Traditional technology also implied isolation, to some extent at least. Language labs as well as traditional computer laboratories used to isolate learners from others while giving all of them a rigid seating order. Portable computers and laptops started to change the situation, which, thanks to cellular phones and datacards is utterly different from what it used to be.

Virtual reality is not yet here to a tangible extent but it is not difficult to grasp what thought-provoking opportunities it will give to, say, foreign language learning as soon as virtual excursions to various target countries become feasible. One step onwards will most probably be virtual computing which, according to some researchers (e.g., Naisbitt 1994) will lead to ubiquitous computing in the 21st century.

The Question of Cost/Effectiveness

"Education has by far the lowest level of investment in technology of any major sector of the economy. (Education invests an average of $ 100 per worker per year in technology, compared to an average of $ 50,000 per worker per year in many industries.)"

Educational technology has also been handicapped by economic restrictions submitted to schools. The question, basically, is about how costly or how affordable certain communications media are. For the time being, communication via satellites is costly while video conferencing, especially desktop video, such as CU-SeeMe type of software, is becoming affordable at various levels of schooling. What this basically boils down to are the videophones which give full connectivity to the Internet but cost just roughly 10 % of a full-scale video conferencing system.

The Kilpisjärvi Project (Husu et al. 1994), however, clearly demonstrates that a full video conference system using ISDN lines can also be fairly affordable.

Audio conferencing and telephony in general have been studied in quite a few countries for years now. Audio conferencing, when combined with audio-graphics, for instance, has proved a success even if in the conventional solution two telephone lines are needed.

At the most affordable end of the scale, educators have had recourse to videotapes, audiotapes, cassettes, minidiscs, etc. These represent conventional if not widely and universally available technology which few educators fight against.

MODERN INFORMATION AND COMMUNICATION TECHNOLOGIES

What are or what is meant by modern information and communication technologies? Historically speaking, first there was ADP (automatic data-processing), soon to be replaced by computer-based education (CBE), which was further divided into CAI (computer-assisted instruction) or CAL (computer-assisted learning) and into CMI (computer-managed instruction).

The general construct so far has been IT (information technology, sometimes technologies). In a larger perspective, IT is no longer enough, although it is still used occasionally in educational contexts as well. For instance, in the English National Curriculum, IT is said to provide a natural medium for creating, storing, retrieving and communicating information and thus being an ideal resource in language learning (Modern Languages 1992, F1). Information as such is not enough; what is needed is communication. Therefore it is easily understood why a lot of researchers have started talking about communication and information technologies (les technologies de communication et d'information), abbreviated as CIT.

This construct is often used in UNESCO documents as well. However, in order to avoid any embarrassing connotations due to the pronunciation of that abbreviation in English, it is generally considered wiser to talk about ICT (information and communication technologies) or NICT (new information and communication technologies). Speaking of "new" information and communication technologies is, in the final analysis, somewhat misleading, as many of the applications are based on rather old technology, i.e., on the telephone network. If "new" is used, it should be understood to imply the latest services, especially telematic and electronic. In this article, these technologies will be referred to as MICT (modern information and communication technologies), as it can be considered a wide enough construct to cover all up-to-date technologies and, more importantly, all pedagogical applications of earlier IT.

The classification is meant to give a general outline on different ways of using computer applications in education. It enumerates some of the main technological developments (left column), with a few references to possible educational applications or emphases (right column). The two columns are interdependent and many components overlap as they tend to have features in common, which also means that emphases mentioned in the right column belong to several technologies on the left and vice versa. The temporal dimension covered by the left-column is fairly long, reaching up to the 21st century (e.g., ubiquitous computing).

As new applications keep on being launched, many educators, no doubt, whole-heartedly agree with Collis & Verwijs's (1995, 5) statement that "we seem now to have moved from a time of comparative simplicity to one of a bewildering range of developments and terminology".

At the moment it is easy to understand that a computer which is not logged on to a communications network, is a stand-alone machine, still useful for many purposes, but with no real asset regarding a networked learning environment. From an educational point of view, it could best be described as specific to and within a given computer application. Broadly speaking, computer-based training in its conventional form can also be regarded as a general educational application.

Audio conferencing and audio-graphics rely heavily on the conventional telephone network, although cordless microphones and other equipment can also be used. Audio-graphics has made it possible to transmit graphs and pictures to remote locations, and to use an optic tablet for drawing purposes. Audio conferencing represents traditional distance education technology, still widely used.

Telefax is a special problem from an educational point of view. It certainly represents a user-friendly technology when compared to e-mail, for instance. Besides, practically all fax machines communicate with each other, which is not true of e-mail systems. Naisbitt (1994) sees the difference between telefax and e-mail as the difference between evolutionary and revolutionary developments. Telefax is "a bridge between the old and new. Paper is slid into the fax machine much like being slid into an envelope. And the fax machine is dialed the same way the phone is. It is familiar and comfortable. Electronic mail, on the other hand, is revolutionary and does not relate to paper, only to electronics" (Naisbitt 1994, 96). However, Naisbitt (1994) believes that as people play more and more to e-mail's strength, it will start to gain on faxes.

Computer conferencing has widened the educational perspective by giving more open access to distance and multi-mode (2) educational solutions. In fact, computer-mediated communication and distance education have a lot in common. In both of them, technology can take students into otherwise inaccessible environments. In distance education, the teacher's role is usually fairly active, while in computer conferencing teachers tend to become consultants or co-learners. One of the key issues to be studied further is whether some factual information or knowledge is being transferred through computer conferencing or distance education or whether more attention ought to be paid to interactional effort and process-led collaboration.

Saying that audio conferencing is largely based on listening comprehension, while computer conferencing leans back on written skills and reading comprehension is a simplification because the limits of the traditional language skills (reading, speaking, listening, writing) overlap extensively in the field of MICT. It has been pointed out elsewhere (e.g., Tella 1992) that e-mail, and computer-mediated chat in particular (e.g., communication in real time via computers), emulates the use of oral language though making use of a written mode.

In fact, it is slightly surprising to notice that while oral proficiency is being underscored in many walks of life, at the same time some of the latest developments of MICT, such as cellular phones when connected to data transmission cards, have started using written messagerie (short written messages typed on the tiny screen of the phones).

From the research point of view, e-mailing and computer conferencing give ample opportunity to gather data electronically. Some of the traditional data analysis techniques, however, cannot be used when computer-mediated communication is analysed. Nordenbo (1990) points out some of the difficulties connected to these kinds of data analyses. Some analysis techniques and classifications are given in Tella (1994b, 52--62).

Computer-mediated communications systems apparently offer different kinds of educational opportunities. Boyd (1987), for instance, underlines (i) epistemological viewpoints, connected to discursive flexibility facilitated by electronic mail systems, e.g., bi-or multidirectional (from one/many to one/many) communication vs. unidirectional communication (from one to many only), represented by mass media; (ii) affiliative viewpoints (e.g., peer tutoring and long-term affiliations between students and their school, or among students), and (iii) the physical flexibility offered by computer-mediated communications systems (e.g., opportunities to study in more convenient places and at more convenient times).

The main focus in CAI and CAL and in traditional computer-based software intended for educational purposes used to be on the proceduralisation of the formal elements of the target language, while in computer-mediated communication and in e-mail in particular, the computer serves not only as a learning tool but also as a tool for communication and information retrieval. As to the position of e-mail in a broader context, Naisbitt (1994) foresees, somewhat paradoxically, that there will be a shift of emphasis towards "virtual tribes" or "electronic tribes", as e-mail is a tribe-maker. Electronics makes us more tribal at the same time it globalises us. This vision refers to the fact that e-mail and communications networks are likely to make communication more networked but laying at the same time more emphasis on telelogic communication, i.e., on small group or specifically targeted group communication. At the moment, CD-ROMs are gaining ground in the educational sector. More and more schools are purchasing CD-ROM or CD-

I players and most of the modern microcomputers already have a CD-ROM player installed when shipped to the users. Basically, a CD-ROM gives an individual learner access to an enormous amount of hypertext-based information. On the other hand, users of communications networks also access CD-ROMs without paying much attention to it. For instance, many library databases are in fact on CD-ROMs which the user accesses through communications networks.

Multimedia and hypermedia are words which mean different things to different people. Lane (1993) describes how computer, video, and audio can be combined to multimedia in an interactional model. Chou & Matsuoka (1993) talk about an integrated learning system (ILS), which is used to create a computer-based information rich constructivist learning environment (CIRCLE), in which communications networks are made extensive use of and which involve real experts in the activities of the schools. The ambiguity of the word `multimedia' has also led to mild protestations, like in Braswell (1994), who through a parody points out several problems connected to multimedia at school (the dollar factor; just enough to be dangerous syndrome; the Holy Grail syndrome; you don't need much time; the purpose behind repurposing).

On the other hand, it may be worth while trying to find common features between intrinsic characteristics of multi-or hypermedia and up-to-date or communicative foreign language teaching. Liu (1994, 305), for instance, has identified seven features common to both communicative CALL (computer-assisted language learning) and hypermedia.

EPSS is cautiously taken for a new category of educational software (Collis & Verwijs 1995). Barker & Banerji define EPSS as "a custom-built interactive guidance and information support facility that is integrated into a normal working environment ... with a range of different performance support tools, each one of which will have been selected in order to aid a particular job function". One of the EPSSes could, for instance, include all sorts of tools that would help a writer browse databases on the WWW, then retrieve relevant information with key words, integrate all necessary items into a piece of writing, and then write up a complete article, to be finalised and printed out. While these kinds of tools are being built, Collis & Verwijs (1995, 13) consider it most important to advance from a systems approach towards a human approach, which would include questions like "What are the user's activities and needs?", "How can electronic support help?"; "Balance between human and technological aspects?", etc. Finally, EPSSes should be integrated with electronic tools and environments the end user already is using for his on-going tasks (Collis & Verwijs 1995, 20).

Desktop video (= a PC plus a video camera on top of it) is probably going to be substituted for ordinary video conferencing systems in situations where only a few persons are interacting with one another. One of the assets of desktop video software is that communication is possible on the Internet, while ordinary videoconference systems use ISDN lines. Still, both add the visual channel to the interaction between different sender and recipient.

Not much will be said in this connection about the last categories i.e., virtual reality, virtual computing, and ubiquitous computing. What seems to characterise all these technologies is learning becoming more and more experiential. Ubiquitous computing is a certain ideal concept (Naisbitt 1994), which implies that by the time this ideal has come true, computing will have been wholly integrated into all educational systems. Naisbitt (1994, 56) also argues that in the global economic network of the 21st century, information technology will drive change just as surely as manufacturing drove change in the industrial era.

10

The Power of Participatory Media and Social Change

To promote a more participatory society, it is important to promote participatory media and to challenge, replace and eventually abandon mass media. In order to better understand the mass media's inherent lack of democracy, it is useful to imagine a communication system that allows and fosters participation by everyone. David Andrews did this with his concept of" information routing groups" or IRGs. His discussion predated the vast expansion of computer networks and is worth outlining in its original form. He imagined a computer network in which everyone is linked to several interest groups, with each group having anywhere from perhaps half a dozen up to several hundred people.

An interest group might deal with anything from growing apples to racism. Each time a person makes a contribution on a topic, whether a short comment, a picture or a substantial piece of writing, they send it to everyone in the group. A person receiving a message could, if they wished, post it to other groups to which they belonged. Andrews called each of the groups an IRG. In a network of IRGs, everyone can be a writer and publisher at the same time. But there are no guaranteed mass audiences. If a contribution is really important or exciting to those who receive it, they are more likely to post it to other groups. In this way, a piece of writing could end up being read by thousands or even millions of people.

But note that this requires numerous individual decisions about circulating it to further groups. In the case of the mass media, a single editor can make the decision to run or stop an item. In the case of IRGs, lots of people are involved. By deciding whether or not to forward an item to another group, each person acts somewhat like an editor.

If a group has too many active members, then each one might be bombarded with hundreds of messages every day. Some might opt out, as long as there was someone who would select pertinent messages for them. This person then acts as a type of editor. But note that this "editor" has little of the formal power of editors in the mass media. In an IRG system, anyone can set themselves up as an editor of this sort. Members of this editor's IRG can easily look at the larger body of contributions, should they so wish. One of the main reasons why the IRG editor has relatively little formal power is that there is no substantial investment in terms of subscriptions, advertisers, printing equipment or salaries.

Participating in an IRG is something that can easily be done in a few hours per week. Investments are lower and positions are less entrenched. An IRG editor will maintain an audience only as long as the editing is perceived to be effective. Similarly, quitting is relatively painless.

To anyone familiar with computer networks, especially the Internet, it may seem that to talk about IRGs is simply an awkward way of describing what is actually taking place on existing networks. Indeed, Andrews' account of IRGs can be interpreted as a description of what later took place on the Internet.

While parts of the Internet operate like IRGs, it is unwise to assume that cyberspace is or will remain a model participatory medium. There are ongoing pressures, inequalities and struggles involving access, cost, commercial uses, censorship and surveillance.

IRGs do not have to be based on Computers

Again, this already happens with a number of discussions that operate by post, where each member adds a page or so of comment on the current topic and sends it to the group coordinator, who then makes copies of all contributions for all members. For those who have the technology and know how to use it, computer networks make this process far easier and faster.

Another medium that is inherently participatory is the telephone. Phones are very easy to use—only speaking, not writing, is required—and are widely available. Certainly it is possible for a person to dominate a telephone conversation, but only one person is at the other end of the line, or occasionally more in the case of a conference call. In the mass media, one person speaks and thousands or millions hear. Ivan Illich proposed the concept of " convivial tools." This includes technologies that foster creative and autonomous interactions between people. Convivial technologies in the case of the media are the ones that foster participation. The postal system, the telephone system, computer networks and short-wave radio are examples of convivial media.

The implication of this analysis is straightforward. To promote a more participatory society, it is important to promote participatory media and to challenge, replace and eventually abandon mass media. Jerry Mander, in his case against television, gave as one of his four main arguments corporate domination of television used to mould humans for a commercial environment. But all mass media involve centralised power. Mander's argument should be extended: all mass media should be abandoned.

Saying "mass media should be superseded" is easy. Working out practical implications is the hard part. In my view, although a world without mass media may be a long-term goal, the mass media will be around for quite some time. Therefore, it is necessary to have a strategy to challenge them, from inside and outside, as well as to promote alternatives.

There are already plenty of challenges to the mass media, of course. But these challenges are not to the existence of the mass media, but only to the way they are run. In a way, media criticism is a form of loyal opposition.

Wait—before looking at strategies, what if the mass media are being whittled away anyway?

Are cable television and the Internet making mass media obsolete by providing more communication channels and creating niche markets?

Will newspapers be replaced by net-based news services that can be individually tailored?

Is the mass audience a relic of the modernist age, while fragmentation of audiences and perspectives is characteristic of the new postmodern era? It would be unwise to trust in "natural" processes to cause the demise of mass media. There is nothing automatic about technological and social change.

Powerful groups are doing everything they can to control markets and opinions in the changing information order. Another scenario is that mass media will continue to have a major influence and that governments and corporations will extend their influence into the more fragmented channels. After all, television, video cameras and cassettes did not lead to the collapse of Hollywood and large-scale movie-making.

If the mass media are ever replaced, it will be due to lots of people taking action to help it happen. Hence the need for strategies, both individual and collective.

Strategies

Here I outline a number of possible strategies, focusing on what can be done by individuals and small groups to challenge mass media and replace them by participatory network media. It would be easy to make some sweeping recommendations about what should be done, especially by governments. But to be compatible with the goal of a participatory communication system, the methods should be participatory too.

The following ideas are meant to encourage discussion.

Change one's own media consumption patterns: Many people are such regular and insistent consumers of the mass media—television, radio and newspapers—that it's possible to speak of an addiction. This also includes many of those who are strongly critical of the mass media.

Cutting down on consumption can be part of a process of imagining and fostering a participatory communications system.

Some people may object to this recommendation. Surely, they will say, it's quite possible to be an avid mass media consumer—or to work for the media—while still maintaining a critical perspective and also using and promoting alternative media. True enough. Analogously, a factory worker can certainly remain critical of capitalism and promote alternatives.

My view is not that cutting back mass media consumption is necessary, but that it can be a useful way to change people's consciousness. It is similar to animal liberationists reducing their consumption of animal products and environmentalists riding bicycles and composting their organic wastes. Such individual acts cannot by themselves transform the underlying structures of factory farming, industrial society or centralised media: collective action for structural change is needed.

Nevertheless, changes in individual behaviour serve several important purposes:

a) they change the perspectives of individuals,

b) they reinforce concern about the issue and

c) they provide an example (of consistency) for others.

Changing media habits can be incredibly difficult. Watching the news on television is, for many people, a ritual. For others, reading the daily paper is an essential part of each day. Although Jerry Mander's book Four Arguments for the Elimination of Television has become a classic in alternative circles, no social movement has developed to abolish TV. There are only some small groups, such as the Society for the Elimination of Television, producing a few newsletters.

One reason may be that—according to one argument—watching television changes one's brain waves, reducing the number of fast waves characteristic of thinking and increasing the number of slow waves characteristic of relaxed states.

This explains why watching television seems so relaxing: it allows the brain to switch off. It also explains why television is so effective at communicating commercial messages. Images go into the brain without processing; the images cannot be recalled, but they can be recognised, for example in a supermarket. Another reason why switching off the television is so difficult is that it becomes part of the household. It seems voluntary, and it is to some extent.

Action must begin at home: It is easier to oppose "alien" technologies such as nuclear power, which are not part of people's everyday lives. Challenging technologies that are personal possessions, used routinely—such as television and cars—is far more difficult. Except for some people who must monitor the media as part of their work, mass media consumption is, from a time management view, quite inefficient. Think back on all the television you watched during the past ten years. How much of it was genuinely necessary to be fully informed, or was even genuinely informative? A similar calculation can be made for reading newspapers.

But what if the aim is not efficiency but simply enjoying life and occasionally learning something along the way? This brings the discussion back to lack of participation. Most people have been turned into passive consumers of the media. This will not change until some people take the initiative to break the pattern.

Learn how the media construct reality: If it is essential to consume products of the mass media, a useful antidote is to learn how these media products are created. It is illuminating to spend time with a television film crew or in a newspaper office. It quickly becomes apparent that of the many possible things that could be treated by the media, and of the many possible ways that this could be done, only certain ones actually are chosen.

It is also useful to gain some experience on the receiving end of media construction of reality, by joining a rally or media conference and seeing how it is reported, or by being interviewed oneself.

Another way to gain insight into media construction of reality is to undertake a detailed study of some topic, whether it is child rearing, banking, crime or East African politics. This could involve reading books and in-depth articles, investigating alternative viewpoints and consulting with experts and concerned groups. With a good grounding in a range of perspectives and an ability to think confidently about the topic, it is then possible to make an informed assessment of mass media treatments, including biases and omissions.

It is important to be aware of how the media constructs reality, but that alone does not change the dynamics of the media. Therefore it is valuable to communicate what one learns about media constructions to others.

Participate in a group to change media consumption patterns: In a group of two or more people, it can be easier to make some of the individual changes. Individuals can be assigned the task of monitoring particular media and reporting on issues that are important to the group.

Others can do the same with alternative media. In this way, individuals don't need to worry so much that they have missed some important item. More important, though, is the process of interaction in the group: discussing the issues. This is what is missing in the individual consumption of the mass media. Of course, quite a bit of discussion occurs already among friends and colleagues. By working in a more directed fashion in a group, a greater commitment to participation and participatory media can be fostered. Teachers can contribute to this process by giving guidance on how to analyse the mass media and how to use and develop alternatives.

Use the mass media for one's own purposes: This is the usual approach: writing letters to the editor, putting out press releases, being interviewed, inviting media to meetings, holding rallies to attract media coverage, etc. Numerous action groups, from feminists to farmers, promote their cause this way. Such efforts can shift the emphasis in media coverage, for example from coverage of politicians and business to some attention to social issues and movements. But this does little or nothing to challenge the fundamental lack of participation in the mass media. Furthermore, it can distort social movement agendas. Seeking media attention can be a way of building grassroots support but it can also take priority over building support. Some movement leaders are turned into stars by the media, causing internal stresses and resentments. All in all, this approach, as a means of promoting participatory media, has little to recommend it. Social movements need a strategy on communication, including how to deal with both establishment and alternative media.

Of course, promoting participatory media is not the only goal of social movements. In a great number of cases, using the existing mass media is a sensible and quite justifiable approach. Furthermore, campaigns such as those by Fairness and Accuracy in Reporting to challenge biases in the media are extremely important. But it is important to be aware of the limitations of such campaigns.

Even "fair and accurate" mass media are far from participatory. Participating in the mass media is inevitably limited to only a few people or only to minor contributions. Only a few people have the skills or opportunity to write an article—that will be published—for a large newspaper, or to be interviewed for more than a few seconds on television. Even an occasional article or television appearance is trivial compared to the impact of those who host a television programme or write a regular column in a major paper.

Furthermore, those who are successful in "breaking in" may actually legitimise the media in which they appear. This is analogous to the way that worker representatives on company boards can legitimise both the decisions made and the hierarchical structure of the company. Many progressives want to use the media, or go into it as journalists or producers, to help the causes in which they believe. The intention is good, and the work many of them do is superb. But it should be remembered that this approach perpetuates unequal participation. It needs to be asked whether the aim is mainly to promote a favoured viewpoint or to foster a discussion involving ever more people. These two aims are not always compatible.

Participate in alternative media: This is an obvious strategy. Possibilities include:

- o subscribing to alternative magazines and supporting small presses
- o writing material for newsletters and small magazines
- o publishing one's own newsletter, magazine or books
- o organising meetings of friends to discuss issues of significance
- o doing community organising with techniques such as public meetings and door-to-door canvassing
- o listening to and producing programmes for community radio and television
- o participating in computer discussion groups
- o producing, collecting and using micrographics (microfiche, microfilm), especially to distribute and save nonstandard works
- o using short-wave radio
- o running workshops on developing skills for network media
- o developing campaigns that help build skills in using alternative media and don't rely on mass media
- o participating in self-managing media enterprises.

These and other initiatives are going on all the time. They need more support and development. This strategy is fully compatible with the goal of participatory media, so there are fewer internal contradictions and traps.

Use nonviolent action to challenge the mass media: Activists have more often used than challenged the mass media. Yet there are numerous methods of nonviolent action that can be used to confront and change mass media, as well as to promote network media. For example, boycotts can be organised of particularly offensive publications or shows. Small shareholders can use direct action to present their concerns at shareholders' meetings. Activists can occupy media offices. However, it is usually extremely difficult for consumers of the media to organise challenges. The best prospects are for media workers. They can challenge and subvert management by publishing or showing items without permission, allowing humorous mistakes to slip through, resigning as a group, working in against orders, and even taking over media operations and running them participatively. Such initiatives can only succeed if there is considerable support from the users of the media. Hence, links between workers and users are essential, for example between journalists and public interest groups.

Undermine institutional support for mass media: This is a big one. It roughly translates into "undermine monopoly capitalism and the state." The mass media would not be able to maintain their dominant position without special protection. Television is the best example. In most countries, governments own and run all channels. In liberal democracies there are some commercial channels, but these must be licensed by the government. Without government regulation, anyone could set up a studio and broadcast at whatever frequency they wanted. For cable systems, government regulations control who gains access.

The power of commercial television comes, of course, from corporate sponsorship, typically via advertisements. Without sponsorship from wealthy corporations, a few channels would be unlikely to be able to maintain their dominant positions. If a society of small enterprises is imagined—whether run by owners or worker collectives—there would be no basis or reason for large-scale sponsorship of mass media. Corporations and governments also are crucial in maintaining the position of large-circulation newspapers. In many countries the dominant newspapers are government owned and produced. In capitalist societies, advertisements are essential to keep the purchase price down.

Without advertisements, the size of the papers would shrink and the price would jump, leading to a decline in circulation. This would make the newspapers more similar to current-day alternative newspapers and magazines, which typically require contributions above and beyond subscription fees in order to stay afloat. Governments also help maintain large-circulation commercial newspapers in various indirect ways, including high postal rates for alternative media, defamation law (which can bankrupt small publishers), and copyright (which enables monopoly profits).

Governments and large corporations support the mass media, and vice versa. Of course, there are many conflicts between these powerful groups, such as when the media criticise particular government decisions or corporate actions, and when government or corporations try to muzzle or manipulate the media. But at a more fundamental level, these institutions reinforce each other.

Without government and corporate support, the mass media would disintegrate. With participatory media instead of mass media, governments and corporations would be far less able to control information and maintain their legitimacy. In terms of strategy, the implication of this analysis is that challenges to the mass media, and the strengthening of network media, should be linked to challenges to monopoly capitalism and the state. To bring about true participatory media, it is also necessary to bring about participatory alternatives to present economic and political structures.

PARTICIPATORY COMMUNICATION OF MEDIA FOR SOCIAL CHANGE

Participation involves the more equitable sharing of both political and economic power, which often decreases the advantage of certain groups. Structural change involves the redistribution of power. In mass communication areas, many communication experts agree that structural change should occur first in order to establish participatory communication policies. Mowlana and Wilson (1987), for instance, state:

Communications policies are basically derivatives of the political, cultural and economic conditions and institutions under which they operate. They tend to legitimize the existing power relations in society, and therefore, they cannot be substantially changed unless there are fundamental structural changes in society that can alter these power relationships themselves.

Therefore, the development of a participatory communication model has to take place in relation with overall societal emancipation processes at local, national as well as international levels. Several authors have been trying to summarize the criteria for such a communication model. The Latin American scholar Juan Somavia (1977, 1981) sums up the following (slightly adapted) components as essential for it:

(a) *Communication is a human need:* the satisfaction of the need for communication is just as important for a society as the concern for health, nutrition, housing, education and labour. Together with all the other social needs, communication must enable the citizens to emancipate themselves completely. The right to inform and to be informed, and the right to communicate, are thus essential human rights and this both individually and collectively.

(b) *Communication is a delegated human right*: within its own cultural, political, economic and historical context, each society has to be able to define independently the concrete form in which it wants to organize its social communication process. Because there are a variety of cultures, there can therefore also arise various organizational structures. But whatever the form in which the social communication function is embodied, priority must be given to the principles of participation and accessibility.

(c) *Communication is a facet of the societal conscientization, emancipation and liberation process.* The social responsibility of the media in the process of social change is very large. Indeed, after the period of formal education, the media are the most important educational and socialization agents. They are capable of informing or disinforming, exposing or concealing important facts, interpreting events positively or negatively, and so on.

(d) *The communication task involves rights and responsibilities/obligations.* Since the media in fact provide a public service, they must carry it out in a framework of social and juridical responsibility that reflects the social consensus of the society. In other words, there are no rights without obligation.

The freedom and right to communicate, therefore, must be approached from a threefold perspective: *first,* it is necessary for the public to participate effectively in the communication field; *secondly,* there is the design of a framework in which this can take place; and, *thirdly,* the media must enjoy professional autonomy, free of economic, political or whatever pressure. In sum, participatory communication for social change sees people as the nucleus of development. Development means lifting up the spirits of a local community to take pride in its own culture, intellect and environment. Development aims to educate and stimulate people to be active in self and communal improvements while maintaining a balanced ecology. Authentic participation, though widely espoused in the literature, is not in everyone's interest. Due to their local concentration, participatory programmes are, in fact, not easily implemented, nor are they highly predictable or readily controlled.

DIFFERENT 'TYPES' OF PARTICIPATORY COMMUNICATION PROJECTS

In spite of the widespread acceptance of the ideas of Freire and UNESCO by development organizations and communication researchers, there is still a very wide range of projects calling themselves 'participatory communication projects'. There is an evident need for clarification in descriptive and normative theories of participatory media. What does it mean to be participatory? It is necessary to make further distinctions and arguments to deal with a wide variety of actually existing experiences and political intentions.

A review of the literature turns up the following *types* :

(1) participatory media are internally organized on democratic lines (as worker co-operatives or collectives);

(2) participatory media are recognized by their opposition to cultural industries dominated by multinational corporations;

(3) participatory media may be traced to the liberation of linguistic and ethnic groups following a major social transformation;

(4) the strong existence of participatory media may be explained in terms of class struggle within the society;

(5) participatory media may be identified as "molecular" rather than "molar" (a collectivity of individual autonomous units rather than one that is homogenized and one-dimensional);

(6) participatory media (like the montage of Eisenstein and the theatre of Brecht) by design requires a creative and varied reception from its audience.

Reyes Matta (1986) argues that participatory communication is first and foremost an alternative to media dominated by transnational corporations. This is the context in which any alternative must operate. To succeed is to have won against the culture industries that are dominated by multinational corporations. The line of thought developed by CINCO (1987) is a development of this because it involves above all a structural analysis of communicative institutions. For the CINCO researchers media are alternative if they have a democratic institutional structure. Here the issue is one of ownership and control that is external to the community against access and participation in the media organization.

Legitimacy and political credibility can be fostered by the establishment of what is called *participatory democracy*, the building in of actual participation from the public. This is only possible when the communication system is decentralized. The control over communication and information may not be monopolized by one or a few segments of the society. Unfortunately, most of the time structural aspects stand in the way of the ideal of democracy. In most developing countries, the first stone for bridging the gap between the ruling elite and the masses has still to be laid. For the establishment of participatory democracy, therefore, dialogue must be made possible between the authorities and the public, nationally, regionally, and locally. In the political sector, this can be done through political parties, pressure groups, civil action groups, environmental movements, and the like. Thus political credibility as well as social and cultural identity of the population and an awareness and support of the development goals are needed. The concept of Community Media (CM) has shown to be, in its long theoretical and empirical tradition, highly elusive. The multiplicity of media organizations that carry this name has caused most mono-theoretical approaches to focus on certain characteristics, while ignoring other aspects of the identity of community media. This theoretical problem necessitates the use of different approaches towards the definition of community media, which will allow for a complementary emphasis on different aspects of the identity of community media. For a more elaborate description of the different domains of alternative/ participatory media.

By Way of Summary

The above-described changes in the field of communication for development could be summarized as follows.

The growth of a deeper understanding of the nature of communication The perspective on communication has changed. Early models in the '50s and '60s saw the communication process simply as a message going from a sender to a receiver (that is, Laswell's classic S-M-R model). The emphasis was mainly sender-and media-centric; the stress laid on the freedom of the press, the absence of censorship, and so on. Since the '70s, communication has become more receiver-and message-centric.

The emphasis now is more on the process of communication (that is, the exchange of meaning) *and on the significance of this process* (that is, the social relationships created by communication and the social institutions and context which result from such relationships). As a result, the focus has moved from a 'communicator' to a more 'receiver-centric' orientation, with the resultant *emphasis on meaning sought and ascribed rather than information transmitted.*

A new understanding of communication as a two-way process With this shift in focus, one is no longer attempting to create a need for the infirmation one is disseminating, but one is rather *disseminating information for which there is a need.* The emphasis is on information exchange rather than on the persuasion in the diffusion model. The 'oligarchic' view of communication implied that freedom of infirmation was a one-way right from a higher to a lower level, from the centre to the periphery, from an institution to an individual, from a communication-rich nation to a communication-poor one, and so on. Today, the interactive nature of communication is increasingly recognized. It is seen as fundamentally two-way rather than one-way, interactive and participatory rather than linear.

A new understanding of culture: The cultural perspective has become central to the debate on communication for development. Culture is not only the visible, non-natural environment of a person, but primarily his/her normative context. Consequently, one has moved away from a more traditional mechanistic approach that emphasized economic and materialistic criteria to a more *multiple appreciation of holistic and complex perspectives.*

The trend towards participatory democracy: The end of the colonial era has seen the rise of many independent states and the spread of democratic principles, even if only at the level of lip service. Though often ignored in practice, democracy is honoured in theory. Governments and/or powerful private interests still largely control the world's communication media, but they are more attuned to and aware of the democratic ideals than previously. At the same time, literacy levels have increased, and there has been a remarkable improvement in people's ability to handle and use communication technology. As a consequence, *more and more people can use communication media and can no longer be denied access to and participation in communication processes for the lack of communication and technical skills.*

Recognition of the imbalance in communication resources or the digital divide: The disparity in communication resources between different parts of the world is increasingly recognized as a cause of concern. As the centre nations develop their resources, the gap between centre and periphery becomes greater. *The plea for a more balanced and equal distribution of communication resources can only be* *discussed in terms of power at local, national and international levels.* The attempt by local power-elites to totally control the modern communication channels –press, broadcasting, education, and bureaucracy– does no longer ensure control of all the communication networks in a given society. Nor does control of the mass media ensure support for the controlling forces, nor for any mobilization around their objectives, nor for the effective repression of opposition. Some may argue that thanks to the new ICTs, especially the Internet and, one has to readdress the debate on the digital divide; however, others remain sceptical and less optimistic.

The growing sense of globalization and cultural hybridity: Perhaps the greatest impetus towards a new formulation of communication freedoms and the need for realistic communication policies and planning have come from the realization that the international flow of communication has become the main carrier of cultural globalization. This cultural hybridity can take place without perceptible dependent relationships.

A new understanding of what is happening within the boundaries of the nation-state: One has to accept that "internal" and "external" factors inhibiting development do not exist independently of each other. Thus, in order to understand and develop a proper strategy one must have an understanding of the class relationships of any particular peripheral social formation and the ways in which these structures articulate with the centre on the one hand, and the producing classes in the Third World on the other. To dismiss Third World ruling classes, for example, as mere puppets whose interests are always mechanically synonymous with those of the centre, is to ignore the realities of a much more complex relationship. The very unevenness and contradictory nature of the capitalist development process necessarily produces *a constantly changing relationship.*

Recognition of the 'impact' of communication technology: Some communication systems (e.g., audio-and video-taping, copying, radio broadcasting, and especially the

Internet) have become *cheap* and so simple that the rationale for regulating and controlling them centrally, as well as the ability to do so, is no longer relevant. However, other systems (for instance, satellites, remote sensing, trans-border data flows) remain *very expensive*. They are beyond the means of smaller countries and 'have-nots'. Moreover, they may not be 'suitable' to local environments.

From an information society to knowledge societies: Information has been seen as the leading growth sector in society, especially in advanced industrial economies. Its three strands –computing, telecommunications and broadcasting– have evolved historically as three separate sectors, and by means of digitization these sectors are now converging.

Throughout the past decade a gradual shift can be observed away from a technological in favour of more socioeconomic and cultural definitions of the Information Society. The term Knowledge Societies (in plural as there are many roads) better coins this shift in emphasis from ICTs as 'drivers' of change to a perspective where these technologies are regarded as tools which may provide a new potential for combining the information embedded in ICT systems with the creative potential and knowledge embodied in people: "These technologies do not create the transformations in society by themselves; they are designed and implemented by people in their social, economic, and technological contexts".

True knowledge is more than information. Knowledge is the sense or meaning that people make of information. *Meaning is not something that is delivered to people, people create/ interpret it themselves.* If knowledge is to be effectively employed to help people, it needs to be interpreted and evaluated by those it is designed to help. That requires people to have access to information on the issues that affect their lives, and the capacity to make their own contributions to policy-making processes. Understanding the context in which knowledge moves –factors of control, selection, purpose, power, and capacity– is essential for understanding how societies can become better able to learn, generate and act on knowledge.

A new understanding towards integration of distinct means of communication: Modern mass media and alternate or parallel networks of folk media or interpersonal communication channels are not mutually exclusive by definition. Contrary to the beliefs of diffusion theorists, they are *more effective if appropriately used in an integrated fashion, according to the needs and constraints of the local context.*

The modern mass media, having been mechanically transplanted from abroad into Third World societies, enjoy varying and limited rates of penetration. They are seldom truly integrated into institutional structures, as occurs in some Western societies. However, they can be effectively combined, provided a functional division of labour is established between them, and provided the limits of the communication media are recognized.

The recognition of dualistic or parallel communication structures: No longer governments or rulers are able to operate effectively, to control, censor, or to play the role of gatekeeper with regard to all communications networks at all times in a given society. Both alternate and parallel networks, which may not always be active, often function through political, sociocultural, religious or class structures or can be based upon secular, cultural, artistic, or folkloric channels. These networks feature a highly participatory character, high rates of credibility, and a strong organic integration with other institutions deeply rooted in a given society.

PARTICIPATORY COMMUNICATION: THE NEW PARADIGM?

The differences between a so-called diffusionist or top-down communication model versus a participatory or bottom-up communication model; two general differences in approach within the participatory model, which lead to different 'types' of participatory communication projects, especially at the community media level; by way of conclusion we identify eleven changes within the communication for social change field which will, in our opinion, further condition and complicate the future of the field.

FROM MODERNIZATION, OVER DEPENDENCY, TO MULTIPLICITY

Development communication in the 1950s and 1960s was generally greeted with enthusiasm and optimism. Building on the American scholar Daniel Lerner's influ-ential 1958 study of communication and development in the Middle East and Wilbur Schramm's 1964 study on the role of media for national development, communication researchers assumed that the introduction of media and certain types of educational, political, and economic information into a social system could transform individuals and societies from traditional to modern.

This optimism was in line with the 'Zeitgeist' after the Second World War and the fall of Nazism and fascism. The founding of the United nations stim-ulated relations among sovereign states, especially the North Atlantic Nations and the developing nations, including the new states emerging out of a colonial past. Though the 'cold war' clouded this stage of enthusiasm, the superpowers –the United States and the former Soviet Union– tried to expand their own interests to the developing countries. They both started to promote opposite versions of 'modern futures' to the so-called Third World.

In fact, the USA was defining development and social change as the replica of its own political-economic system and opening the way for the transnational corporations. At the same time, the developing countries saw the 'welfare state' of the North Atlantic nations as the ultimate goal of development. These nations were attracted by the new technology transfer and the model of a centralized state with careful economic planning and centrally directed development bureaucracies for agriculture, education and health as the most effective strategies to catch up with those industrialized countries.

This mainly economic-oriented view, characterized by endogenism and evolutionism, ultimately resulted in the *modernization and growth* theory. It sees development as an unilinear, evolutionary process and defines the state of underdevelopment in terms of observable quantitative differences between so-called poor and rich countries on the one hand, and traditional and modern societies on the other hand. As a result of the general intellectual 'revolution' that took place in the mid '60s, this Euro-or ethnocentric perspective on development was challenged by Latin American social scientists, and a theory dealing with *dependency and underdevelopment* was born. This dependency approach formed part of a general structuralist re-orientation in the social sciences. The 'dependistas' were primarily concerned with the effects of dependency in peripheral countries, but implicate in their analysis was the idea that development and underdevelopment must be understood in the context of the world system.

This dependency paradigm played an important role in the movement for a New World Information and Communication Order from the late 1960s to the early 1980s. At that time, the new states in Africa, Asia and the success of socialist and popular movements in Cuba, China, Chile and other countries provided the goals for political, economic and cultural self-determination within the international community of nations. These new nations shared the ideas of being independent from the superpowers and moved to form the Non-Aligned nations. The Non-Aligned Movement defined development as political struggle.

Since the demarcation of the First, Second and Third Worlds has broken down and the crossover centre-periphery can be found in every region, there is a need for a new concept of development which emphasizes *cultural identity and multidimensionality*. The present-day 'global' world, in general as well as in its distinct regional and national entities, is confronted with multifaceted crises. Apart from the obvious economic and financial crisis, one could also refer to social, ideological, moral, political, ethnic, ecological and security crises. In other words, the previously held dependency perspective has become more difficult to support because of the growing interdependency of regions, nations and communities in our globalized world.

From the criticism of the two paradigms above, particularly that of the dependency approach, a new viewpoint on development and social change has come to the forefront. The common starting point here is the examination of the changes from 'bottom-up', from the self-development of the local community. The basic assumption is that there are no countries or communities that function completely autonomously and that are completely self-sufficient, nor are there any nations whose development is exclusively determined by external factors. Every society is dependent in one way or another, both in form and in degree. Thus, a framework was sought within which both the centre and the periphery could be studied separately and in their mutual relationship, both at global, national and local levels.

More attention is also being paid to the content of development, which implies a more normative approach. Another development questions whether 'developed' countries are in fact developed and whether this genre of progress is sustainable or desirable. It favours a multiplicity of approaches based on the context and the basic, felt needs, and the empowerment of the most oppressed sectors of various societies at divergent levels. A main thesis is that change must be structural and occur at multiple levels in order to achieve these ends.

DIFFUSION VERSUS PARTICIPATORY COMMUNICATION

The above general typology of the so-called development paradigms can also be found at the communications and culture level. The communication media are, in the context of development, generally used to support development initiatives by the dissemination of messages that encourage the public to support development-oriented projects. Although development strategies in developing countries diverge widely, the usual pattern for broadcasting and the press has been predominantly the same: informing the population about projects, illustrating the advantages of these projects, and recommending that they be supported. A typical example of such a strategy is situated in the area of family planning, where communication means like posters, pamphlets, radio, and television attempt to persuade the public to accept birth control methods. Similar strategies are used on campaigns regarding health and nutrition, agricultural projects, education, and so on. This model sees the communication process mainly as a message going from a sender to a receiver. This hierarchic view on communication can be summarized in Laswell's classic formula, –'Who says What through Which channel to Whom with What effect?'–, and dates back to (mainly American) research on campaigns and diffusions in the late '40s and '50s.

The American scholar Everett Rogers (1983) is said to be the person who introduced this diffusion theory in the context of development. Modernization is here conceived as a process of diffusion whereby individuals move from a traditional way of life to a different, more technically developed and more rapidly changing way of life. Building primarily on sociological research in agrarian societies, Rogers stressed the adoption and diffusion processes of cultural innovation. This approach is therefore concerned with the *process of diffusion and adoption of innovations* in a more systematic and planned way. Mass media are important in spreading awareness of new possibilities and practices, but at the stage where decisions are being made about whether to adopt or not to adopt, personal communication is far more likely to be influential. Therefore, the general conclusion of this line of thought is that *mass communication is less likely than personal influence to have a direct effect on social behaviour*.

Newer perspectives on development communication claim that this is a limited view of development communication. They argue that this diffusion model is a vertical or one-way perspective on communication, and that development will accelerate mainly through active involvement in the process of the communication itself. Research has shown that, while groups of the public can obtain information from impersonal sources like radio and television, this information has relatively little effect on behavioural changes. And development envisions precisely such change. Similar research has led to the conclusion that more is learned from interpersonal contacts and from mass communication techniques that are based on them. On the lowest level, before people can discuss and resolve problems, they must be informed of the facts, information that the media provide nationally as well as regionally and locally. At the same time, the public, if the media are sufficiently accessible, can make its information needs known. Communication theories such as the 'diffusion of innovations', the 'two-step-flow', or the 'extension' approaches are quite congruent with the above modernization theory. The elitist, *vertical or top-down orientation* of the diffusion model is obvious.

The *participatory model*, on the other hand, incorporates the concepts in the framework of multiplicity. It stresses the importance of cultural identity of local communities and of *democratisation and participation at all levels* –international, national, local and individual. It points to a strategy, not merely inclusive of, but largely emanating from, the traditional 'receivers'. Paulo Freire (1983) refers to this as the right of all people to individually and collectively speak their word: This is not the privilege of some few men, but the right of every (wo)man. Consequently, no one can say a true word alone –nor can he say it for another, in a prescriptive act which robs others of their words.

In order to share information, knowledge, trust, commitment, and a right attitude in development projects participation is very important in any decision-making process for development. Therefore, the International Commission for the Study of Communication Problems, chaired by the late Sean MacBride, argued that "this calls for a new attitude for overcoming stereotyped thinking and to promote more understanding of diversity and plurality, with full respect for the dignity and equality of peoples living in different conditions and acting in different ways". This model stresses reciprocal collaboration throughout all levels of participation.

Also, these newer approaches argue, the *point of departure must be the community*. It is at the community level that the problems of living conditions are discussed, and interactions with other communities are elicited. The most developed form of participation is self-management. This principle implies the right to participation in the planning and production of media content. However, not everyone wants to or must be involved in its practical implementation. More important is that participation is made possible in the decision-making regarding the subjects treated in the messages and regarding the selection procedures. One of the fundamental hindrances to the decision to adopt the participation strategy is that it threatens existing hierarchies. Nevertheless, participation does not imply that there is no longer a role for development specialists, planners, and institutional leaders. It only means that the viewpoint of the local groups of the public is considered before the resources for development projects are allocated and distributed, and that suggestions for changes in the policy are taken into consideration.

TWO MAJOR APPROACHES TO PARTICIPATORY COMMUNICATION

There are two major approaches to participatory communication that everybody today accepts as common sense. The first is the dialogical pedagogy of Paulo Freire, and the second involves the ideas of access, participation and self-management articulated in the UNESCO debates of the 1970s. Every communication project that calls itself participatory accepts these principles of democratic communication. Nonetheless there exists today a wide variety of practical experiences and intentions. Before moving on to explore these differences it is useful to briefly review the common ground. The *Freirian argument* works by a dual theoretical strategy. He insists that subjugated peoples must be treated as fully human subjects in any political process. This implies dialogical communication. Although inspired to some extent by Sartre's existentialism –a respect for the autonomous personhood of each human being–, the more important source is a theology that demands respect for otherness –in this case that of another human being. The second strategy is a moment of utopian hope derived from the early Marx that the human species has a destiny which is more than life as a fulfilment of material needs. Also from Marx is an insistence on collective solutions. Individual opportunity, Freire stresses, is no solution to general situations of poverty and cultural subjugation. These ideas are deeply unpopular with elites, including elites in the Third World, but there is nonetheless widespread acceptance of Freire's notion of dialogic communication as a normative theory of participatory communication. One problem with Freire is that his theory of dialogical communication is based on group dialogue rather than such amplifying media as radio, print and television. Freire also gives little attention to the language or form of communication, devoting most of his discussion to the intentions of communication actions. The second discourse about participatory communication is the UNESCO language about *self-management, access and participation* from the 1977 meeting in Belgrade, the former Yugoslavia. The final report of that meeting defines the terms in the following way.

- Access refers to the use of media for public service. It may be defined in terms of the opportunities available to the public to choose varied and relevant programs and to have a means of feedback to transmit its reactions and demands to production organizations.
- Participation implies a higher level of public involvement in communication systems. It includes the involvement of the public in the production process, and also in the management and planning of communication systems.
- Participation may be no more than representation and consultation of the public in decision-making.
- On the other hand, self-management is the most advanced form of participation. In this case, the public exercises the power of decision-making within communication enterprises and is also fully involved in the formulation of communication policies and plans.

Access by the community and participation of the community are to be considered key defining factors, as Berrigan eloquently summarizes: "[Community media] are media to which members of the community have access, for information, education, entertainment, when they want access. They are media in which the community participates, as planners, producers, and performers. They are the means of expression of the community, rather than for the community" (Berrigan, 1979). Referring to the 1977 meeting in Belgrade, Berrigan (1979) (partially) links access to the reception of information, education, and entertainment considered relevant by/for the community: [Access] may be defined in terms of the opportunities available to the public to choose varied and relevant programs, and to have a means of feedback to transmit its reactions and demands to production organizations. Others limit access to mass media and see it as 'the processes that permit users to provide relatively open and unedited input to the mass media' (Lewis, 1993: 12) or as 'the relation to the public and the established broadcasting institutions' (Prehn, 1991). Both the production and reception approaches of 'access' can be considered relevant for an understanding of 'community media'.

These ideas are important and widely accepted as a normative theory of participatory communication: it must involve access and participation (Pateman, 1972). However, one should note some differences from Freire. The UNESCO discourse includes the idea of a gradual progression. Some amount of access may be allowed, but self-management may be postponed until some time in the future. Freire's theory allows for no such compromise. One either respects the culture of the other or falls back into domination and the 'banking' mode of imposed education. The UNESCO discourse talks in neutral terms about 'the public'. Freire talked about 'the oppressed'. Finally, the UNESCO discourse puts the main focus on the institution. Participatory or community radio means a radio station that is self-managed by those participating in it.

ROLE OF SOCIAL MEDIA

With just the weekend between now and the start of the major party conventions, the amazing thing about the New Media is just how little it has impacted so far on the story. No major leaks about the vice presidential nominations, no blogger unmaskings of damaging revelations about the candidates at the top of the ticket, no shaky video of loose talk or surrogates jockeying for position. Is is possible that the campaigns have learned how to contain the new viral media, or is something else going on? With Twitter, Qik, FriendFeed, and other social media platforms now in place and largely battle-tested for the coming storm of pre-baked circuses, why is the news so tightly controlled by the traditional networks? Perhaps the nature of the underlying story of this election undercuts the technology equation. With a disruptive candidate like Barack Obama, people are looking to the media for less, rather than more drama. The shiny object fascination with radical technology change has given way to a more pragmatic mood, where iPhones have become commonplace and the rapid spread of information throughout the day and on the move has let the mainstream media play more to its traditional strengths as not just aggregators but synthesists of the news.

Real time bursts of information over Twitter and IM have changed how we react to events; the edge professionals have with insider notification is being smoothed out and delivered as a service to consumers via intermediaries who give away the data for the ongoing relationship. We use Facebook and other social hubs as early warning systems, insurance against being out of the loop when breaking information makes a difference in how you do your job or finding one.

SOCIAL MEDIA IS SLOWLY CHANGING

Traditionally, political participation has always been highly correlated with income and education. According to a new report, this is still holds true for those who participate in political activities online. According to the Pew Internet & American Life Project, online users with a higher income are still far more likely to participate in political activities online than those with lower incomes. At the same time, though, the Pew study also sees some hints that new forms of civic engagement through social media services could soon change this pattern.

According to this report, 31% of all users on social networking sites engage in some activity "with a civic or political focus." Pew defines this category very broadly, though, and includes relatively simple activities like 'friending' a political candidate as an "activity with political focus." In total, about 10% of all internet users have used social networks for this kind of political activity. A far more interesting statistic is that 15% of all Internet users have left comments on websites about political or social issues, or posted images or written blog posts related to politics or social issues. What is even more interesting, though not surprising, is that young adults between 18 and 29 are far more likely to use social networks as a venue for political and civic engagement than older users. These younger users who engage in political activity online are also far more likely to participate in politics offline.

SOCIAL MEDIA MIGHT LEVEL THE PLAYING FIELD

Social media is mostly the domain of younger Internet users and while young adults (18-24) are, as a group, less interested in political activities online, they are far more likely than any other group to use blogs and social networking sites to engage in political discussions. About 34% of young adults make political use of social networking sites and 34% post political material on the Internet. Users under 35 represent 72% of those users who make political use of social networks. In addition, the income and education gap for those who engage in political activities on social networks is far less pronounced when compared to those who use other forums.

Will these Trends Continue?

What will be interesting to watch, the Pew study points out, is how these younger users will use these existing networks as they get older. It will also be interesting to see if these developments will mean that socioeconomic status will become less of an indicator of civic engagement, or if these new technologies will create new barriers of entry for those with a lower income and education level.

Given that the US just experienced a highly contested election cycle and is in the middle of a heated debate about health care right now, we have to wonder, though, if these numbers will continue to hold true over the next few years or if they were just a blip on the radar.

Bibliography

Arant, David: *Perspectives: Ethics, Issues and Controversies in Mass Media,* St. Paul, Coursewise Publishing, 1999.

Baker, C. Edwin: *Advertising and a Democratic Press,* Princeton NJ: Princeton University Press, 1994.

Berry, David: *Ethics and Media Culture*, Woburn, Focal Press, 2000.

Bruce D. Itule: *Visual Editing: A Graphic Guide for Journalists,* Belmont, CA: Wadsworth, 1990.

Clifford G.: *Media Ethics: Cases and Moral Reasoning,* Boston, Allyn & Bacon, 2004.

Daniel, Webster: *The Media in America,* Santa Barbara, ABC-CLIO, 1995.

David Sloan: *Historical Methods in Mass Communication,* Hillsdale, NJ: Lawrence Erlbaum, 1989.

David, Sloan: *Historical Methods in Mass Communication,* Hillsdale, NJ: Lawrence Erlbaum, 1989.

Day, A: *Ethics in Media Communications*, Belmont, Wadsworth, 2003.

Downing, John: *Ethnic Minority Media: An International Perspective,* Thousand Oaks, CA: Sage, 1992.

Earl R.: *Writing for Mass Communication,* White Plains, NY: Longman, 1996.

Fishkin, James S.: *Democracy & Deliberation*, New Haven CT: Yale University Press, 1991.

Fiske, John: *Media Matters: Everyday Culture and Political Change*, Minneapolis MN: U. Minnesota Pr., 1996.

Graber, Doris A.: *Processing the News,* N.Y., Longman, 1984.

Hiley, H.: *Mainsteams of American Media History,* Needham Heights, MA: Allyn & Bacon, 1997.

John Williams Tebbel: *American Media History,* Belmont, Thomson/Wadsworth, 2005.

Kessler, Lauren: *The Dissident Press,* Newbury Park, CA: Sage, 1984.

Land, Mitchell : *Contemporary Media Ethics*, Spokand, Marquette Books, 2006.

Lucy, Shelton: *Guide to Sources in American Journalism History,* New York, Greenwood Press, 1989.

Merrill, C.: *Journalism Ethics: Philosophical Foundations for News Media,* New York, St. Martin's Press, 1997.

Norris, Pippa: *Women, Media and Politics*, Oxford, Oxford University Press, 1997.

Richard E.: *Mass Politics: The Politics of Popular Culture,* New York, NY: St. Martin's/WORTH, 1999.

Robert V.: *Mass Media,* New York, Garland Publishing, 1987.

Scott, K.: *Human Resource Management in the Electronic Media*, Westport, Quorum Books, 1998.

Shropshire, Kenneth L.: *Black and White: Race and Sports in America*, New York, NY: New York University Press, 1996.

Sohn, Ardyth: *Media Management: A Casebook Approach,* Mahwah, Lawrence Erlbaum Associates, 2003.

Surette, Ray: *Justice and the Media,* Springfield, Thomas Books, 1984.

Ward, Brian: *Radio and the Struggle for Civil Rights in the South.* Gainesville, FL: University Press of Florida, 2004.

West, Darrell M.: *The Rise and Fall of the Media Establishment*, Boston MA: Bedford/St. Martin's, 2001.

Index

□□□